T0321341

THE
ANTI-GLOBLIST
MANIFESTO

THE
ANTI-GLOBLIST
MANIFESTO

ENDING THE WAR
ON HUMANITY

DR. JEROME R. CORSI
FOREWORD BY STEPHEN K. BANNON

WAR ROOM
BOOKS

War Room Books may be purchased in bulk at special discounts for sales promotion, corporate gifts, fund-raising, or educational purposes. Special editions can also be created to specifications. For details, contact the Special Sales Department, Skyhorse Publishing, 307 West 36th Street, 11th Floor, New York, NY 10018 or info@skyhorsepublishing.com.

Skyhorse® and Skyhorse Publishing® are registered trademarks of Skyhorse Publishing, Inc.®, a Delaware corporation.

Visit our website at www.skyhorsepublishing.com.
Please follow our publisher Tony Lyons on Instagram @tonylyonsisuncertain

10 9 8 7 6 5 4 3 2 1

Library of Congress Cataloging-in-Publication Data is available on file.

Cover design by Brian Peterson

Print ISBN: 978-1-64821-110-2
Ebook ISBN: 978-1-64821-111-9

Printed in the United States of America

Dedicated to
Robert F. Kennedy Jr.,
whose courage, skill, and experience as a litigator for the environment
and a defender of children uniquely qualifies him to root out and
destroy the Deep State Evil that killed his father and his uncle while
they were yet in their prime.

CONTENTS

———

FOREWORD

In any generation, only a few authors manage to rise to international recognition during their lifetimes. War Room Books is honored to bring into print what may become Dr. Jerome Corsi's most important book, *The Anti-Globalist Manifesto: Ending the War on Humanity*. I consider Dr. Corsi a patriot warrior with whom I am happy to go into battle to defeat the dark forces trying to drive God from our lives in their Satanic efforts to destroy all that is good about America. Even more important, I consider Dr. Corsi a friend who has championed and won causes I have championed and won as well, including the current battle in which we are both engaged: the battle to vindicate and re-elect President Donald J. Trump.

Reading this essential book, you will see Dr. Corsi draw spiritual inspiration from Archbishop Carlo Maria Viganò, the former papal nuncio to the United States, who Pope Francis is trying to excommunicate from the Catholic Church for his rejection of the Godless woke ideology—the Deep Church—that seeks to join the Deep State in an insane woke attempt to replace traditional moral values with a dark dystopian "utopia" in which we are considered "useless" human beings.

The book you have in your hands is Dr. Corsi's blueprint for creating an Anti-Globalist future in which we turn back to God, restore our traditional families, and engage in the productive process of rebuilding communal life—a life where energy can be bought directly from suppliers, food can be produced and sold locally by farmers in control of their own destinies, and our children can be educated in health learning devoid of the radical woke gender-confusion.

In the first part of Dr. Corsi's book, you will read how the War on Humanity has been waged by a military-industrial-intelligence-media hydra that seeks depopulation and perpetual war as their way to enrich themselves as a transhuman oligarchy seeking to control the world by merging with their AI-enhanced supercomputers. The vision that we are dispensable when robotics are available to produce for the transhuman globalist elite perpetual life extension is truly diabolic. Peacemakers like John and Robert Kennedy gave their lives to elevate human rights to drive and motivate our politics. Dr. Corsi shows the depth of his wisdom and understanding by dedicating this book to Robert Kennedy Jr.—another warrior who has fought in the courts to preserve the environment and to protect our children from the evils of agribusiness conglomerates and BigPharma.

Truly, we are engaged in a spiritual battle whose outcome is uncertain when the Deep State is willing to contemplate nuclear war and Deep Church satanists push a sexual and moral agenda that is shocking in its schizophrenic acceptance of political policies political martyrs like John Kennedy, Robert Kennedy, and Dr. Martin Luther King Jr. could never have imagined would be taught in our schools, infecting students with mind malware from their first years as kindergarten children to their final studies as graduate candidates for higher degrees.

In the second part of his book, he explores the darkness of the evil that seeks to control the world—an evil that commits evil acts, knowing those acts are evil. But I will believe readers will ultimately agree with me that Dr. Corsi continues to champion the human spirit to rise above evil. He explains that we have within our power the ability to join with what Abraham Lincoln called "the better angels of our nature." As Dr. Corsi notes, we defeat Satan by renouncing Satan. We defeat evil by refusing to participate, cooperate, or boy to the globalist elite. As Dr. Corsi continually reminds us, "In the end, God always wins!"

War Room Books is proud to publish this book—a book we believe will play a historic role internationally in inspiring us to rise up and say, "No" to the globalist elite and their nefarious psychological operations. God did not create us to fail. God remains sovereign and the end of this nightmare is now written. I join Dr. Corsi in confidence that together with God-fearing patriots we can end the globalists war on humanity, starting now with our refusal to see God banned from our lives, with our determination to form families and raise children, and with our desire to live in communities that truly serve our needs.

Stephen K. Bannon
June 2024

INTRODUCTION:
THE TERRIBLE TRUTHS
OF OUR EXISTENCE

"Man is unique in organizing the mass murder of his own species."
—Aldous Huxley, *War*[1]

Question: Why are you running for president?
RFK Jr.: Because I don't like the way the country is going. I don't like the wars. I don't like the censorship. I don't like the addiction to war. Both political parties are now the war party. I don't like the corporate capture of our government—corrupt merger of state and corporate power. I think I'm in a unique position to be able to unravel it.
—Source: American Values 2023 Documentary, May 2024

For, *in the final analysis*, our most basic common link is that we all inhabit this small planet. We all cherish our children's future. And we are all mortal.
—President John F. Kennedy, Commencement Address at American University, Washington, DC, June 10, 1963.[2]

---

1 Aldous Huxley, "War," in *Ends and Means: An Enquiry into the Nature of Ideals and Into the Methods employed for their Realization* (London: Chatto & Windus, 1937).
From the 1946 edition, Chapter IX, pp. 89–125, at p. 125.
2 President John F. Kennedy, Commencement Address at American University, Washington, DC, June 10, 1963, https://www.jfklibrary.org/archives/other-resources/john-f-kennedy-speeches/american-university-19630610.

Yet we know what we must do. It is to achieve true justice among our fellow citizens. The question is now what programs we should seek to enact. The question is whether we can find in our own midst and in our own hearts that leadership of human purpose that will recognize the terrible truths of our existence. —Robert F. Kennedy, Remarks to the Cleveland City Club, April 5, 1968[3]

In the godless secular world in which we now live, self-appointed globalist deep-state actors are running naked to the finish line of imposing their totalitarian nightmare upon us. These self-appointed globalists hide deep within the intelligence bureaucracies, within our justice systems, our educational systems, our state and federal bureaucracies, and the editorial offices of our mainstream media.

They are atheists, convinced there is no value in human lives except maybe for their own. Believing their mission is to "save the planet," the World Economic Forum, in conjunction with the United Nations Agenda 2030 and the World Health Organization, are prepared to kill billions of people considered useless to them. This self-appointed globalist elite believes that artificial intelligence, quantum computing, and advanced robotics will allow them to advance to a transhuman status in which they will enjoy perpetual life extension.

Their goal is to extinguish the belief that God as the Creator endowed us as human beings with inalienable rights that no state dared violate. Bizarrely, the androgynous transgender now comes out of the shadows in a "day of visibility," advanced by the nation's head-of-state to an increasingly secular public as the poster child of this New World Order utopia. We have systematically removed God from our schools,

---

3 Robert F. Kennedy, Remarks to the Cleveland City Club, April 5, 1968, https://www. jfklibrary.org/learn/about-jfk/the-kennedy-family/robert-f-kennedy/robert-f-kennedy-speeches/remarks-to-the-cleveland-city-club-april-5-1968.

our public squares, our homes, our marriages, and our lives. Stepping in to fill the void is the androgynous goat-man Satanic god Baphomet.

We are witnessing the triumph of a neo-Marxist ideology only capable of destroying. In 1944, Frankfurt school authors Max Horkheimer and Theodor Adorno published *Dialectic of Enlightenment* (*Dialektik der Aufklärung*). Horkheimer and Adorno's book marked the beginning of neo-Marxists blending Freudian sexual liberation into Marx's call for an economic revolution to end social class oppression.[4] With Antonio Gramsci's prison notebooks written in Italy from 1926–1937, the Marxist revolution morphed into cultural warfare that aimed to destroy God and the family in the celebration of unleashed libido. I consider this current book to be an extension of my thoughts expressed in my previous book, *The Truth About Neo-Marxism, Cultural Maoism, and Anarchy: Exposing Woke Insanity in an Age of Disinformation.*[5] In that last book, I traced the evolution of neo-Marxist critical theory from Immanuel Kant and Georg Wilhelm Friedrich Hegel to Karl Marx and Mao Tse-tung, as influenced by the Frankfurt School, and turned into value relativism by postmodernist thinkers contending all reality is subjective reality. Here, we seek to demonstrate that such a godless ideology can only destroy, turning into a self-loathing that celebrates death, ultimately culminating in a suicidal war on humanity. With Satan free to prey on Earth, his globalist worshipers seek to control us with technology capable of monitoring our every thought and movement.

---

4 Original edition: Max Horkheimer and Theodor W. Adorno, *Dialektid der Aufklärung* (New York: Social Studies Association, 1944). See also: James Schmidt, "The Making and the Marketing of the *Philosophische Fragmente*: A Note on the Early History of the *Dialectic of Enlightenment* (Part I)," PersistentEnlightenment.com, January 9, 2017, https://persistentenlightenment.com/2017/01/09/philfrag1/. See also: Max Horkheimer and Theodor W. Adorno, *Dialektid der Aufklärung* (Amsterdam: Querido Verlag XV, 1947). Page numbers cited in the footnotes come from this edition of the book: Max Horkheimer and Theodor W. Adorno, *Dialectic of Enlightenment*, trans. John Cumming (New York, Continuum Publishing, 1986).

5 Jerome R. Corsi, *The Truth About Neo-Marxism, Cultural Maoism, and Anarchy: Exposing Woke Insanity in an Age of Disinformation* (New York: Post Hill Press, 2023).

In *The Truth About Neo-Marxism, Cultural Maoism, and Anarchy: Exposing Woke Insanity in an Age of Disinformation*,[6] I explained that Horkheimer and Adorno's book remarkably placed the lascivious Marquis de Sade on the pedestal of their revolutionary heroes. I noted:

> In Horkheimer and Adorno's view, the Marquis de Sade was the one person who had cracked the code explaining why the Enlightenment had led to a fascist totalitarian state. More specifically, they noted that Sade understood the capitalist enslavement culture as a "bourgeois individual freed from tutelage."[7] Their point is that Sade understood how the ruling class in advanced capitalist societies created a domination culture to enslave bourgeois and proletariat alike.[8]

Horkheimer and Adorno celebrated Sade's libertine sexual wantonness that attacks the family, promotes incest, and encourages all sexual activities that generate pleasure without placing boundaries.[9] With the cover of the 1961 paperback edition of his 1955 book *Eros and Civilization*, Herbert Marcuse catapulted to become the cultural hero of the new Left's 1960s sex, drugs, rock-and-roll, anti-war youth movement.[10] The cover of the paperback vibrated in shades of purple with images of naked figures celebrating uninhibited sex. Marcuse argued sex will

---

6 Ibid., pp. 196–202.

7 Max Horkheimer and Theodor W. Adorno, "Juliette or Enlightenment and Morality," in *Dialectical Enlightenment*, 81–119, at p. 86.

8 Jerome R. Corsi, The Truth About Neo-Marxism, Cultural Maoism, and Anarchy, op. cit., p. 199.

9 Stephen Coughlin and Richard Higgins, *Re-Remembering the Mis-Remembered Left: The Left's Strategy and Tactics to Transform America, An Unconstrained Analytics Report* (Washington, DC: Unconstrained Analytics, February 2019), version 1.2, updated July 2019, pp. 82–85.

10 Herbert Marcuse, *Eros and Civilization: A Philosophical Inquiry into Freud* (Boston: Beacon Press, 1955). Pagination in footnotes come from the 1955 edition. See also: Herbert Marcuse, *Eros and Civilization: A Philosophical Inquiry into Freud* (New York: Vintage Books, 1961). First paperback edition of *Eros and Civilization* published in the United States.

transform into eros in the non-repressive civilization.[11] He encouraged "polymorphous sex,"[12] railing against the concept that God created sex for procreation, with marriage defined as a union between one man and one woman. He rejected the concept that the sacred gift of procreation extends into a responsibility of both parents—mother and father—to raise their children in a moral education fully aware of God as the source of all life and well-being.

Serious students of postmodern theory have recognized that schizophrenia, customarily considered a psychological disorder, is the psychological state that best describes the subjective nature of postmodern reality. Catherine Prendergast, a professor of English at the University of Illinois at Urbana-Champaign, realized this in a 2008 article entitled "The Unexceptional Schizophrenic: A Post-Modern Introduction," published in the *Journal of Literary & Cultural Disability Studies*.[13] Prendergast noted that postmodern theory destabilized national progress, social order, and identity narratives. She commented, "Crucial texts of postmodern theory have only achieved these destabilizations by stabilizing one identity: that of the schizophrenic."[14] The Mayo Clinic defines schizophrenia as "a serious mental disorder in which people interpret reality abnormally." The medical center notes that schizophrenia "may result in some combination of hallucinations, delusions, and

---

11 Jerome R. Corsi, *The Truth About Neo-Marxism, Cultural Maoism, and Anarchy*, op. cit., p. 238.

12 Herbert Marcuse, Eros and Civilization: A Philosophical Inquiry into Freud, op. cit., p. 201.

13 Catherine Prendergast, "The Unexceptional Schizophrenic: A Post-Postmodern Introduction," *Journal of Literary & Cultural Disability Studies* 2, no. 1 (2008): 55–62, https://www.liverpooluniversitypress.co.uk/journals/article/48277. The article was also published here: Catherine Prendergast, "The Unexceptional Schizophrenic: A Post-Postmodern Introduction," in Lennard J. Davis, ed., *The Disability Studies Reader* (New York: Routledge, 4th ed., 2013), 236–245. Quotations are identified by page numbers from the publication of Prendergast's paper in this book.

14 Ibid, 236.

extremely disordered thinking and behavior that impairs daily functioning and can be disabling."[15]

The Frankfurt School blended Gramsci and Freud into Marxism, giving birth to Georg Lukács's *aufheben der Kultur* (in English, "negate the culture")[16] admonition to destroy the culture. However, critical theory has brought forth not utopia but a confused, nightmarish world where the "lure of androgyny"[17] is the operating principle. The neo-Marxist critical theory produces a world of ambiguous sexuality in which we discard God, dismantle capitalism, and abandon the monogamous nuclear family. The Hegelian dialectic is an ingenious algorithmic formula for destruction, but the algorithm has no similarly effective counterpoint formula for creation.

* * *

On April 5, 2023, Revolver News published an article entitled "Biden regime just proved once and for all that the US government is the most corrupt organization in the world, and it isn't even close." The article highlighted the Biden administration's Justice Department's decision to prosecute a J6 grandmother who dared pray inside the Capitol. Revolver began the piece as follows:

> Our justice system is a goner. The writing was on the wall the moment Douglass Mackey got a federal prison slot for posting an anti-Hillary meme. Then, seeing J6 patriots branded as domestic terrorists and political prisoners sealed the deal. And when they threw a parade of

---

15 "Schizophrenia: Overview," Mayo Clinic, MayoClinic.org, n.d., https://www.mayoclinic.org/diseases-conditions/schizophrenia/symptoms-causes/syc-20354443.

16 Georg Lukács, *History and Class Consciousness: Studies in Marxist Dialectics*, trans. Rodney Livingstone (Cambridge, MA: MIT Press, 1971).

17 Mary Eberstadt, "The Lure of Androgyny," *Commentary*, October 2019, https://www.commentary.org/articles/mary-eberstadt/the-lure-of-androgyny/.

sham indictments at President Trump, also known as "election interference," well, that was the cherry on top.[18]

Revolver continued:

> The woman affectionately dubbed the "J6 Grandma," Rebecca Lavrenz, found herself in the spotlight for all the wrong reasons. Captured on video praying outside the Capitol on January 6th, she ventured inside for about ten minutes, where she was recorded having a peaceful exchange with a police officer. Yet astonishingly, in what's supposed to be the "land of the free," she was put on trial, found guilty, and now stares down the barrel of federal prison time and up to a quarter-million fines.[19]

Revolver concluded that the US justice system has become hypocritically political in claiming to champion "democracy" and "election integrity." Was it an "insurgency seeking to overthrow a legitimate election" when Democrats complained the Supreme Court decision ended the Florida recount in a manner that denied Vice President Al Gore the presidency to his GOP contender George W. Bush? Revolver continues:

> At seventy-two, this Christian grandmother from Colorado embodies the harsh truth: The United States, for all its lofty claims of moral superiority, operates with a level of tyranny that rivals the most oppressive regimes, all while convincing much of the world it's the bastion of "freedom," brimming with liberty and justice. At least with tyrants in North Korea and similar regimes, the situation is pretty clear-cut; you

---

18 "Biden regime just proved once and for all that the US government is the most corrupt organization in the world, and it isn't even close ..." Revolver.news, April 5, 2024, https://revolver.news/2024/04/biden-regime-just-proved-once-and-for-all-that-the-us-government-is-the-most-corrupt-organization-in-the-world-and-its-not-even-close/.
19 Ibid.

know exactly what you're dealing with. But the US government lays the game with a more cunning and evil twist. It's not just that dissent is crushed and voices silent; it's how it's done—with a wide smile and draped in layers of propaganda so thick, you'd need a shovel to find your way out. This approach makes the US government's tactics not just oppressive but insidiously deceptive. We're the most dangerous kind of villain: the kind that masquerades as a hero.[20]

Even more outrageous is the prosecution under the FACE Act of eighty-seven-year-old Eva Edl, a survivor of a communist concentration camp in Yugoslavia, for daring to stand outside the door of an abortion clinic where she joined others to sing hymns and pray to end abortion in an incident in Tennessee on March 5, 2021. The Freedom of Access to Clinical Entrances Act (FACE Act), 18 U.S.C. Section 248 prohibits any physical obstruction outside an abortion clinic. The relevant text of the FACE Act prohibits anyone "by force or threat of force or by physical obstruction, intentionally injures, intimidates or interferes with or attempts to injure, intimidate or interfere with any person because that person is or has been, or in order to intimidate such person or any other person or class of persons from, obtaining or providing reproductive health services." The *Washington Examiner* reported the following:

> Not Edl, or any of the other activists ever engaged in any violent behavior, they simply sat and stood in the hallway praying and singing. The DOJ [Department of Justice] claims that because a woman saw the group and chose not to enter the clinic, the group obstructed the entrance in violation of the law.[21]

---

20 Ibid.
21 Jeremiah Puff, "A vote for Biden is a vote for the persecution of the pro-life movement," *Washington Examiner*, WashingtonExaminer.com, April 4, 2024, https://www.washingtonexaminer.com/opinion/beltway-confidential/2953100/a-vote-for-joe-biden-is-a-vote-for-the-persecution-of-the-pro-life-movement/.

The *Washington Examiner* article continued to point out the Biden administration's actual purpose in prosecuting Edl:

> The prosecution of Edl and her compatriots is the latest act of vengeful retaliation by the Biden administration for the Supreme Court placing the legality of abortion in the hands of the voters and their elected representatives. Since the *Dobbs* ruling, Biden and his Department of Justice have made persecution of pro-life voices a prosecutorial priority. And in this vile campaign to shut down dissent through politically motivated prosecutors and show trials, Biden has turned the FBI and the Department of Justice into a kind of modern-day Stasi that has more in common with the secret police of communist regimes than the American tradition of law and order.[22]

* * *

Archbishop Viganò has been particularly articulate in his profound understanding of the neo-Marxist war on humanity—a war that aims to silence, restrain, and eradicate Christianity from the face of the earth. In a message delivered on January 2, 2024, to the "Medical Doctors for Covid Ethics" international Zoom meeting participants, Archbishop Viganò made clear that today, we are facing a globalist plan to achieve world depopulation. He said:

> For the past four years we have been witnessing the implementation of a criminal plan of world depopulation, achieved through the creation of a false pandemic and the imposition of a false vaccine, which we now know to be a biological weapon of mass destruction, designed with the aim of destroying the immune system of the entire population, causing sterility and the onset of deadly diseases. Many of our friends

---

22 Ibid.

and acquaintances have died or been severely damaged by the adverse effects of this experimental gene serum. Many have discovered, too late, that they have been the victims of a global plan with a single script under a single direction.[23]

He named the most visible participants in this evil cabal:

What is even more serious is that this neo-Malthusian project of mass extermination, to which is added the will to control each of us through graphene oxide nanostructures, has been announced to us for some time by those in the World Health Organization and the World Economic Forum who conceived and implemented it. The rulers of all Western states, hostage to Bill Gates and Klaus Schwab, have become accomplices to this crime, demonstrating their malice and premeditation by their behavior: falsifying data on alleged infections, doctoring statistics that attribute deaths and adverse effects to Covid-19 but not to the gene serum, prohibiting effective treatments, imposing harmful protocols that have no scientific basis, banning autopsies, and preventing or thwarting accurate reports to health authorities.[24]

Archbishop Viganò continued, arguing that we must bring this evil cabal to justice before international tribunals:

This global coup d'état must be denounced, and those responsible must be tried and judged by an international court. But above all, it is necessary for all of us to understand that this all-out war against humanity

---

23 Archbishop Carlo Maria Viganò, "Message to the participants of the Medical Doctors for Covid Ethics International," ExSurgeDomine.it, January 2, 2024, https://exsurgedomine.it/240103-medical-doctors-eng/.
Archbishop Viganò's message to the Medical Doctors for Covid Ethics International is printed at the back of this book in its entirety as Appendix A.
24 Ibid.

is not motivated only by the lust for wealth and power, but mainly by a religious motive—a *theological* reason. This reason is Satan's hatred: hatred of God, hatred of God's Creation, and hatred of man, who is created in the Image and Likeness of God. Bill Gates, Klaus Schwab, George Soros, and the hundreds of servants whom they blackmail in governments all hate God. They hate life, which only God can give. They hate love, which comes only from God. They hate peace, which can reign only where Christ reigns. As Tucker Carlson said a few days ago, we are facing people who serve Satan and the demons of hell, just as normal people worship and serve God. [25]

Archbishop Viganò concluded with the confidence that in the end, God always wins:

> This, then, is a battle in which body and soul, matter and spirit are made the object of a mortal attack by men and spiritual powers. But let us not forget that, if our enemy avails himself of the help of infernal spirits, we have on our side the Lord God of the armies arrayed—Dominus Deus Sabaoth—and all the hosts of Angels and Saints, infinitely more powerful. God is Almighty: let us never forget that. And He is Father: He does not abandon His children in times of trial.[26]

What the globalists forget is that God is sovereign. The final act of this dark end-days drama has already been written. In the end, God always wins—and God will win here too!

Truthfully, *in the final analysis*, God has already won. God is sovereign here and everywhere, now and for all eternity. Satan is doomed to lose.

As rightly said in the Latin Mass of the Catholic Church: *"Erat in*

---

25 Ibid.
26 Ibid.

Principio et Nunc, et Semper, et in Saecula Seculorum" [*"He Was in the Beginning, Is Now, and Always Will Be, onto the Age of the Ages"*].

In the spirit of 2 Chronicles 7–14, please join me in getting down on my knees and asking God to forgive us for letting this godless woke insanity reign. God has given us the opportunity of an historic Great Awakening. If we commit ourselves to a global revival, God will do the heavy lifting of locking Satan back within the confines of Hell where evil belongs.

PART I:
THE WAR ON HUMANITY

CHAPTER 1

TRANSGENDER DAY OF VISIBILITY

All humanity is awakening from a slumber that has lasted far too long.
—Archbishop Carlo Maria Viganò, Declaration, Easter,
March 31, 2024[27]

In 2024, Easter fell on March 31. Easter is considered the most sacred of days—the day celebrating Jesus Christ's Resurrection. In Christianity, Easter is the defining moment that proves Jesus's divinity. "He has Risen!" is celebrated worldwide as proof that our existence on Earth is not the end. If there is an afterlife, as Jesus proved, our behavior here has consequences for what is to come.

Since 2009, March 31 has been pre-designated to be an annual global celebration of a day known as the "Transgender Day of Visibility," commonly abbreviated "TDOV." Psychotherapist Rachel Crandall-Crocker, noted for founding the 501(c)3 nonprofit group Transgender Michigan in 1997, created TDOV.[28] Like many "woke" secular dog-

---

27 Archbishop Carlo Maria Viganò, "Dichiarazione Del 31 Marzo 2024," ExSurgeDomine.it, https://exsurgedomine.it/240331-biden-ita/. In English, see: Archbishop Carlo Maria Viganò, "Statement of March 31, 2024, on the scandalous proclamation of March 31 as 'Transgender visibility day' by 'president' Joe Biden," ExSurgeDomine.it, https://exsurgedomine.it/240331-biden-eng/.
28 TDOV: https://www.transgendermichigan.org

mas, comprehending this peculiar neo-Marxist ideology demands an excursion into language perversion. "Why would transgenders need a day of visibility?' we ask. The answer is simple. Transgender sex has traditionally been considered a sexual perversion best reserved for the shadows of society. But today, a "day of visibility" means transgenders are now encouraged to display publicly their sexual preference fetish, regardless how bizarre. The point of the exercise goes beyond normalizing men who wear dresses and women of male sexuality. A day of transgender visibility demands we see and celebrate transgenders who are encouraged to act out publicly on this "Day of Visibility." The woke demand to consider transgender sex as normal goes even beyond celebration. Those of us who fail to celebrate the unique and privileged nature of transgender sexual attraction are not just politically incorrect. In woke moral terms, those of us who see transgender sex as sinful are the ones who have acted unjustly. We must now say "transgender persons" to acknowledge we embrace transgender sex. At the same time, any verbalization that characterizes transgender sex as a psychological disorder is a "hate crime," making the person who utters such thoughts subject to criminal prosecution.

On Saturday, March 30, 2024, the day before Easter, Biden himself went to a microphone to make a national announcement proclaiming that this year, on Easter, we would honor not only the lesbians, gays, and bisexuals designated in the acronym "LGBT," but transgenders. Biden said:

> On Transgender Day of Visibility, we honor the extraordinary courage and contributions of transgender Americans and reaffirm our Nation's commitment to forming a more perfect Union—where all people are created equal and treated equally throughout their lives. I am proud that my Administration has stood for justice from the start, working to

ensure that the LGBTQI+ community can live openly, in safety, with dignity and respect.[29]

Biden said, "I, Joseph R. Biden, Jr., president of the United States of America, by virtue of the authority vested in me by the Constitution and laws of the United States, do hereby proclaim March 31, 2024, as Transgender Day of Visibility."[30] Biden's address made no mention of Jesus Christ or his resurrection. In a world that celebrates TDOV, we Christians are the ones who must hide in the shadows.

Former Papal Nuncio for the USA, Archbishop Carlo Maria Viganò, a Catholic critic of Pope Francis and a spiritual force against godless woke insanity, was quick to take notice. In a proclamation issued on Easter day, Archbishop Viganò said the following:

> The word Apocalypse, in Greek, means unveiling, revelation. This revelation in Sacred Scripture concerns, first and foremost, the objective reality of Good and Evil, that is, the collective awareness of the ongoing war between God and Satan, between the children of Light and the children of darkness.
>
> The unprecedented and scandalous proclamation of March 31 as 'Transgender Visibility Day' by self-styled US President Joe Biden—who dares to proclaim himself a Catholic—constitutes a most serious offense to God and to millions of Catholics and Christians in America and around the world, before which it is impossible to react with due firmness.[31]

---

29 "A Proclamation on Transgender Day of Visibility, 2024," White House, WhiteHouse.gov, March 29, 2024, https://www.whitehouse.gov/briefing-room/presidential-actions/2024/03/29/a-proclamation-on-transgender-day-of-visibility-2024/.
30 John Levine, "Biden slammed over proclamation that Easter Sunday is 'Transgender Day of Visibility' as Trump calls for president to 'issue an apology,'" *New York Post*, NYPost.com, March 30, 2024,
31 Archbishop Carlo Maria Viganò, "Statement of March 31, 2024, on the scandalous proclamation of March 31 as 'Transgender visibility day' by 'president' Joe Biden," op. cit.

Biden's proclamation made clear that in this world of "woke sensibility," Christians no longer have the religious freedom to characterize transgender sexual activity as sinful behavior violating God's law. Suddenly, we Christians who abhor transgender sex are bigots whom law enforcement has a right to silence. In this world of "through the looking glass" reality, transgender sex rules. Woke moral reversal demands that Joe Biden proclaim Easter as TDOV without mentioning Jesus Christ or his Resurrection.

Archbishop Viganò urged the immediate excommunication of President Biden from the Catholic Church. He proclaimed, "I call on Catholics and all Christians to pray that, on this solemn Easter Day, the Risen Lord will have mercy on the United States of America and put an end to the onslaught of the infernal forces unleashed today more than ever."[32]

Satanic Androgyny

We should not be surprised that woke sexual ideology demands that Biden replace Jesus Christ at Easter with TDOV celebrating transexuals. Viewing LGBT as a sexual deviance hierarchy, "T" stands for transexuals as an advanced stage of sexual perversion. Fundamental to the attack of male and female sex understood as a binary duality is the concept of the androgyny.

In the occult Hermetic teachings of the Kabbalah, known as "black magic," transgenderism plays a central role. Lucifer is portrayed as a grotesque androgynous combination, as suggested by the tarot card number fifteen, "The Devil." Éliphas Lévi described Baphomet and transcendental magic in his 1854 book *Dogme et Rituel de la Haute Magie* (in English, *Dogma and Ritual of High Magic*)[33] and his 1860

---

32 Ibid.
33 Éliphas Lévi, *Transcendental Magic, Its Doctrine and Ritual: A Complete Translation of "Dogme et Ritual de la Haute Magie,"* with a Bibliographical Preface, trans. Arthur Edward Waite (London: George Redway, 1896).

book *Histoire de la Magie* (in English, *History of Magic*).[34] Lévi portrayed the Kabbalistic Satan as Baphomet, the androgynous "Goat of Mendes." In Kabbalistic lore, Baphomet is a grotesquely androgynous figure, represented as a male humanoid with a goat's head, the wings of a bat, and a woman's breasts. In both books, Lévi explained that the doctrine of transcendental magic involved an initiation into Satanism that confers on humans the occult knowledge of good and evil. The result is that the initiated receive superhuman powers.[35]

John R. Clarke, a professor of art history at the University of Texas at Austin, in his 1998 book *Looking at Lovemaking: Constructions of Sexuality in Roman Art 100 B.C.—A.D. 250*, notes that the ancient Greek and Roman god Hermaphroditus was a combination of male and female sexes joined together in one person, creating an androgynous male-female unity. "Hermaphroditus is biologically both sexes at once and forever, a sign of gender confusion," he wrote.[36]

Occult transcendental black magic is at the heart of Lucifer's promise to Adam and Eve in the Garden of Eden that eating the apple would convey the secret of good and evil. The twisted subtheme of the serpent in the garden is that the God of the Bible is an "oppressive God" who wanted to keep humanity in obedient ignorance.[37] The serpent claims to be the true savior of humanity, offering enlightenment if only Adam and Eve disobey God. Unlocking the secret knowledge of good and evil in occult transcendental magic produces the androgynous utopian

---

34 Éliphas Lévi (Alphonse Louis Constant), *The History of Magic: Including a Clear and Precise Exposition of Its Rites and Mysteries*, trans. Arthur Edward Waite (London: Rider & Co., 1913).

35 This paragraph and the next four paragraphs are drawn from my previous book: Jerome R. Corsi, *The Truth About Neo-Marxism, Cultural Maoism, and Anarchy*, op. cit., pp. 286–287.

36 John R. Clarke, *Looking at Lovemaking: Constructions of Sexuality in Roman Art 100 B.C.—A.D. 250* (Berkeley, CA: University of California Press, 1998), p. 49.

37 Ken Ammi, The Occult Roots of Postgenderism: And a History of Changes to Psychiatry and Psychology (Self-Published, freethinker.com, 2017), p. 5.

union of opposites. For Hermetic Kabbalists and Frankfurt School atheists, we can only accomplish this feat of transcendental magic by venturing into the secret of good and evil that demands the dialectical negation of all dualities.

The transhuman condition is presumed to involve evolving a transcended consciousness beyond good and evil. Artificial intelligence to merge the human mind will endow the transhuman with the thinking power of quantum computing. In this elevated state, transhumans can aspire to achieve permanent life extension, robotic machines doing the menial manual labor necessary for daily living. Transhumans experiencing reality in a metaverse will create subjective utopias by applying their particular value judgments to produce their specific pleasures, fulfilling all carnal desires, regardless of how base. But how do we unlock that secret?

As noted earlier, the key that unlocks the occult secret for Marcuse is polymorphous-perverse sexuality in the here-and-now, or for Wilhelm Reich, the peak experience of orgasmic ecstasy. Through the Marquis de Sade's perverse sex, as Horkheimer and Adorno suggested, we unlock the door to good and evil, giving birth to Postgenderism (i.e., the state where gender is self-determined and infinitely variable).[38] If there are no limits on polymorphous sex, is it possible the progression of lesbian, gay, bisexual, and transgender could extend the hierarchy of perversion ultimately to include pedophilia, bestiality, cannibalistic rituals cooking and consuming babies, sadomasochistic sex culminating in snuff films, chains, whips, bondage, etc., finally ending in necrophilia? Will these dark fetishes also come out of the shadows? If we ever reach the point of normalizing necrophilia, sex as procreation will have transformed into masturbation with death. Is this Satan's end goal, to have the life force

---

38 I explore these concepts more thoroughly in "The Lure of Androgny," in *The Truth About Neo-Marxism, Cultural Maoism, and Anarchy,* op. cit., pp. 280–287, at pp. 286–287.

that God has bestowed to us devolve into a force that reaches sexual pleasure embracing death?

The sexual mutilation of gender-confused youth is already exhibiting itself in our public schools, as is the transgender story hour for preschool toddlers. Only a few years ago, it was hard to imagine pedophilia and child pornography woud become normalized. But already the woke language perversion recasts pedophiles with a patina of legitimacy by branding pedophiles as "minor attracted persons." Today monster pedophiles who conceptualize themselves as "minor-attracted adults" achieve their peak sexual experience by sexualizing children who have no comprehension of sex because they have not reached the age of puberty. Transgender predators justify destroying the innocence of youth with transexual gender performance and accompanying language perversion that reaches peak sexual experience by conducting preschool story hours. Once we open the pandora's box by normalizing what previous generations. have considered to be sexual perversions, where do we stop?

The postmodern abandon to libertine sexuality eschews the end goal of progenerating. Instead, the goal is to give rebirth to ourselves as transcendent, self-actualized Nietzschean *Übermensch* (in English, "above man," or, more commonly, "superhuman") beyond good and evil. In the Frankfurt School's occult neo-Marxism, Horkheimer, Adorno, Marcuse, and Reich stand united that God plays no role in transforming human beings into Nietzschean *Übermensch*. Polymorphic-perverse sex is the transformative secret sauce required to bring forth in history Kant and Hegel's triumph of spirit in which the transhuman Nietzschean *Übermensch* actualizes God.

The neo-Marxists of the Frankfurt School embraced Lucifer's agenda "to corrupt and debauch God's children through the merging of opposites so that at Christ's second advent, none of them are found fit for God's eternal family household."[39] Lucifer, the "Bearer of Light," is worshiped as the Divine Androgyne on the principle that we can perfect human nature on Earth once we resolve to transcend good and evil, fully embracing the godless, transhuman, transgender, transracial, transnational new world order.

Marketing Sexual Deviance

The LGBT+ community generally regards June 28, 1969, when the New York Police Department raided the Stonewall Inn, a gay bar in Greenwich Village, as the day the queer revolt started. The five days of rioting that followed the NYPD raid led to a game-changing strategy in which angry gays and lesbians decided to come out of the closet to fight mainstream American disdain. However, a sober reflection on the consequences of LGBT+ aggression led thoughtful gays and lesbians to realize that a violent approach to traditional scorn was doomed to failure. Gay rights activists Marshall Kirk and Hunter Madsen, PhD, laid bare their strategic thinking in their 1989 book entitled *After the Ball: How America Will Conquer Its Fear and Hatred of Gays in the 90's.*[40] Kirk and Madsen wrote:

> Unfortunately, solving your problems with your fists, though exhilarating, is ill advised unless your fists are awfully big indeed. An eight-hundred-pound gorilla sits wherever it wants; we, however, are not seen

---

39 Steve Barwick, "Lucifer: The Divine Androgyne, Ancient God of the Modern Transgender Movement," Have Ye Not Read? an independent Christian Bible study ministry unaffiliated with any church or denomination, HaveYeNotRead.com, no date, https://haveyenotread.com/wp-content/uploads/2018/04/Lucifer-the-Divine-Androgyne-Ancient-God-of-the-Modern-Transgender-Movement.pdf.
40 Marshall Kirk and Hunter Madsen, PhD, *After the Ball: How America Will Conquer Its Fear and Hatred of Gays in the 90's* (New York: Doubleday, 1989). I explored the marketing of LGBTQ+ sexual behavior more thoroughly in my previous book on the American Civil Liberties Union. See: Jerome R. Corsi, *Bad Aamaritans: The ACLU's Relentless Campaign to Erase Faith from the Public Square* (Nashville, TN: Thomas Nelson, 2013), pp. 150–152.

as eight-hundred-pound gorillas. Rather, we're seen by straights as a submicroscopic population of puny freaks, and for us to raise our fists on TV and shout, "You'd better give us our rights or else!" can elicit only amusement and disgust.[41]

"It's time to learn from Madison Avenue, to roll out the big guns," Kirk and Madsen continued. "*Gays must launch a large-scale campaign—we've called it the Waging Peace campaign—to reach straights through the mainstream media.* We're talking about propaganda."[42] Citing Sigmund Freud's observation that "Groups are subject to the truly magical power of words," Kirk and Madsen urged gays to talk about homosexuality openly, often, and positively. Under the principle that constant talk builds the impression that public opinion is divided and that a sizable block accepts or even practices homosexuality, they advised, "The main thing is to *talk about gayness until the issue becomes thoroughly tiresome.*"[43] They suggested that gays should portray themselves as victims in need of protection "so straights will be inclined by reflex to adopt the role of protector."[44] They urged that the message be kept simple—gay rights—calculating that potential protectors needed to perceive that homosexuals had a just cause.

They wrote:

In Conversion, the bigot, who holds a very negative stereotypic picture, is repeatedly exposed to literal picture/label pairs. In magazines, and on billboards and TV, of gays—explicitly labeled as such!—who not only don't look like his picture of a homosexual, but are carefully selected to look either like the bigot and his friends, or like any one of

---

41 Ibid., p. 140.
42 Ibid., p. 162. Italics in original.
43 Ibid., p. 178.
44 Ibid., p. 183.

his other stereotypes of all-right guys—the kind of people he already likes and admires. This image must, of necessity, be carefully tailored to be free of absolutely every element of the widely held stereotypes of how 'faggots' look, dress and sound. He—or she—must not be too well or fashionably dressed; must not be too handsome—that is, mustn't look like a model—or too well groomed. The image must be that of an icon of normality—a good beginning would be to take a long look at Coors beer and Three Musketeers candy commercials. Subsequent ads can branch out from that solid basis to include really adorable, athletic teenagers, kindly grandmothers, avuncular policemen, *ad infinitem.*[45]

Kirk and Madsen were merely following Edward Bernays's transformation that began with his 1928 book *Propaganda: The Public Mind in the Making*[46] and ended with his turning the pejorative term "propaganda" into a much more acceptable term, culminating in his 1952 book *Public Relations.*[47] Following Bernays's advice, Kirk and Madsen resolved to engage in the psychological legerdemain that takes language perversion to an entirely new level. They decided to employ Bernays's ideas to create a "public mind" desensitized to the point where the LGBT+ community could convert hatred into acceptance, with the goal of normalizing LGBT+ sexual performances. Doing so, Kirk and Madsen knew they were lying.

Predictably, Kirk and Madsen justified their lying:

The objection will be raised—and raised, and raised—that we would "Uncle Tommify" the gay community; that we are exchanging one false stereotype for another equally false; that our ads are lies; that that is *not*

---

45 Ibid., p. 154.
46 Edward L. Bernays, *Propaganda: The Public Mind in the Making* (New York: Horace Liveright Inc., 1928).
47 Edward L. Bernays, *Public Relations* (Norman, OK: University of Oklahoma Press, 1952).

how *all* gays actually look; that gays know it, and bigots know it. Yes, of course—we know it, too. But it makes no difference that the ads are lies; not to us, because we're using them to ethically good effect, to counter negative stereotypes that are every bit as much lies, and far more wicked ones; not to bigots, because the ads will have little effect on them whether they believe them or not.[48]

Kirk and Madsen fully understood the power of this particular lie. "In Conversion, we take the bigot's good feelings about all-right guys, and attach them to the label 'gay,' either weakening or eventually, replacing his bad feelings toward the label and the prior stereotype," they explained.[49]

The authors presented a "portfolio of pro-gay advertising."[50] They criticized one ad because "it showcases a couple that reinforces an unappealing stereotype—suggesting, perhaps, two leathery old dykes from tobacco road who bark at each other with gin-cracked voices, and who first met at a motorcycle roundup."[51] Another ad—this one showing two gay male sailors in uniform locked in an intimate kiss—the authors criticized because instead of "offering potential friends the ideal of Love as a just cause worth defending, this ad offers the ideal of Gay Lust, which isn't half so compelling or legitimate to straights. Overall, the ad's effect is not to desensitize, jam, or convert: it merely reinforces revulsion and inflames homo hatred. Not recommended."[52] An ad the authors liked showed a photo of a gay man smiling. The ad, captioned "Someone You'd Like to Know," was scored positively for employing the following strategy: "Strategy: *Conversion.* Compensate

---

48 Marshall Kirk and Hunter Madsen, PhD., After the Ball: How America Will Conquer Its Fear and Hatred of Gays in the 90's, op.cit., p. 154.
49 Ibid., p. 155.
50 Ibid, Part 5 of the book, beginning at p. 215.
51 Ibid., page 232-233.
52 Ibid., page 230-231.

straights' lack of familiarity with gay people by presenting them with 'solid citizens'—likable individuals who defy uncomplimentary stereotypes. The interviewee talks about his conventional gay life in a relaxed, low-key, matter-of-fact way, undercutting several myths as he talks."[53]

The public relations strategy the authors proposed carefully avoided any explicit discussion of what sexual practices gays, lesbians, bisexuals, and transgender individuals want us to view as normal. Explicit presentations of actual LGBT+ sexual practices would risk offending a majority heterosexual audience by providing too much information. Instead, the authors merely advise against a list of rather explicitly discussed behaviors they characterize as "homosexual misbehaviors"[54]— practices that range from aggressive homosexual sex displayed in public to openly practiced homosexual promiscuity involving multiple partners and seemingly little or no emotional attachment. "Self-indulgent, self-destructive behavior is lamentable enough when it occurs, so to speak, 'within the family,' but when Brother Gay trots out his unsavory shenanigans for the consumption of the general public, the rest of us are dragged down with him," the authors admonished.[55] However, a successful public relations campaign professionally managed with the right messages properly delivered, Kirk and Madsen envisioned, could not only turn public opinion positive toward homosexuality but also prove lucrative in the process. "If the ads project a new, resolutely positive, all-American image with which most gays can identify, we think that, in no time, millions will be so eager to perpetuate these good works that they'll begin to donate money to our appeals on TV

---

53 Ibid., pages 244–245. Italics in original. This and the following paragraph are drawn from my previous book *Bad Samaritans: The ACLU's Relentless Campaign to Erase Faith from the Public Square*, op. cit., pp. 129–158, at pp. 150–152.
54 Ibid., pp. 312–332.
55 Ibid., page 307.

as though their social salvation depended on it. Which it does," the authors advised with great anticipation.[56]

How we got from accepting lesbians, gays, and bisexuals to the significant leap of accepting transexual gender performances involves understanding the influence of the Frankfurt School that sought to combine Freud with Marx to create a sexual revolution designed to erase all boundaries. Pornography today presents beautiful "women" exposing their male sexual organs, as well as older adults cozying up to intentionally seductive, sexually advanced, underage children. Simply normalizing LGBT+ sex was not sufficient to get to this point. What was necessary was to abolish the traditional definitions and boundaries subconsciously built into our traditional paradigm understandings of "male" and "female."

Queer Critical Theory

The celebration of transexual behavior traces back to Judith Butler's seminal 1990 book, *Gender Trouble: Feminism and the Subversion of Identity*.[57] Butler distinguished that sex and gender were two different terms with separate meanings. For Butler, "sex" was a biological term that specified whether a person was born with male or female sex organs. However, "gender" was a cultural term that traditionally divided people into "male" and "female" categories. Butler rebelled against all "binary" designations. She questioned what a woman was for herself and others. Butler insisted that "gender" could only be determined by how a person performs in sex. Butler emphasized that gender involved a spectrum of possible sexual orientations.

In the convoluted prose typical of postmodern critical theory, Butler writes: "Assuming for the moment the stability of binary sex, it does

---

56 Ibid., page 263.
57 Judith Butler, *Gender Trouble: Feminism and the Subversion of Identity* (New York: Rutledge, 1990).

not follow that the construction of 'men' will accrue exclusively to the bodies of males or that 'women' will interpret only female bodies."[58] Thus, for Butler, the particular nature of a person's sexual inclinations as performed in sexual activity is what defines a person's gender, regardless of whether their sex is male or female. In the postmodern world, subjective perception determines "right" and "wrong." To Butler, all statements point to the nearly infinite ability of humans to decide on their sexual identity. In a world where all judgments of right and wrong are relative, there can be no God. The concept of God implies natural right and natural law—a set of fixed rules by which reality functions. Arguments proceeding from moral relativism lose the ability to assert certain sexual activities must remain taboo because they violate fundamental human rights. Atheistic moral relativism reaches a new plateau where there is no God to bestow inalienable human rights. If life has no meaning or inherent value, than why should sexual acts that harm or kill another person be forbidden?

When we add the critical theory concept of "intersectionality," Butler's concept of gender becomes unlimited. In set theory, intersectionality involves overlapping sets. Thus, in set theory, if the set of race grievances overlaps the set of gender grievances, a black woman transexual has doubled their intersectional grievance score. If the transsexual black woman was born in a colonial country, she adds one more discrimination to her intersectionality score. So, if a black colonial transexual woman conceptualizes "their" sex as feline, animal gender performance is added to the intersectionality score. In traditional psychology, such thinking would be characterized as schizophrenic.

DEI: Malware of the Brain

In critical queer theory, compounding an initial confusion about sex

---

58 Ibid., p. 9.

and gender demands a dizzying list of discriminations that can elevate a person's value in the hierarchy of the oppressed. The result is that pronouns like "he" and "she" no longer apply. Instead, we have to invent a new pronoun language to avoid committing a microaggression, the ultimate critical race theory sin in a world that demands we avoid gender-bound pronouns relating to male and female sex organs. Then we encounter the woke demand for DEI (diversity, equity, and inclusion). The DEI standard demands that we give positions of privilege, including admission to schools and employment, according to the dictates of identity politics, while disregarding the person's qualification to attend the school or do the job. With a nearly infinite array of sexually bizarre identities created when the concept of intersectionality is applied to gender uncertainty, how could all genders possibly be represented among those admitted as students or accepted for employment?

When we understand this, we realize the goal of DEI was never to achieve full inclusion in a world of infinitely possible schizophrenic sexual identities. The goal was to degrade education and employment by applying an identity standard to override ability qualifications. Finally, we are forced to remember that the goal of neo-Marxism and cultural Maoism is to destroy the traditional order to replace it with a new world order conceptualized as a transhuman utopia.

Thus, the inevitable conclusion is that DEI standards were created to destroy educational institutions and to degrade the employment environment. Those demons who first conceptualized DEI knew what they were doing. We have now appointed to the Supreme Court a judge who evidently does not know what a woman is. Why should we be surprised when the Supreme Court decisions start throwing out decades of "equal rights" legal precedents in favor of DEI privileges? In a US Navy where a transgender admiral wears a dress, why should we be startled that West Point has now changed the curriculum to teach the cadets "Uniformed Perspectives: The Evolution of Cross-Dressing in the Military and Gender Norms"?[59] We have to wonder whether the woke cross-dressing Pentagon is planning to defend the nation by conducting a transgender parade down Fifth Avenue in New York City.

Lost in this gender confusion is the elevated status Christianity gives women in that all humans are born from the womb. Yet, not to be refuted, critical gender theory insists men can menstruate, conceive babies, and lactate to nourish their children. The National Health Service in Great Britain has adopted gender-neutral terms to avoid offending woke patients. So, "chestfeeding" has been substituted for "breastfeeding" and "breast milk" has become "human milk." The NHS asking men if they are pregnant before they get an X-ray or MRI has become standard for an NHS seeking to be "inclusive, respectful, and relevant." Menopause is no longer when a woman stops having a period; in woke-speak, menopause has become "when *your* periods stop." Mothers and fathers are now "birthing parents." Ovarian cancer is no longer referred to as "one of the most common causes of cancer in women." Instead, the NHS now explains that "anyone with ovaries can get ovarian cancer."[60] The result is that women are being quietly removed from woke medicine, just as transgender men seek to dominate traditional women's sports. Archbishop Viganó is correct: as Satan hates life which only God can give, Satan hates women because all human life births through women.

As noted, all neo-Marxist creations are created to be destructive. If we

---

59 Jim Hoft, "US Military Academy Introduces Woke Curriculum Courses on Deconstructing Patriotism, Cross-Dressing in the Military, Gender Norms, and Representation in the Ranks," Gateway Pundit, GatewayPundit.com, May 5, 2024, https://www.thegatewaypundit.com/2024/05/us-military-academy-introduces-woke-curriculum-courses-deconstructing/.

60 John Ely, "From 'chestfeeding' to 'human milk' and 'birthing PARENTS': How NHS language is going woke—with women quietly being scrubbed out of 'inclusive' advice pages,'" *Daily Mail*, DailyMail.co.uk, July 1, 2022, https://www.dailymail.co.uk/health/article-10968271/How-NHS-language-going-woke-quietly-scrubbing-women-inclusive-advice-pages.html.

apply the Biblical standard of judging a tree by knowing its fruits, woke critical theory is malware of the brain. Once a brain is infected by woke ideology, the brain's everlasting confusion prevails. The woke brain malware makes the human mind malfunction. The output becomes verbal garbage as the brain goes into endless confusing language loops that create a metaverse in which women cease to exist as such. Men become she-men wearing dresses to cover their penises. The Kirk/Madsen propaganda reduces to dribble once tampons are put into restrooms for men. What type of surgeon performs a sex change operation when the man in question assumes a feline feminine identity? Veterinarians are trained to neuter animals, not to make male cats into female cats. But woke is right on target when the brain malware neuters the ability of a person to think logically or behave productively. Contemplating this sexual mish-mash, we are forced to realize the point of creating queer critical theory was to end procreation, not to foster it.

The Sexual Mutilation of Children

In woke lingo, transgender and gender-nonconforming (abbreviated TGNC) youth who suffer from "gender dysphoria" are prime targets for the LGBTQ+ acolytes who dominate public education as "teachers." Labeled as "gender-affirming care," hormone blockers may start being administered at the onset of puberty, which can begin around age ten to eleven years. The University of California, San Francisco's (UCSF) "Transgender Care" webpage lists a number of "gender-affirming" surgical procedures. UCSF notes:

> Transgender people may seek any one of a number of gender-affirming interventions, including hormone therapy, surgery, facial hair removal, interventions for the modification of speech and communication, and behavioral adaptations such as genital tucking or packing, or chest

binding. All of these procedures have been defined as medically necessary by the World Professional Association for Transgender Health.[61]

Among the gender-affirming surgical interventions the UCSF transgender care website recommends for changing male sexual organs to female sexual organs, and vice versa are:

1. feminizing vaginoplasty, i.e., the removal of the penis, scrotal sac, and testes to create a vagina and vulva (including mons, labia, clitoris, and urethral opening)[62]; and
2. masculinizing phalloplasty/scrotoplasty, i.e., the removal of all or part of the vagina in a vaginectomy, the creation of a scrotum in a scrotoplasty, and the placement of testicular prostheses, along with increasing the length of the clitoris in a metoidioplasty to create a penis via phalloplasty.[63]

Sex change operations are further complicated by the need to eliminate breasts or create breasts, the removal or addition of facial hair, and any number of other adjustments which, in the world before woke, made a man masculine and a woman female.

The complications of reengineering the human body are enormous. The male and female internal organs, not just the obvious sexual apparatus,

---

61 Madeline B. Deutsch, M.D., MPH, "Overview of gender-affirming treatments and procedures," University of California, San Francisco, UCSF Transgender Care & Treatment Guidelines, TransCare.UCSF.edu, June 17, 2016, https://transcare.ucsf.edu /guidelines/overview#:~:text=Surgical%20interventions&text=Surgeries%20specific%20 to%20transgender%20populations,enlargement%2C%20may%20include%20 urethral%20lengthening.
62 "What is the procedure for vaginoplasty?" Denver Health, DenverHealth.org, no date, https://www.denverhealth.org/conditions/v/vaginoplasty#:~:text=Vaginoplasty%20 is%20a%20gender%2Daffirming,penis%2C%20scrotal%20sac%20and%20testes.
63 "Masculinizing surgery," Mayo Clinic, MayoClinic.org, no date, https://www.mayoclinic .org/tests-procedures/masculinizing-surgery/about/pac-20385105#:~:text=Surgery%20 to%20remove%20all%20or,create%20a%20penis%2C%20called%20phalloplasty.

differ in many fundamental ways. Removing a penis to create a vagina or creating a penis from tissue removed from the arm while enlarging the clitoris fail to address the fundamentally different ways a male and female body operate. It should be obvious, but God did not build men to grow babies in wombs, nor did God create women to inject sperm. But to the woke-mind virus, these biological fundamentals are irrelevant. What's relevant is that with proper encouragement, a ten-year-old child can be made to feel confused about their gender. This confusion is probably predictable when transgender story hour masters begin explaining to preschoolers that parents of this girl are both men, and the parents of that boy are both women, or the parents of all the boys and girls in LGBT+ "marriages" are suffering from gender dysphoria their "children" must certainly feel.

Not only are gender-affirming and gender-transitioning medical interventions expensive, but surgical interventions are also generally irreversible. We should not be surprised that 82 percent of transgender individuals have considered killing themselves, while 40 percent have attempted suicide, with the suicide rates highest among youth.[64] But again, we should not be confused. The truthful goal in sexually mutilating youth is obviously to create sexual monsters who would never be able to produce children. Remember: Satan hates life. The point of the woke sexual mutilation mind virus is that those fetuses lucky enough to escape abortion get to enter an evil world where demons convince them to alter their sex organs such that they will never be able to reproduce. Born trusting that adults are there to nourish them, sexually innocent children go to kindergarten and elementary school only to find queer demons supervising them as teachers and principals, waiting to grab their young souls with evil sexual intent. In the Satanic cult

---

64 Ashley Austin, et. al., "Suicidality Among Transgender Youth: Elucidating the Role of Interpersonal Risk Factors," *Journal of Interpersonal Violence*, Volume 37, Number 5–6, (March 2022), https://pubmed.ncbi.nlm.nih.gov/32345113/.

of queer critical theory, the real purpose of transitioning ideology is to transform bright life-bearing children into confused, suicidal perverts. Brainwashed to mutilate themselves sexually, our children turn themselves into he-she or she-he Frankensteins incapable of procreating.

Without Parental Consent

> The idea that children are the property of the state repulses every human person. In the Christian social order, the civil authority exercises its power to guarantee its citizens that the natural well-being is ordered toward the spiritual good. The common good pursued by the state in temporal things therefore has a well-defined object that cannot and must not be in conflict with the Law of God, the Supreme Legislator. Every time that the State infringes on this eternal and immutable Law, its authority is diminished, and its citizens ought to refuse to obey it.
> —Archbishop Carlo Maria Viganò, "Letter to Mothers: Against Globalist Dictatorship," August 15, 2020[65]

When we venture into the morass of state law, we find California law (SB-107, signed into law by Governor Gavin Newsom in 2022) to be the most permissive. Under California law, a judge may terminate the custody of parents if a child shows up in California seeking gender transition treatments without parental knowledge. So, under this law, a child from another state who flees or is transported to California can even get gender reassignment surgery without the knowledge or consent of the parents. The effect of this law is to give California jurisdiction over the parental rights to determine medical care for their minor children in all fifty states.[66] What is at stake here is the right of parents to control the

---

65 Archbishop Carlo Maria Viganò, "Letter to Mothers: Against Globalist Dictatorship," August 15, 2020, in Archbishop Carlo Maria Viganò, Brian M. McCall, ed., *A Voice in the Wilderness* (Brooklyn, NY: Angelico Press, 2021), pp. 300–309, at. p. 302.
66 Family Freedom Project, "California Law Would Help Children Get Gender Transition Surgery Without Parental Consent," FamilyFreedomProject.org, no date, https://familyfreedomproject.org/ca-law-would-help-children-get-gender-transition-surgery/#:~:text=Under%20this%20law%2C%20a%20child,the%20child's%20 parents%20back%20home.

medical care given their minor children. At the most extreme, queer critical theory ideologues would insist that children desiring gender-affirming medical care, including gender transition surgery, need to be protected by the state from parents who do not understand the need of nonbinary and transgender children to determine their own sexuality. This premise negates the natural right God bestowed upon parents to bear the primary responsibility for raising their children with a moral education. Children under the age of thirteen lack the development of a mature mind that can evaluate the health risks of hormone therapy and the irreversible physical damage inherent to transition surgery.

Not satisfied with driving God out of the public schools, queer critical theorists seek to replace the right of parents to raise their children with a state whose stated intention is to create an environment for children in which nonbinary and transexual desires to transition gender are the norm—the rights held to be inviolate to the point where parents have no say in the state's ability to brainwash their emotionally vulnerable and sexually innocent children into making decisions in the early years of life to poison and disfigure themselves in a manner that physically and psychologically dooms futures a moral education could have saved. In this twisted Satanic world of gender confusion, how many Christian parents will think twice about birthing children the state may rip from their arms to sexually confuse and abuse?

Conclusion: Orgasm with the Dead

We are well served to ponder why Imperial Rome, a nation that established an empire unequaled in antiquity, converted to Christianity after Constantine's mystical experience before the Battle of the Milvian Bridge in 312 AD. Among the many possible answers, we must appreciate that Christianity survived brutal persecutions before Constantine legalized Christianity in the Edict of Milan in 313 AD. I have always believed that the spiritual power that allowed Christianity to flourish in the dark was the power of mothers determined to protect their children. After up to nine months of pregnancy, a difficult and painful childbirth, and several years of caring for born children unable as infants to care for themselves, ancient Roman mothers were loath to see pagan monsters pervert their children for sexual pleasure. In his "Letter to Mothers: Against Global Dictatorship," Archbishop Viganò appears to have come to the same conclusion. There he wrote: "Dear mothers, never fail in your duty to protect your children not only in the material order but also, even more important, in the spiritual order."[67]

That the Transgender Day of Visibility should supplant Easter as the celebration of Christ's Resurrection makes clear that the evil globalist cabal understands the importance of destroying the traditional family to the achievement of their dystopian, Satanic goals. We conclude this chapter with an essential teaching from Archbishop Viganó:

> First of all, the systematic effort to demolish the family, the foundation of society, must be denounced, with the multiplication of ferocious attacks not only against conjugal life, which Christ elevated to a sacrament, but also against its natural essence, against the fact that marriage is by nature constituted between a man and a woman in an indissoluble bond of fidelity and reciprocal assistance.[68]

He stressed:

> The presence of a father and a mother is fundamental in the upbringing of children, who need a male and female figure as reference for their integral and harmonious development; nor can it be permitted that children, during the most delicate phase of their infancy and

---

67 Archbishop Carlo Maria Viganò, "Letter to Mothers: Against Globalist Dictatorship," op. cit., p. 308.
68 Ibid., p. 300.

adolescence, be used. to advance partisan ideological claims, with serious damage for their psychosomatic equilibrium, by those who with their own rebellious reflect the very idea of nature. You can easily understand the impact of the destruction of the family on the civil consortium: today we have right before our eyes the results of decades of unfortunate policies that inevitably lead to the dissolution of society.[69]

God created male and female to bring forth life on Earth. A society that considers the primary purpose of sex to be bringing and keeping a man and woman together in matrimony to birth and raise children for the glory of God is a functional society. Of all the Satanic ideas that do not work, the separation of sex from gender may be one of the most dangerous. Those accepting Satan's lie that gender is nonbinary doom themselves to a Baphomet-like existence, half human and half beast, half male and half female. This grotesque androgynous being is nothing but a confused combination that would be laughable were it not so sinfully tragic. Unfortunately, the ultimate queer critical theory gender performance may be necrophilia—where the impulse God blessed to create life is mocked in a perverse and evil ritual designed to reach orgasm with the dead.

---

69 Ibid., pp. 300–301.

CHAPTER 2

NUCLEAR WAR ON
THE HORIZON

———

"I am not such a fool as to believe that war is a thing of the past. I know the people do not want war, but there is no use in saying we cannot be pushed into another war.

Looking Back, Woodrow Wilson was re-elected president in 1916 on a platform that he had 'kept us out of war' and on the implied promise that he would 'keep us out of war.' Yet, five months later he asked Congress to declare war on Germany.

In that five-month interval the people had not been asked whether they had changed their minds. The four million young men who put on uniforms and marched or sailed away were not asked whether they wanted to go forth to die.

Then what caused our government to change its mind so suddenly? Money."

—Brigadier General Smedley Darlington Butler,
War Is a Racket[70]

The Clintons did not invent the game, but they took it to a new level. Actually, the crime is ancient. Bribery involves paying money to influence a favorable political outcome. With Hillary Clinton as secretary

———

70 Brigadier General Smedley Darlington Butler, *War Is a Racket* (New York: Skyhorse Publishing, 2016), p. 39. The book was originally published in 1935. See: Brigadier General Smedley Darlington Butler, *War Is a Racket* (New York: Round Table Press, Inc., 1935).

of state and former president Bill Clinton as head of the Clinton
Foundation, the Clintons had a game on. Hillary Clinton established
a private email server so she could parlay her State Department pol-
icy-making role to conduct Clinton Foundation fund-raising with
wealthy foreign nationals. Hillary planned to kept her private email
server secret, knowing that establishing this Clinton Foundation back
channel to the office of the secretary of state was in obvious violation
of federal law regarding the handling of national security documents.

Partners in Crime

In my 2016 book, *Partners in Crime: The Clinton's Scheme to Monetize
the White House for Personal Profit*,[71] I described the scheme. Founded in
2001, the year Bill Clinton left the White House, the Clinton Foundation
flourished in 2009, when Hillary became Obama's secretary of state.
Expecting to win the 2016 election, Hillary knew that with her as president and with Bill as ex-president, there was no limit to the amount of
money the foundation might rope in from a gullible public, but more
importantly, from criminal oligarchs seeking political favor.

On January 26, 2001, six days after Bill Clinton left the presidency,
the western part of India suffered one of the worst earthquakes in history. The Clinton Foundation criminal enterprise smelled cash, just as
the foundation did nine years later when a 7.0 magnitude earthquake
hit Haiti. Allied with the United Nations UNITAID and the blessing
of Nelson Mandela, the Clinton Foundation delivered to Africa defec-
tive HIV/AIDS medications fraudulently manufactured in India. After
star-studded bashes with Canadian mining financier Frank Giustra,
Bill Clinton decided to seize a huge uranium deal in Kazakhstan from
the grasp of Russia.

The Clinton Foundation was all about money for the Clintons, while

---

71 Jerome R. Corsi, *Partners in Crime: The Clinton's Scheme to Monetize the White House
for Personal Profit* (Washington, DC: WND Press, 2016).

federal and state regulators turned a blind eye to enforcing charitable giving rules and regulations that would have been severely enforced on conservatives. While the Clintons may have thought the game was only about running a fraudulent foundation to enrich themselves, the Deep State had another agenda. The CIA and the State Department's goal was to push NATO to the border of Russia, even if it meant going to war with Putin. Ukraine is noted for its rich fields of grain and its abundant oil and natural gas resources. Russia's access to the Atlantic Ocean depends on its access to the Black Sea through Ukraine and its access to the Baltic Sea from St. Petersburg with the cooperation of Finland.

At the heart of the evil perpetrated by the Clinton Foundation was the constant touting of philanthropic purposes that induced millions of donors to give the Clintons their hard-earned dollars, without realizing the Clintons were always only exploiting, with the mendacity of a grifter, the pain and suffering of an earthquake victim in India or Haiti, or the uncertain future of an HIV/AIDS human being in Africa for their own financial gain. As in case of Ukraine, the Clintons found their best marks—oligarchs who had enriched themselves in a kleptocracy masquerading as a nation. As it turned out, the greed of the Clintons played into the secret Deep State schemes put in motion through the clandestine maneuvers of the CIA working in consort with the US State Department. The US intelligence agency, military industrial complex, diplomatic core, and government-control media aimed to advance NATO to the border of Russia. While the American Left and a large faction of the Democratic Party had been enamored with Russia since the 1917 revolution, the fall of the Berlin Wall in 1989 and Russia's subsequent renouncement of Communism made Russia the Enemy Number One of the Deep State globalists who are now in control of our government.

In 2023, Hillary Clinton's net worth was estimated at $120 million,[72]

---

72 Timan Wainaina, "Hillary Clinton's Net Worth: How She Became One of America's

much resulting from the $2 billion global empire[73] into which she, Bill, and Chelsea built the Clinton Foundation, including the years when Hillary was secretary of state.   In the aftermath of the January 2010 earthquake in Haiti, Secretary Clinton's State Department pledged $1 billion in aid to Haiti through USAID. Bill Quigley, then an associate legal director at the Institute for Justice and Democracy in Haiti, and his co-author, Amber Ramanauskas, a lawyer and a human rights researcher, wrote an article titled "Haiti: Where Is the Money?" published by the *Arkansas Journal of Social Change and Public Service* on February 26, 2012. They estimated that international donors had given Haiti some $2 billion in relief aid by then. "But two years later, over half a million people remain homeless in hundreds of informal camps, a majority of the tons of debris from destroyed buildings still lays where it fell, and cholera, a preventable disease, was introduced into the country and is now an epidemic killing thousands and sickening hundreds of thousands more," they noted. "Haiti today looks like the earthquake happened two months ago, not two years."[74]

As I pointed out in *Partners in Crime*, the specific violation of state and federal criminal laws regarding the operation of a charity is inurement—a scheme designed by the operators of a philanthropy to personally enrich themselves and their associates. The Clintons took inurement to a different level, extending their political influence by opening the Clinton Foundation doors to foreign criminal oligarchs who had

Wealthiest Politicians," Capitalism.com, updated July 6, 2023, https://www.capitalism. com/hillary-clintons-net-worth/.

73 David A. Fahrenthold, Tom Hamburger, and Rosalind S. Helderman, "The inside story of how the Clintons built a $2 billion empire," *Washington Post*, June 2, 2015, https://www.washingtonpost.com/politics/the-inside-story-of-how-the-clintons-built-a-2 -billion-global-empire/2015/06/02/b6eab638-0957-11e5-a7ad-b430fc1d3f5c_story.html.

74 Bill Quigley and Amber Ramanauskas, "Haiti: Where is the Money?" *Arkansas Journal of Social Change and Public Service*, University of Arkansas at Little Rock, UAIR. edu, February 26, 2012, https://ualr.edu/socialchange/2012/02/26/haiti-where-is-the -money/.

amassed fortunes through their influence with corrupt regimes. The Clintons found Ukraine a target rich environment, one that ultimately attracted the Biden crime family to participate. The dirty secret is that both the Clintons and the Bidens were operating with the full but secret cooperation of the CIA, the Department of State, and the Department of Justice. Both the Secretary of State Hillary Clinton and Vice President Joe Biden found their positions in the Obama administration were nothing more than a license to steal.

Hillary Courts Ukraine

The NATO- and US-backed war against Russia began in 2000 when Clinton courted New York's large Ukrainian American constituency in her run for the US Senate. Hillary openly exploited the Ukrainian hatred of Stalin over his plan to starve millions of anti-Russian Ukrainian peasants to death in his 1932-33 communist collective farming disaster. As a senator, she campaigned on admitting Ukraine to the World Trade Organization (WTO) and promised to advance the legislative agenda to admit Ukraine to NATO.

In 2010, Secretary of State Clinton was warmly welcomed in Kyiv by Ukraine's pro-Russian President Viktor Yanukovych.[75] During that visit, Clinton told Yanukovych that "NATO's door remains open"[76] despite Yanukovych's evident retreat from pursuing NATO membership. The battle lines between Hillary and Trump trace back to 2004 when Paul Manafort agreed to become a paid advisor to Yanukovych. Manafort was a top-level Republican operative who had previously worked with Presidents Ronald Reagan and George H. W. Bush.

---

75 "File: Secretary Clinton is Greeted By Ukrainian President Yanukovych.jpg," Commons.Wikimedia.org, July 2, 2010, https://commons.wikimedia.org/wiki/File:Secretary_Clinton_Is_Greeted_By_Ukrainian_President_Yanukovych.jpg.
76 Radio Free Europe/Radio Liberty, "Clinton Tells Ukraine that Door to NATO Remains Open," RFERL.org, July 2, 2010, https://www.rferl.org/a/Clinton_Tells_Ukraine_That_Door_To_NATO_Remains_Open/2089237.html.

Yanukovych was a former governor of Donetsk, a major city in one of Ukraine's two Russian-speaking provinces close to the border with Russia. The Russian-majority Republics of Donetsk and Luhansk in eastern Ukraine have been allied with Russia for centuries, with residents speaking predominantly Russian even today.

Billionaire Ukrainian Joins Forces with Hillary

In 2016, when Hillary was running for president, the *Wall Street Journal* reported that Victor Pinchuk was a Ukrainian oligarch who owned Interpipe Group, a Cyrus-incorporated manufacturer of seamless pipes used in the oil and gas sector. Pinchuk, a former member of the Ukrainian Parliament, was the son-in-law of Leonid Kuchma, who was president of Ukraine from 1994–2005. He also owned Credit Dnipro Bank. The newspaper reported that Pinchuk had contributed $8.6 million to the Clinton Foundation while Hillary Clinton was secretary of state, making him the largest contributor to the Clinton Foundation while Hillary held that position.[77] On February 12, 2014, the *New York Times* reported that as president of Ukraine Kuchma "led a government criticized for corruption, nepotism, and the murder of dissident journalists."[78] As president, Kuchma privatized a giant state steel factory and sold it to Pinchuk's consortium for the low price of approximately $800 million. The *New York Times* article also reported that between 2006 and 2014, Pinchuk donated roughly $13.1 million to the Clinton

---

77 Peter Nicholas, "As Secretary of State, Hillary Clinton Hosted at Dinner a Ukrainian Donor to Family Foundation," *Wall Street Journal*, August 23, 2016, https://www.wsj.com/articles/as-secretary-of-state-hillary-clinton-hosted-at-dinner-a-ukrainian-donor-to-family-foundation-1471995857.

78 Amy Chozick, "Trade Dispute Centers on Ukrainian with Ties to Clintons," *New York Times*, February 12, 2014, https://www.nytimes.com/2014/02/13/us/politics/trade-dispute-centers-on-ukrainian-executive-with-ties-to-clintons.html.

Foundation.[79] Pinchuk strongly advocated Ukraine joining the EU, a cause he championed with Secretary of State Clinton.[80]

In November 2014, then Republican congressman from Texas, Steve Stockman, wrote the US Department of Treasury with evidence suggesting Pinchuk had violated US sanctions by selling pipes to Iran that could be used in Iran's nuclear weapons program.[81] Despite Representative Stockman's documented complaint, the Department of Treasury took no apparent action against Pinchuk or Interpipe.

Douglas Schoen, a New York–based Democratic Party pollster and political operative, introduced Bill Clinton to Pinchuk in 2004. Schoen registered as a lobbyist and set up an office in Washington, DC, after Pinchuk offered to pay him $40,000 a month to set up meetings that were almost exclusively held with senior officials in Secretary Clinton's State Department.[82] The *Wall Street Journal* reported that the purpose of the State Department meetings that Schoen arranged was "to encourage the US to pressure Ukraine's then-President Viktor Yanukovych to free his jailed predecessor, Yulia Tymoshenko."[83] The newspaper also reported that Ukraine topped the list of contributions by individuals of more than $50,000 to the Clinton Foundation from 1999 to 2014, with Ukrainians contributing $10 million total.[84]

In 2004, Pinchuk created the Yalta European Strategy (YES), an

---

79 Ibid.

80 Isobel Koshiw, "Viktor Pinchuk: Friend or foe of Ukraine?" *Kiev Post*, October 14, 2016, https://www.kyivpost.com/post/7810.

81 Rory Ross, "Hillary Clinton's Big Benefactor Has Trade Links with Iran, *Newsweek*, April 18, 2015, https://www.newsweek.com/2015/04/24/hillary-clinton-runs-white-house-and-row-over-ukrainian-benefactors-trade-322253.html. See also: Garth Kant, "Did Clinton-Iran Ties Boost Nuke Program?" World Net Daily, WND.com, April 23, 3025.

82 Amy Chozick, "Trade Dispute Centers on Ukrainian with Ties to Clintons," loc. cit.

83 James V. Grimaldi and Rebecca Ballhaus, "Clinton Charity Tapped Foreign Friends," *Wall Street Journal*, March 19, 2015, https://www.wsj.com/articles/clinton-charity-tapped-foreign-friends-1426818602.

84 Ibid.

annual international forum organized to connect Ukraine with leading
European business leaders and heads of state (including Bill Clinton)
with the goal of integrating Ukraine into the European Union's economy.[85] In 2013, Pinchuk welcomed then presidential candidate Hillary
Clinton to the stage of the Yalta European Strategy meeting, calling her
"a real megastar." Pinchuk was also on the international advisory board
of the Atlantic Council, aptly described as a "NATO-aligned American
think tank" among whose prominent members was Victoria Nuland,
the 18th US Ambassador to NATO from 2005–2008 and Assistant
Secretary of State for European and Eurasian Affairs from 2013–2017.

The Deep State Goes to War with Russia Over Ukraine

The decisions that led Obama/Clinton/Biden to go to war against
Russia in today's proxy Ukraine-Russia war trace back to November 30,
2013, the day Yanukovych announced he was suspending preparations
for signing an agreement to join NATO that had been scheduled to
occur at an EU summit held that day in Vilnius, Lithuania.[86] The State
Department's efforts to remove Yanukovych from power in Ukraine
began with the Soros-funded and State Department-organized Orange
Revolution in 2004.[87] The crux of the Orange Revolution was the
Soros-fostered suspicion in Ukraine that the November 2004 presidential election had been rigged to favor Yanukovych. Ukraine's Supreme
Court intervened, ordering a revote that was won by Victor Yuschenko.
In the subsequent 2010 election, Yanukovych's win was considered fair.
Yanukovych succeeded Yuschenko in an inauguration held on February
25, 2010.

---

85 "Yalta European Strategy," Victor Pinchuk Foundation, no date, PinchukFund.org,
https://pinchukfund.org/en/projects/21/.
86 "Ukraine protests after Yanukovych EU deal rejection," BBC News, November 20,
2013, https://www.bbc.com/news/world-europe-25162563.
87 "US campaign behind the turmoil in Kiev," *The Guardian*, TheGuardian.com,
November 24, 2004, https://www.theguardian.com/world/2004/nov/26/ukraine.usa.

An argument can be made that the war against Russia had its origin in a State Department/Pentagon plan developed early in Obama's first term as president to take control of Ukraine. A goal of that plan appears to have been to gain control of Sevastopol in Crimea, a crucial Russian naval port on the Black Sea. Crimea is another predominantly Russian-speaking part of Ukraine. The Obama administration apparently coveted transforming Sevastopol into a US naval base. Obama's State Department also pushed for Ukraine to join the EU as a first step to Ukraine joining NATO. With Ukraine in NATO, Obama could place nuclear weapons on the doorstep of Russia.[88] On July 21, 2009, Vice President Joe Biden said the following after a meeting with Ukrainian President Yushchenko: "If you choose to be part of Euro-Atlantic integration, which I believe you have, then we strongly support that."[89] On July 21, 2009, Ellen Berry reporting for the *New York Times* wrote:

> Mr. Biden's visit to the region taking place only two weeks after President Obama's summit meeting with President Dmitri A. Medvedev of Russia was intended to ease fears in Georgia and Ukraine over whether the Obama administration might withdraw support for their pro-Western governments to improve ties with Russia. Russian officials have been increasingly angered by deepening Western alliances in what it terms its "zone of privileged interests," and especially the proposed expansion of NATO to include Ukraine and Georgia, which were once part of the Soviet Union. Mr. Biden made it clear that the United States remained enthusiastic about the proposal.[90]

---

88 Eric Zuesse, "How the War in Ukraine Started," TheDuran.com, November 9, 2019. Article currently archived on the Internet here: https://robscholtemuseum.nl/eric-zuesse-how-the-war-in-ukraine-started/.
89 Ellen Barry, "Biden says US Still Backs Ukraine in NATO," *New York Times*, July 21, 2009, https://www.nytimes.com/2009/07/22/world/europe/22biden.html?_r=1&ref=world.
90 Ibid.

Antony J. Blinken, then Vice President Biden's personal national security advisor, expressed caution over Biden's enthusiasm that Ukraine would want to join NATO. "I don't have any guarantee that that's how it's going to play out," Blinken noted, adding that Viktor Yanukovych was likely to beat Yuschenko in the upcoming January 2010 presidential election. Blinken was right: Yanukovych, aligned with Russia, won the presidency in 2010. As noted, Yanukovych ultimately balked at concluding negotiations for joining NATO.

The US Deep State, apparently eager to reignite tensions with Russia, never wavered on the importance of bringing Ukraine into the EU/NATO sphere. Zbigniew Brzezinski, former national security advisor to President Jimmy Carter, wrote: "It cannot be stressed strongly enough that without Ukraine, Russia ceases to be an empire, but with Ukraine suborned and then subordinated, Russia automatically becomes an empire."[91] In his 2008 book *America and the World* published the year Obama won the presidency, there is a discussion of US administrations desiring to push NATO to include Ukraine. The discussion is raised in the context of the Monroe Doctrine—a discussion that prompts recalling the reaction of President Kennedy to Nikita Khrushchev's decision to put nuclear weapons in Cuba in 1962. Brzezinski commented that "if Ukraine moves to the West, first to the EU, eventually maybe to NATO, the probability that Russia will move toward Europe is far greater than if Ukraine is told in advance that it can never be part of the EU and NATO because Moscow doesn't want it to be."[92]

---

91 Zbigniew Brzezinski, "The Premier Partnership," *Foreign Affairs*, Volume 73, Number 2, March/April 1994, p. 76.
92 Zbigniew Brzezinski and Brent Scowcroft, *America and the World:: Conversations on the Future of American Foreign Policy* (New York: Basic Books, 2008), pp. 172–174, at p. 174.

The Maidan Revolution Coup d'État

In December 2013, three hundred thousand Ukrainians took to the streets in the largest protests since the Orange Revolution, this time demanding Yanukovych resign over his refusal to pursue discussions with the EU.[93] These protests developed into the State Department[94] and Soros-funded Maidan Revolution,[95] which ultimately led to Yanukovych fleeing to Russia in February 2014. The Maidan protest events were organized from inside the US embassy in Kiev, starting in March 2013,[96] such that the Maidan Revolution was in reality a coup d'état orchestrated by the CIA and the US State Department, with Soros funding anti-Russian NGOs (Non-Government Organizations) in Ukraine.

The Maidan Revolution was soon taken over by Oleh Tyahnybok of the Svoboda party, an ultra-nationalist party that is openly neo-Nazi.[97] The symbol logo of the Svoboda party is the Nazi "wolfsangel" rune—a symbol that resembles a swastika and was worn by the Waffen SS, a branch of the SS that included volunteers and conscripts from Nazi-conquered countries, including Ukraine.[98] During World War II,

---

93 "Ukrainians call for Yanukovych to resign in protests sparked by EU u-turn," *The Guardian*, TheGuardian.com, December 2, 2013, https://www.theguardian.com/world/2013/dec/01/ukraine-largest-street-protests-orange-revolution.

94 Ted Galen Carpenter, "America's Ukraine Hypocrisy," Cato Institute, Cato.org, August 6, 2017, https://www.cato.org/commentary/americas-ukraine-hypocrisy.

95 George Soros, "Keep the Spirit of the Maidan Alive," Open Society Foundations, OpenSocietyFoundations.org, April 7, 2014, https://www.opensocietyfoundations.org/voices/keep-spirit-maidan-alive.

96 Eric Zuesse, "New Video Evidence of America's Coup in Ukraine—and What It Means," WashingtonsBlog.com, February 8, 2015, https://web.archive.org/web/20191010061137/https://washingtonsblog.com/2015/02/new-video-evidence-americas-coup-ukraine-means.html.

97 Aaron Maté, "What 10 Years of US Meddling in Ukraine Have Wrought (Spoiler Alert: Not Democracy," Real Clear Investigations, RealClearInvestigations.com, April 24, 2024, https://www.realclearinvestigations.com/articles/2024/04/30/what_10_years_of_us_meddling_in_ukraine_have_wrought_spoiler_alert_it_wasnt_democracy_1027411.html.

98 "Ukrainian Svoboda party links to neo-Nazism," Question for written Answer

the Waffen SS participated in the murder of over one million Jews, killed mostly in the years 1941–1942.[99] In 2004, Tyahnybok was thrown out of President Yushchenko's cabinet for urging Ukrainians to fight against a "Muscovite-Jewish mafia."[100] One of the most crucial divisions in Ukraine is that the western part of the country, the center of power for the Ukrainian government, currently led by Ukrainian President Volodymyr Zelenskyy, is allied with Germany, while the east of Ukraine and Crimea are aligned with Russia. Openly neo-Nazi brigades still operate in western Ukraine, while the eastern provinces yearn to become independent republics with close ties to Russia.

The Maidan Revolution ended in violence, following a script the CIA, the State Department, and George Soros had been utilizing since the so-called "Color Revolutions." This trio of the CIA, the State Department, and George Soros developed a set of tactics designed to engineer Color Revolutions among the countries leaving the Soviet bloc from 2000 to 2004, after the fall of the Berlin Wall, and in the Arab Spring uprisings, in the Middle East and North Africa, from 2010–2013.[101] The Deep State has become well versed in prolonging "peaceful demonstrations" long enough that they can be mobilized into coup d'état movements, as has been demonstrated by the Tahir Square protests in 2011 that led to Egyptian president Mubarak being deposed in an Arab Spring action—tactics the CIA, the State Department, and Soros replicated to cause the Maidan uprising in Ukraine in 2014.

Parliamentary Question E-003446-14," European Parliament, Europarl.Europa.EU, March 21, 2014, https://www.europarl.europa.eu/doceo/document/E-7-2014-003446_EN.html.

99 Nadine Yousif, "Canada Nazi row puts spotlight on Ukraine's WWII Past," *BBC News*, BBC.com, September 23, 2023, https://www.bbc.com/news/world-us-canada-66914756.

100 David Stern, "Svoboda: The rise of Ukraine's ultra-nationalists," *BBC News*, BBC.com, December 26, 2012, https://www.bbc.com/news/magazine-20824693.

101 Glenn Beck, "The Democrats Hydra," GlennBeck.com, November 14, 2019, https://www.glennbeck.com/specials/glenn-beck-presents-the-democrats-hydra--glenn-tv.

On February 20, 2014, to bring the protests to the level of intensity needed to spur crowd violence, a group of "snipers" began shooting protesters. When the tear gas and smoke cleared, four police officers and forty-eight protesters were dead. The snipers were believed to be paramilitary forces loyal to President Viktor Yanukovych.[102] While the debate has raged, extensive forensic analysis of the shootings has left the identification of the shooters unresolved, leaving open the possibility the "snipers" could have been hired by Soros forces, in a "false flag" operation that had the tacit support of the Obama State Department. Buttressing this suspicion was an intercepted phone call involving Estonian Foreign Minister Urmas Paet that suggested the snipers were tied not to the Yanukovych government, but to the Maidan activists backed by the US government and Soros.[103] Two days after the shootings, Yanukovych fled to Russia.

On September 21, 2019, investigative journalist Lee Stranahan reported that Soros funded the International Renaissance Foundation that worked closely with Hillary Clinton's State Department in Ukraine and contributed at least $8 million to Hillary-affiliated super-PACs in her 2016 presidential campaign cycle.[104]

After Hillary left the State Department in 2014, Assistant Secretary of State, Bureau of European and Eurasian Affairs Victoria Nuland

---

102 Aaron Maté, "What 10 Years of US Meddling in Ukraine Have Wrought (Spoiler Alert: Not Democracy)," loc. cit.

103 "Breaking: Estonian Foreign Minister Urmas Paet and Catherine Ashton discuss Ukraine over the phone," posted by Michael Bergman, YouTube, 2014, https://www.youtube.com/watch?v=ZEgJ0oo3OA8. See also: Ivan Katchanovski, "Buried trial verdict confirms false-flag Maidan massacre," CanadianDimension.com, February 20, 2024, https://canadiandimension.com/articles/view/buried-trial-verdict-confirms-false-flag-maidan-massacre-in-ukraine-2024.

104 Jim Hoft, "All Eyes on Ukraine: Deep State and Hillary Operatives Worked with Ukrainian Government to Take Down Trump," Gateway Pundit, TheGatewayPundit.com, September 21, 2009, https://www.thegatewaypundit.com/2019/09/all-eyes-on-ukraine-deep-state-and-hillary-operatives-worked-with-ukrainian-government-to-take-down-trump/.

took up the cause of getting Ukraine into NATO. On December 13, 2013, as the Maidan Revolution was beginning to develop, Nuland gave a speech to the US-Ukraine Foundation. In that speech, she said, "When Ukrainians say they are European, this is what they mean. And as one very prominent Ukrainian businessman said to me, 'The Maidan Movement's greatest achievement is that it has proven that the people of Ukraine will no longer support any president—this one [i.e., Yanukovych] or a future one—who does not take them to Europe.'"[105] In February 2014, a leaked transcript of a telephone call between Nuland and Geoffrey Pyatt, then US ambassador to Ukraine, Nuland said, "F... the EU!" in apparent frustration the EU was not equally as enthusiastic as was the State Department in supporting the Maidan Revolution's push to for Ukraine to join NATO.[106]

Russia Invades Crimea

In March 2014, following the Maidan Revolution that ousted Yanukovych, Russian troops invaded and annexed the Crimea peninsula for Russia. Obama stood by, allowing Russia to annex Crimea and take control of Sevastopol without opposition. The Ukrainian government, however, in retaliation against Russia for invading Crimea, sent military troops to attack Russian-backed armed separatists[107] that supported Russia-aligned provinces in eastern Ukraine who wished to be independent states aligned with Russia. Among these military attacking

105 Victoria Nuland, Assistant Secretary, Bureau of European and Eurasian Affairs, US Department of State, "Remarks at the US-Ukraine Foundation Conference, Washington, D.C., December 13, 2013," State.gov, https://2009-2017.state.gov/p/eur/rls/rm/2013/dec/218804.htm.
106 Bob Dreyfuss, "The Not-So-Secret Ukraine Phone Call," The Nation, TheNation.com, February 10, 2014, https://www.thenation.com/article/archive/not-so-secret-ukraine-phone-call./
107 Oksana Grytsenko, "Armed pro-Russian insurgents in Luhansk say they are ready for police raid," Kyiv Post, April 12, 2014, https://web.archive.org/web/20140412131249/http://www.kyivpost.com/content/ukraine/armed-pro-russian-insurgents-in-luhansk-say-they-are-ready-for-police-raid-343167.html.

the separatists in eastern Ukraine were the Azov battalion—a neo-Nazi group associated with neo-Nazi ideology and insignia. Originally acting as an autonomous media, the Azov battalion was fully integrated into the Ukrainian National Guard.[108]

On February 18, 2023, NATO Secretary General Jens Stoltenberg stepped in front of microphones for an impromptu press conference following a meeting of the NATO Defense Ministers at NATO headquarters in Brussels, Belgium. Stoltenberg openly admitted to the Western media that NATO has been at war with Russia since 2014. "Since 2014, NATO allies have provided support to Ukraine with training and equipment. Ukrainian forces were much stronger in 2022 than they were in 2014."[109] This admission acknowledges the reality. Billed as a proxy war between the Zelenskyy government in Ukraine and Putin in Russia, the Ukraine war has all along been a US/NATO war against Russia, thinly disguised as a proxy war.

Enter Hunter Biden

In his 2018 book, *Secret Empires: How the American Political Class Hides Corruption and Enriches Family and Friends*, Peter Schweizer, cofounder and president of the Government Accountability Institute, documented how Biden and then-Secretary of State John Kerry pulled off what Ukrainian anti-corruption watchdog Nashi Groshi ("Our

---

108 Tara John and Tim Lister, "A far-right battalion has a key role in Ukraine's resistance. It's neo-Nazi history has been exploited by Putin," CNN World, CNN.com, March 30, 2022, https://www.cnn.com/2022/03/29/europe/ukraine-azov-movement-far-right-intl-cmd/index.html.
109 "NATO Secretary General—Doorstep statement at Defense Ministers Meeting, NATO News, YouTube, February 14, 2023, https://www.youtube.com/watch?v=b7fyj DyhHp8&t=392s. See also: The Last Refuge, "He Did It Again—General Secretary Admits NATO Has Been at War with Russia in Ukraine Since 2014," posted by Sundance, TheConservativeTreehouse.com, February 18, 2023, https://theconservativetreehouse .com/blog/2023/02/18/he-did-it-again-general-secretary-admits-nato-has-been-at-war -against-russia-in-ukraine-since-2014/.

Money") described as "an asset siphoning operation."[110] Schweizer documented that on April 16, 2014, Devon Archer, the college roommate of Kerry's stepson, H. J. Heinz, visited the White House to meet with Vice President Biden.

Less than a week later, on April 22, 2014, there was a public announcement Burisma Holdings, based in Kyiv, Ukraine, had asked Devon Archer to join the board. Three weeks later, on May 12, 2014, Burisma asked Hunter Biden to join the board. Burisma was a giant Ukranian natural gas company with ties to Ihor Kolomoisky, reputedly the third-wealthiest man in Ukraine with an estimated net worth of $24 billion. Kolomoisky had managed to seize the largest reserves of natural gas in Ukraine. Kolomoisky also owned PrivateBank. Zelensky, an actor by profession, became famous portraying a president on a television show, "Servant of the People," that aired on Kolomoisky's television network. In 2012, Zelensky's production company entered into a deal with Kolomoisky's media group, with Zelensky's production company alledgedly receiving $41 million in funding from PrivatBank. When Zelinsky ran for president, Kolomoisky provided him security services. Kolomoisky, at the time he supported Zelensky, was accused of embezzling $5.5 billion through a PrivatBank subsidiary in Cyprus. In addition to providing financial backing for Zelensky's presidential campaign, Kolomoisky also funded the neo-Nazi Azov Battalion.[111]

Schweizer commented, "Neither Biden nor Archer had any

---

110 Peter Schweizer, *Secret Empires: How the American Political Class Hides Corruption and Enriches Family and Friends* (New York: Harper, 2018), pp. 65–66, at p. 66.
111 Richard Abelson, "It All Comes Together: Hunter, Burisma, Kolomoisky, Zelensky, and the 'Children Burned Alive in Donetsk,'" RightEdition.com, March 22, 2022, https://rightedition.com/2022/03/25/it-all-comes-together-hunter-burisma-kolomoisky-zelensky-and-the-children-burned-alive-in-donetsk/ The article was also published by the Gateway Pundit, TheGatewayPundit.com, March 25, 2022, https://www.thegatewaypundit.com/2022/03/comes-together-hunter-burisma-kolomoisky-zelensky-children-burned-alive-donetsk/

background or experience in the energy sector."[112] Schweizer noted Archer was part of the Heinz family foundation, a former senior advisor to John Kerry in his 2004 presidential bid, and the cofounder and managing director of Rosemont Seneca Partners, where he partnered with Hunter Biden.

The day before Archer's appointment to the Burisma board, Vice President Biden arrived in Kyiv to deliver a USAID program to assist the Ukrainian natural gas industry. Soon after, the United States worked with the International Monetary Fund (IMF) to get $1.8 billion in taxpayer loans pumped into the Ukrainian economy courtesy of the IMF.[113] In August 2015, the Centre for Research on Globalization in Montreal disclosed that $1.8 billion in International Monetary Fund (IMF) aid to Ukraine had been deposited into a Cyprus bank account controlled by Ukrainian oligarch Ihor Kolomoisky. The Center for Global Research reported the following:

> Ihor Kolomoisky, the former governor of Dnipropetrovsk, is one of Ukraine's richest businessmen, with a business empire that includes holdings in the energy, media, aviation, chemical and metalwork industries. At the center of Kolomoisky's wealth is PrivatBank, Ukraine's largest financial institution, which claimed the bulk—40 percent—of the [IMF] bailout money which had been earmarked for stabilizing the banking industry.[114]

In 2014, after the Maidan Revolution had deposed Yanukovych, the

---

112 Peter Schweizer, *Secret Empires: How the American Political Class Hides Corruption and Enriches Family and Friends*, op. cit., p. 61.
113 Ibid., p. 65.
114 Centre for Research on Globalization, "$1.8 Billion IMF Ukraine Bailout Money Deposited in Ukraine Oligarch Kolomoyskyi's Offshore Bank Account," GlobalResearch.ca, August 29, 2015, https://www.globalresearch.ca/1-8-billion-imf-ukraine-bailout-money-deposited-in-ukraine-oligarch-kolomoyskyis-cyprus-offshore-bank-account/5472971.

West "propped up the Ukraine government with $15 billion from the International Monetary fund," only to find the money vanished "allegedly through oligarch-held banks like PrivatBank."[115]

Hillary Clinton played a crucial role in the background of the Kolomoisky story. Kolomoisky financed anti-Russian units operating in the Ukrainian civil war in Donbas (started in 2014, expanding into Russia's invasion of Ukraine, currently ongoing).[116] For his support of Petro Poroshenko's government in Kyiv and the Obama administration's drive to get Ukraine into NATO, Kolomoisky received strong support from Secretary of State Hillary Clinton and her assistant secretary for European affairs, Victoria Nuland. Clinton and Nuland dominated the IMF, led by then-managing director Christine Lagarde. Journalist John Helmer explained:

> Following the US regime change [the Maidan Revolution] which installed Poroshenko's regime in the spring of 2014, the IMF voted massive loans for Ukraine to replace the Russian financing on which the regime of Victor Yanukovych [the Ukrainian president favorable to Russia who fled to Moscow in the aftermath of the Maidan Revolution] had depended. More than a third of the fresh IMF money was paid out by the National Bank of Ukraine (NBU), the state's central bank, into PrivatBank controlled by Kolomoisky and his partner, Gennady Bogolyubov.[117]

Obama, Clinton, Nuland, Lagarde, and the IMF ignored the evidence

---

115 Richard Abelson, "It All Comes Together: Hunter, Burisma, Kolomoisky, Zelensky and the 'Children Burned Alive in Donetsk,'" loc. cit.

116 John Helmer, Moscow, "The Kolomoisky Pyramid Started with Hillary Clinton and Victoria Nuland of the State Department Plus Christine Lagarde of the IMF," JohnHelmer.net, June 30, 2019, https://johnhelmer.net/the-kolomoisky-pyramid-started-with-hillary-clinton-and-victoria-nuland-of-the-state-department-plus-christine-lagarde-of-the-imf/.

117 Ibid.

piling up that Kolomoisky had stolen the IMF money through a pyramid of front companies that never intended to pay it back.[118]

Biden had become so accustomed to cashing in on his office that he lost his ethical compass. In a now-infamous recorded appearance at the Council on Foreign Relations on January 23, 2018, Biden made a joke about pressing then-President of Ukraine Petro Poroshenko to fire the country's top prosecutor, who was then investigating Hunter Biden's financial arrangement with Burisma or face the withdrawal of a $1 billion US loan guarantee. "I said, 'You're not getting the billion.' . . . I looked at them and said, 'I'm leaving in six hours. If the prosecutor is not fired, you're not getting the money.'"[119] Making threats of that nature is, under US law, a form of criminal assault.[120] But, acting like a gangster thug, Biden got what he wanted. "Well son of a b****, he got fired. And they put in place someone who was solid at the time." As always, the Biden family has practiced the art of self-justifying their pursuit of politics for money.

In 2021, Secretary of State Antony Blinken designated Kolomoisky and members of his immediate family as ineligible to return to the US due to "his involvement in significant corruption."[121] On January 20,

118 John Helmer, Moscow, "Stress Test for IMF in Ukraine—Igor Kolomoisky's Privatbank is the Biggest Beneficiary of the IMF's Emergency Liquidity Assistance (ELA), JohnHelmer.net, June 24, 2014, https://johnhelmer.net/stress-test-for-imf-igor-kolomoiskys-privatbank-is-the-biggest-beneficiary-of-the-imfs-emergency-liquidity-assistance-ela/.

119 Council on Foreign Affairs, "Foreign Affairs Issue Launch with Former Vice President Joe Biden," CFR.org, January 23, 2018, https://www.cfr.org/event/foreign-affairs-issue-launch-former-vice-president-joe-biden.

120 Rebecca Pirius, Attorney, Mitchell Hamline School of Law, "Criminal Threats: Laws and Practices," CriminalDefenseLawyer.com, updated May 26, 2022, https://www.criminaldefenselawyer.com/crime-penalties/federal/Criminal-Threats.htm.

121 Antony J. Blinken, Secretary of State, "Public Designation of Oligarch and Former Ukraine Public Official Ihor Kolomoyskyy Due to Involvement in Significant Corruption," US Department of State, Press Release, State.gov, March 5, 2021, https://www.state.gov/public-designation-of-oligarch-and-former-ukrainian-public-official-ihor-kolomoyskyy-due-to-involvement-in-significant-corruption/.

2022, the Department of Justice filed a criminal complaint in the US District Court for the Southern District of Florida alleging "that more than $6 million in proceeds from the sale of commercial real estate in Dallas, Texas, which property was maintained and improved using the proceeds of embezzlement and fraud from PrivatBank in Ukraine, are subject to forfeiture based on violations of federal money laundering statutes."[122] Fleeing back to Ukraine, Kolomoisky has not been brought to trial in the United States, nor have Hillary Clinton or Joe Biden been charged with any criminal involvement in the theft of the IMF funds.

On March 21, 2024, Representatives James Comer, chairman of the House Committee on Oversight and Accountability, and Jim Jordan, chairman of the House Committee on the Judiciary, wrote a letter to CIA Director William J. Burns alleging that a whistleblower claimed the CIA had intervened in the investigation of Hunter Biden to prevent the Internal Revenue Service (IRS) and the DOJ from interviewing a witness.[123] The implications of the letter were that Hunter Biden and his father as vice president may have been acting in concert with the CIA to bolster a State Department plan to fund Burisma to compete with Russia's state-owned energy company Gazprom.

Metabiota

Hunter Biden's Rosemont Seneca Technology Partners invested $500,000 in the San Francisco bioresearch firm Metabiota, which subsequently received a $23.9 million contract from the Pentagon.

122 Office of Public Affairs, US Department of Justice, "United States Files Civil Forfeiture Complaint for Proceeds of Alleged Fraud and Theft from PrivatBank in Ukraine," Press release, Justice.gov, January 22, 2022, https://www.justice.gov/opa/pr/united-states-files-civil-forfeiture-complaint-proceeds-alleged-fraud-and-theft-privatbank.
123 Letter from Representatives James Comer, chairman of the House Committee on Oversight and Accountability, and Jim Jordon, chairman of the House Committee on the Judiciary to CIA Director William J. Burns, March 21, 2024, https://judiciary.house.gov/sites/evo-subsites/republicans-judiciary.house.gov/files/evo-media-document/2024-03-21%20JDJ%20JC%20to%20CIA.pdf.

Metabiota's head Nathan Wolfe also worked with EcoHealth's Peter Daszak on SARS-based coronavirus research.[124] On March 26, 2022, the *New York Post* confirmed that Hunter Biden "played a role in helping a California defense contractor analyze killer diseases and bioweapons in Ukraine."[125] Russia's Chairman of the State Duma, Vyacheslav Volodin, followed this two days later with a statement: "US President Joe Biden is involved in the creation of biolaboratories in Ukraine. An investment fund run by his son Hunter Biden funded research and the implementation of the United States military biological program. It is obvious that Joe Biden, as his father and head of state, was aware of that activity." Volodin asserted that involved with the Metabiota bioweapons program in Ukraine was George Soros, "the notorious mastermind of color revolutions, who openly calls for changing government in our country."[126]

On March 9, 2022, in testimony before the Senate Foreign Relations Committee, Victoria Nuland, speaking on behalf of the US Department of State, acknowledged that Ukraine possessed biological research facilities. She added that the US State Department was "quite concerned that Russian troops, Russian forces, may be seeking to gain control of [those labs], so we are working with the Ukrainians on how they can prevent any of those research materials from falling into the hands of

---

124 Richard Abelson, "MORE: Hunter Biden's Biolab Firm Metabiota Linked to EcoHealth, World Economic Forum—Russia Claims 20,000 Biolab Documents," Gateway Pundit, TheGatewayPundit.com, February 1, 2023, https://www. thegatewaypundit.com/2023/02/hunter-bidens-biolab-firm-metabiota-linked-ecohealth-world-economic-forum-russia-claims-20-000-biolab-documents/.
125 John Levine and Jesse O'Neill, "Hunter Biden helped secure funds for US biolab contractor in Ukraine: e-mails," *New York Post*, March 26, 2022, https://nypost. com/2022/03/26/hunter-biden-played-role-in-funding-us-bio-labs-contractor-in-ukraine -e-mails/.
126 Biden must explain his son's involvement in biolabs operations in Ukraine— Duma speaker," Tass, Russian News Agency, Tass.com, March 24, 2022, https:// tass.com/politics/1427005?utm_source=google.com&utm_medium=organic&utm_ campaign=google.com&utm_referrer=google.com.

Russian forces should they approach."[127] This was a surprisingly truthful answer to Senator Marco Rubio's question whether the US had a biological weapons program in Ukraine. Nuland's testimony confirmed not only that the US did have "biological research laboratories" operating in Ukraine, but also that the US failed to secure potentially deadly pathogens in those labs before the Russian invasion began. Nuland's testimony exposed the extensive efforts that the US intelligence agencies had expended in willing cooperation with the mainstream press to dismiss claims Hunter Biden's involvement with Metabiota in Ukraine as disinformation. Nuland's surprisingly candid answer also confirmed Russia had been telling the truth.

Did the Biden administration really expect Russia would ignore the Biden crime family–funded bioweapons labs performing gain-of-function research on deadly, highly contagious pathogens? How is Russia supposed to act today when the CIA has operations centers in Ukraine on the Russian border—CIA stations capable of monitoring Russian military activity while gaining intelligence on Russian military weapons and technology? Both the Obama and Biden administrations have implemented Ukrainian foreign policies that Moscow has no choice but to regard as provocative.

In reaction to the US and NATO supplying Ukraine with long-range cruise missiles that Ukraine has used to hit infrastructure targets within Russia, the Russian forces in Ukraine have begun a massive attack on Ukrainian infrastructure in the remaining Ukraine-controlled part of the country. Russia's strategy in the Ukraine war has been to destroy Ukrainian infrastructure such that without electricity, heat, and water, millions of Ukrainians have been forced to flee, leaving behind them bombed out buildings and largely abandoned cities. If the US

---

127 Glenn Greenwald, "Victoria Nuland: Ukraine Has 'Biological Research Facilities,' Worried Russia May Seize Them," Greenwald.Substack.com, March 9, 2022, https://greenwald.substack.com/p/victoria-nuland-ukraine-has-biological.

and NATO persist in ramping up war efforts to defeat Russia, the likelihood is that Russia will advance into western Ukraine, ultimately threatening to take the capital city of Kiev, as a measure to end the war with Russia taking control of the entire nation. So far, the US, the EU, and NATO have chosen to ignore repeated Russian overtures indicating Russia is willing to negotiate a settlement that would limit Russian gains in Ukraine to territory currently under Russian control.

Surrogate Mothers and Child Trafficking

With the Russian-Ukraine war in its third year, the Ukrainian economy is in shambles. Thousands of young women have turned to baby factories to become commercial surrogate mothers.[128] Globally, the commercial surrogate motherhood market has been riddled with sexual exploitation, child trafficking, and pedophilia abuses.[129] In war-torn country of Ukraine,the situation is so dire that desperate women turn to surrogate motherhood as a means of survival. For women fleeing their homes, often seperated from their families, the prospect of being a surrogate money offers "a potentially life-altering sum of money."[130]

Ukraine is a country where some 60 percent of the population identifies as Orthodox Christian.[131] The pre-war population of Ukraine was estimated at 43.5 million. But the US State Department calculated that

---

128 Stephanie Hegarty and Eleanor Layhe, "Ukraine: Impossible choices for surrogate mothers and parents," BBC.com, March 21, 2022, https://www.bbc.com/news/world-europe-60824936.
129 Christopher White, "Surrogate Parenthood for Money Is a Form of Human Trafficking," Forbes.com, April 4, 2014, https://www.forbes.com/sites/realspin/2014/04/04/surrogate-parenthood-for-money-is-a-form-of-human-trafficking/.
130 Susan Dominus, "It's a Terrible Thing When a Grown Person Does Not Belong to Herself," *New York Times Magazine*, May 3, 2022, updated May 4, 2022, https://www.nytimes.com/2022/05/03/magazine/surrogates-ukraine.html.
131 US Department of State, "2022 Report on International Religious Freedom: Ukraine," State.gov, https://www.state.gov/reports/2022-report-on-international-religious-freedom/ukraine/#:~:text=The%20survey%20found%20another%208.7,with%2018.8%20percent%20in%202021.

by 2022, approximately 7.8 million people had fled the country as war refugees. The concept of a woman being willing to submit her body to be implanted with the sperm of an unknown, but wealthy foreign donor is repugnant to those who see conception as a sacred gift of God meant to enrich the lives of a man and a woman who have intertwined their lives in matrimony. That a woman gives birth to an unknown stranger's child, only to have the child snatched from her arms at the moment of birth, invites psychological damage which will likely plague that young woman's psyche for life. Instead of rearing the child with a moral education, the surrogate mother sends a child born from her own body and blood off into an uncertain world to be raised in a setting whose origin violates the sanctity of sex. Clearly, for Ukraine to have a thriving surrogate mother business would be unimaginable except for the war with Russia, in which the destruction of homes, apartment complexes, and basic infrastructure facilites providing for energy, water, and sanitation continues unabated.

Given the chaos of Ukraine's wartime legal system, surrogate mothers who are abused during or after their pregnancy have little or no legal recourse. In a special report on Ukrainian baby factories, *Politico* reported the following: "But the concerns resonate because of the extent of the surrogacy business in Ukraine—which produces hundreds of babies per year—and the anxiety and desperation of the people involved. There's also the not insignificant factor that the entire process is being carried out amid an epic military clash in which the fate of the country hangs in the balance."[132]

Manuel Fontaine, Director of Emergencies at the United Nations Children's Fund (UNICEF), has expressed alarm that "nearly two thirds

---

132 "Inside a Ukrainian baby factory," *Politico*, Special report, Politico.com, July 23,, 2023, https://www.politico.com/news/2023/07/23/ukraine-surrogates-fertility-00104913#:~:text=The%20requirements%20to%20use%20a,from%20as%20little%20as%20%2440%2C000.

of all Ukrainian children have been displaced since the conflict began." He echoed "reports of sexual violence and other forms of gender-based violence."[133] The US State Department reports that as of July 2023, more than 6 million people have fled Ukraine since the start of the war, with another 5.1 million displaced internally. Experts estimate that 90 percent of those who fled were women and children, and more than half of Ukraine's children were displaced. "These refugee and displaced populations are especially vulnerable to human trafficking," the State Department report stressed. "There are reports of Ukrainian citizens being recruited, including through online means, for sex trafficking abroad and for forced labor, and reports of suspected traffickers targeting women and children fleeing the war at transit points and reception centers."[134] The BBC reported that trafficking rings "are notoriously active in Ukraine and neighboring countries in peace time. The fog of war is perfect cover to increase business."[135]

Nuclear War on the Horizon

The Trump impeachment hearings over Ukraine revealed a clear double standard. While the DOJ took no steps to begin a serious criminal investigation into Hunter Biden's activities in Ukraine, the House of Representatives impeached Trump for daring to ask President Zelenskyy about the status of a criminal investigation in Ukraine. Bolstered by a Government Accountability Office (GAO) report,

---

133 "Mounting Reports of Crimes against Women, Children in Ukraine Raising 'Red Flags' over Potential Protection Crisis, Executive Director Tells Security Council," United Nations, 9013th Meeting (AM), SC/14857, April 11, 2022, https://press.un.org/en/2022/sc14857.doc.htm.
134 Office to Monitor and Combat Trafficking in Persons, US Department of State, "Trafficking in Persons Fact Sheet—Ukraine," State.gov, July 2023, www.state.gov/wp-content/uploads/2023/10/Trafficking-in-Persons-Fact-Sheet-Ukraine-Accessible-Oct-5-2023.pdf.
135 Katya Adler, "How the sex trade preys on Ukraine's refugees," *BBC News,* BBC.com, March 27, 2022, https://www.bbc.com/news/world-europe-60891801.

Democrats in Congress charged that President Trump illegally withheld from Ukraine $214 million in funds that Congress had appropriated to the Department of Defense for security assistance to Ukraine. The allegation was that Trump withheld the funds to bludgeon Ukraine into investigating Biden, the Democrat that Trump was most likely to face as his presidential rival in the 2020 presidential election. That argument did not develop to be decisive in the Senate removal from office trial. Pentagon spokesman Jonathan Hoffman countered, saying, "Our goal with regard to Ukraine aid, has always continued to be, to ensure that anti-corruption measures were in place and that the money would be well spent."[136]

During the House hearings in the run-up to the impeachment vote, numerous State Department officials made clear that Obama administration policy was aimed at getting Ukraine to join the EU and NATO, while providing military assistance to Ukraine to repel the Russian invasion. On October 11, 2019, in her opening statement to the House Permanent Select Committee on Intelligence, the Committee on Foreign Affairs, and the Committee on Oversight and Reform former US Ambassador to Ukraine Marie L. Yovanovitch made clear that State Department policy called for integration of Ukraine into the EU. She testified as follows: "Supporting Ukraine's integration into Europe and combatting Russia's efforts to destabilize Ukraine have anchored US policy since the Ukrainian people protested on the Maidan in 2014 and demanded to be part of Europe and live according to the rule of law. That was US policy when I was appointed Ambassador in August 2016, and it was reaffirmed as the policy of the current administration in early 2017."[137]

---

136 Dan Mangan and Kevin Breuninger, "Trump administration broke law withholding Ukraine aid, watchdog says as Senate prepares for impeachment trial," CNBC.com, January 16, 2020, https://www.cnbc.com/2020/01/16/trump-administration-broke-law-in-withholding-ukraine-aid.htm.l
137 "Opening Statement of Marie L. Yovanovitch to the House of Representatives

Yovanovitch was closely aligned with the Democratic National Party. In 2019, investigative reporter John Solomon revealed that during the 2016 presidential campaign, Yovanovitch gave Ukranian prosecutor General Yuriy Lutsenko a "do not prosecute" list that was designed to protect the Anti-Corruption Action Centre (AntAC), a Soros-funded organization operating in Ukraine. Yovanovitch's goal was to stop Lutsenko's probe into whether $4.4 million in US funding to AntAC had been improperly diverted.[138] On October 3, 2019, Trump fired Yovanovitch, reportedly for blocking the Biden probe and bad-mouthing Trump.[139] John Solomon reported that Yovanovich "believed she was unjustly fired despite the fact that she was an Obama holdover, was speaking out against President Trump and she was colluding with the DNC [Democratic National Committee] and Hillary Clinton to undermine the US presidential election."[140] Yovanovitch was fired because the State Department in Ukraine was a rogue US embassy that violated the Geneva Convention by becoming directly involved in the internal politics of Ukraine to protect Biden, Soros, and Hillary Clinton. The official policy of the Democrats in the State Department since the Obama administration has involved taking many affirmative

---

Permanent Select Committee on Intelligence, Committee on Foreign Affairs, and Committee on Oversight and Reform," October 11, 2019, published by the *New York Times*, https://int.nyt.com/data/documenthelper/1888-yovanovitch-opening-statement/48cf6b834149b4867fb5/optimized/full.pdf.

138 John Solomon, US Embassy pressed Ukraine to drop probe of George Soros group uring 2016 election," The Hill, TheHill.com, March 26, 2019, https://thehill.com/opinion/campaign/435906-us-embassy-pressed-ukraine-to-drop-probe-of-george-soros-group-during-2016./

139 Rebecca Ballhaus, Michael C. Bender, and Vivian Salama, "Trump Ordered Ukraine Ambassador Removed After Complaints from Giuliani, Others," *Wall Street Journal*, October 3, 3019, https://www.wsj.com/articles/trump-ordered-ukraine-ambassador-removed-after-complaints-from-giuliani-others-11570137147.

140 Jim Hoft, "John Solomon Exposes Fired Ukrainian Ambassador's Links to Radical Soros Group," The Gateway Pundit, October 11, 2019, https://www.thegatewaypundit.com/2019/10/john-solomon-exposes-fired-ukrainian-ambassadors-links-to-radical-soros-group-video./

steps, including working with Soros to fund the Maidan Revolution, to eliminate Russian influence in Ukraine and to bring Ukraine into both the EU and NATO—moves which Moscow predictably viewed as provocative. Despite being a State Department employee, Yovanovitch continued to take her direction on Ukraine from Obama and Hillary, even after Trump was elected president.[141]

In May 2022, then British Prime Minister Boris Johnson visited Kiev to encourage President Zelenskyy to reject a negotiated deal with Russia that would have included a promise from Ukraine not to join NATO. Johnson's two main arguments were that Putin could not be trusted in negotiations, and the West was not ready to end the war.[142] In his televised interview with Putin on February 10, 2024, Tucker Carlson asked him why he thought Boris Johnson intervened to prevent Ukraine from negotiating a settlement with Russia. Putin answered, "For some reason, everyone had the illusion that Russia could be defeated on the battlefield."[143]

Putin rejected the US/EU contention that Russia has aggressive ambitions to move back into the eastern European territories that were formerly part of the Soviet Union. Putin dismissed this as absurd: "It is absolutely out of the question. You don't have to be any kind of analyst; it goes against common sense to get involved in some kind of global war. And a global war will bring all of humanity to the brink of extinction."[144] Putin continued, emphasizing the following: "They [the

141 Tyler Durden, "'The Real Ukraine Controversy; John Solomon Exposes How Rogue US Embassy Conducted Foreign Policy," ZeroHedge.com, October 13, 2019, https://www.zerohedge.com/political/real-ukraine-controversy-john-solomon-exposes-how-rogue-us-embassy-conducted-foreign.

142 Connor Echols, "Diplomacy Watch: Did Boris Johnson help stop a peace deal in Ukraine?" ResponsibleStatecraft.org, September 2, 2022, https://responsiblestatecraft.org/2022/09/02/diplomacy-watch-why-did-the-west-stop-a-peace-deal-in-ukraine/.

143 "Full Text Transcript of Tucker Carlson Putin Interview," MirageNews..com, February 10, 2024, https://www.miragenews.com/full-text-transcript-of-tucker-carlson-putin-1171489/.

144 Ibid.

US and EU] have been scaring everyone with us all along. Tomorrow Russia will use tactical nuclear weapons, tomorrow Russia will use that, no, the day after tomorrow. So what? These are just horror stories for people in the street in order to extort additional money from US tax-payers in the confrontation with Russia in the Ukrainian theater of war. The goal is to weaken Russia as much as possible."[145]

On January 26, 2024, the *Guardian* in London reported that the US is planning to station nuclear weapons in the UK "for the first time in 15 years amid a growing threat from Russia."[146] On February 25, 2023, into the third year of the Russia-Ukraine War, the *New York Times* revealed that the CIA over the last eight years had supported a network of twelve spy bases along the Russian border.[147] In March, Russia released a thirty-eight-minute audio recording of an intercepted conversation in which German air force officers discussed striking infrastructure in Crimea with advanced German-made Taurus missiles capable of hitting targets 300 miles away.[148] Dmitry Medvedev, the former president of Russia who now is deputy chair of Russia's security council, has been warning that the aggressive use by Ukraine of advanced US/NATO weaponry capable of hitting targets inside Russia risks a Russian nuclear response.[149]

---

145 Ibid.
146 "US planning to station nuclear weapons in UK amid threat from Russia—report," , January 26, 2024, https://www.theguardian.com/uk-news/2024/jan/26/us-planning-to-station-nuclear-weapons-in-uk-amid-threat-from-russia-report.
147 Adam Entous and Michael Schwirtz, "Spy War: How the C.I.A. Secretly Helps Ukraine Fight Putin," *New York Times*, February 28, 2024, https://www.nytimes.com/2024/02/25/world/europe/cia-ukraine-intelligence-russia-war.html.
148 *Le Monde* with AFP, "Germany to investigate a confidential army recording 'intercepted' by Russia," Le Monde, LeMonde.fr, March 2, 2024, https://www.lemonde.fr/en/international/article/2024/03/02/germany-to-investigate-a-confidential-army-recording-intercepted-by-russia_6579045_4.html#:~:text=The%20'intercepted'%20file%2C%20a,the%20state%2Dbacked%20RT%20channel.
149 "Medvedev says aim of nuclear exercises is to work out response to attacks on Russian Soil," Reuters, May 10, 2024, https://www.reuters.com/world/europe/medvedev-says-aim-nuclear-exercises-is-work-out-response-attacks-russian-soil-2024-05-10/.

On May 6, 2024, Putin ordered the practicing of tactical nuclear weapon deployment as part of planned military exercise after what Moscow said were threats from France, Britain, and the United States to get more directly involved with French, British, and US armed forces—a move that would quickly transform the current US/EU proxy war on Russia into a direct military confrontation.[150] On April 23, 2024, UK Prime Minister Rishi Sunak said the country is putting its defense industry on a "war footing" by increasing defense spending to 2.5 percent of gross domestic product (GDP) by the end of the decade, pledging to send arms worth $620 million dollars to Ukraine.[151] On April 28, 2024, Biden signed into law another spending bill sending $61 billion to Ukraine, with the bulk of the money being passed through US arms manufacturers.[152] So far, the only winners in the Russia-Ukraine war are the arms manufacturers and the bankers who finance them. Meanwhile, the Pentagon, according to the Government Accountability Office, failed its sixth audit in a row in November 2023, unable to account for 63 percent of the Department of Defense nearly $4 trillion in assets.[153]

There is no way the NATO countries are going to dislodge Russia

---

150 Guy Faulconbridge, "Putin orders tactical nuclear weapon drills to deter West," Reuters, May 6, 2024, https://www.reuters.com/world/europe/russia-practice-tactical-nuclear-weapon-scenario-deter-west-defence-ministry-2024-05-06/.

151 Venessa Gera and Sylvia Hui, "UK puts its defense industry on 'war footing' and gives Ukraine $620 million in new military aid," Associated Press (AP), APnews.com, April 23, 2024, https://apnews.com/article/poland-uk-nato-ukraine-sunak-military-aid-be9fa8b106eda83c2da140e0f2774fcb.

152 Ben Wershkul, "Biden is sending $61 billion to Ukraine. Much of it will pass through the US economy first," Yahoo News, April 28, 2024, https://finance.yahoo.com/news/biden-is-sending-61-billion-to-ukraine-much-of-it-will-pass-through-the-us-economy-first-162914531.html?guce_referrer=aHR0cHM6Ly93d3cuZ29vZ2xlLmNvbS88&guce_referrer_sig=AQAAAAbZ-LYWzm7V1DWnFuNtYIzzAtZq1S2BS5WMykTI2mHL2ZUbaJED.

153 Julia Gledhill, "Pentagon can't account for 63% of nearly $4 trillion in assets," Reasonable Statecraft, ReasonableStatecraft.org, December 4, 2023, https://responsiblestatecraft.org/pentagon-audit-2666415734/.

from Ukraine with a conventional war. Already, the Ukraine battle-ground has become like a video game, with sophisticated electronics directing drones and missiles via satellites in space. According to a *New York Times* report, Ukraine's much touted offensive failed given Russia's superior defenses which fortified natural obstacles with "miles of Russian defenses—trenches, tank traps and mines—that only allow Ukraine's troops to make incremental progress at best."[154] In 2023, the US Department of Defense anounced plans to spend $2.6 billions on unmanned weapons systems, with more money going to the development of arial drones than in any other category.[155] A decision by the NATO countries to spend more billions with weapons of ever-increasing sophistication and lethal power only accelerates a decision to make the Ukraine battlefield nuclear.

Finally, we come to the recognition that Ukraine is a failed state because that is exactly the way the US/EU/NATO Deep State wants it to be. The Russia-Ukraine conflict did not have to be fought, had the US/EU/NATO intelligence and military industrial complexes acceded to Putin's wish to keep Ukraine out of NATO. Had Ukraine been run by honest government officials and honest business executives, the Clinton and Biden crime families could never have stolen such a huge amount of money. To assume that the CIA and other military intelligence agencies, including the National Security Agency (NSA) and the US Treasury, were not watching the moral degradation of Ukraine society is naive. What is becoming all too apparent is that the war between Russia and Ukraine is edging toward nuclear war because that is what the US/EU/NATO Deep State demons appear willing to risk, if not

154 Thomas Gibbons-Neff, Josh Holder, and Marco Hernandez, "21 Miles of Obstacles," New York Times, July 28, 2023, https://www.nytimes.com/interactive/2023/06/28/world/europe/ukraine-counteroffensive-obstacles.html.
155 Miriam McNabb, "How Much Will the US Department of Defense Spend on Drones in 2023?" DroneLife.com, January 17, 2023, https://dronelife.com/2023/01/17/how-much-will-the-u-s-department-of-defense-spend-on-drones-in-2023-auvsis-report/.

desire, despite the insanity of a global thermonuclear war for the future of civilization.

As noted earlier, before he became president of Ukraine, Volodymyr Zelenskyy was an actor and comedian who played the role of Ukraine's president in a popular television show, *Servant of the People*.[156] Today, Zelenskyy wears trendy combat fatigues, feigning military prowess for an actor who now gets to play the real role of a wartime president.

Special Counsel Robert Hur found evidence that Vice President Biden "willfully" retained and shared highly classified materials as a private citizen. Hur, however, declined to indict Biden, concluding that Biden was suffering senior memory loss. "Biden will likely present himself to the jury, as he did during his interview with our office, as a sympathetic, well-meaning, elderly man with a poor memory," the special counsel wrote in his final report.[157] The obvious question is why Biden remains president if he is suffering some form of senior dementia. That Zelenskyy and Biden are both actors in a US/EU/NATO Deep State *Truman Show* movie is becoming all too apparent, even to the puppet masters pulling the strings.

On May 14, 2024, the Ukrainian government extended martial law, announcing that all elections, including a presidential election originally scheduled for March–April 2024, would be cancelled until "all Ukrainians" could vote. US Secretary of State Antony Blinken made

---

156 Lisa Respers, France, CNN, "Volodymyr Zelenskyy's acting career prepared him for the world stage," CNN Entertainment, CNN.com, updated March 4, 2022, https://www.cnn.com/2022/03/04/entertainment/volodymyr-zelensky-acting-career/index.html.
157 Associated Press, "Read the full Joe Biden classified documents special counsel report," APNews.com, February 8, 2024, https://apnews.com/joe-biden-special-counsel-report. For the original document, see: US Special Counsel's Office, US Department of Justice, "Report of the Special Counsel on the Investigation Into Unauthorized Removal, Retention, and Disclosure of Classified Documents Discovered at Locations Including the Pen Biden Center and the Delaware Private Residence of President Joseph R. Biden, Jr.," Justice.gov, February 5, 2024, www.justice.gov/storage/report-from-special-counsel-robert-k-hur-february-2024.pdf.

clear that "all Ukrainians" included those in the Ukrainian eastern provinces held by Russia.

John Daniel Davidson, a senior editor for *The Federalist*, correctly noted Blinken's comments amounted to a permanent suspension of elections in Ukraine. "This [Blinken's comments] means no elections even if a ceasefire or peace plan is in place, so long as Russia controls any Ukrainian territory," Davidson wrote. "It's a recipe for the permanent suspension of elections in Ukraine, since any ceasefire or negotiated peace process will inevitably see Russia in control of at least some Ukrainian territory." Davidson noted the irony that Ukraine cancelled the presidential election in the name of "democracy." Davidson recalled that cybersecurity agent Mike Benz had explained on a Tucker Carlson podcast in February 2024[158] that Blinken and Zelenskyy were really "protecting the institutions of democratic society and insulating them from reform—institutions like the CIA, FBI, IMF, and the World Bank." Davidson stressed that "if it comes down to a contest between the two, the institutions must be protected from the voters—that is 'democracy' must be protected from the threat of free and fair elections." Davidson began his commentary with a title that declared the real problem Ukraine had in holding presidential elections as planned was that the Ukrainians might vote to end the war.[159]

President Trump has claimed he could end the Ukraine war in twenty-four hours.[160] Putin has repeatedly signalled that he is willing to stop

---

158 Tucker Carlson, TC Network, Episode 75, "The national security state is the main driver of censorship and election interference in the United States. 'What I'm describing is military rule,' says Mike Benz. 'It's the inversion of democracy,'" Twitter.com (now "X"), February 16, 2024, https://twitter.com/TuckerCarlson/status/1758529993280205039?s=20.

159 John Daniel Davidson, "The real problem with holding presidential elections in Ukraine right now is that Ukrainians. might vote to end the war," The Federalist, TheFederalist.com, May 16, 2024, https://thefederalist.com/2024/05/16/whatever-u-s-elites-are-defending-in-ukraine-it-isnt-democracy/. All John Daniel Davidson quotes in this paragraph come from this source.

160 Andrew Carey and Victoria Butenko, "'Very Dangerous'; Zelinsky on Trump's claim

the war in Ukraine, having secured freedom from the government in Kiev for the two eastern provinces with a history alligned to Russia going back centuries in the past. But the Biden administration and the State Department have remained committed to the Obama policy to move Ukraine into the EU and NATO—a determination that does not seem deterred by the increasingly real possibility that the increasingly direct US or NATO involvement in the war could lead to the use of nuclear weapons. Why is the Biden administration seemingly willing to follow a potentially suicidal foreign policy that already threatens the possible use of tactical nuclear weapons on the batlefield? Why is the Deep State hell-bent on going to conquering Russia even if it means a thermonuclear World War III global apocalypse?[161]

That we appear to be rapidly heading into World War III is another sign Satan sits at the helm of a Deep State-controlled US government that without God is capable only of perpetual war, not perpetual peace. As General Smedley Butler came to realize, the only winners in waging war are the bankers and the arms manufacturers. In a country as corrupt as Ukraine, all the rest is a lie.

---

could end Russia-Ukraine war within 24 hours," CNN.com, January 20, 2024, https://www.cnn.com/2024/01/20/europe/zelensky-trump-end-russia-ukraine-war-intl-hnk/index.html.
161 Posted by Austrian Peter, "The Financial Jigsaw, Part 2—The Global Chessboard—WW3 Update," TheBurningPlatform.com, June 22,2024, https://www.theburningplatform.com/2024/06/22/the-financial-jigsaw-part-2-the-global-chessboard-ww3-update-le-petit-roi-sitrep-ukraine-genocide-cuba-redux-h/.

CHAPTER 3

NOVEMBER 22, 1963: THE DAY
THE MUSIC STOPPED

With every paper I'd deliver
Bad news on the doorstep
I couldn't take one more step
I can't remember if I cried
When I read about his widowed bride
But something touched me deep inside
The day the music died.

—Don McLean, "American Pie," *American Pie*[162]

The Germans were defeated in World War II ... but not the Nazis.
They were simply forced to move. They scattered to the four corners
of the world. Many of them came to the United States and penetrated
what President Dwight D. Eisenhower termed "the military-industrial
complex."

—Jim Marrs, *The Rise of the Fourth Reich*[163]

After November 22, 1963, the day President John F. Kennedy was assassinated in Dallas, Texas, everything about America seemed to change.
In retrospect, the Eisenhower years had been years of innocence.

---

162 Don McLean, Lyrics to his song "American Pie," Track One on the *American Pie* album, 1971, Genius.com, May 26, 1971, https://genius.com/Don-mclean-american-pie -lyrics.
163 Jim Marrs, *The Rise of the Fourth Reich: The Secret Societies That Threaten to Take Over America* (New York: William Morrow, 2008), p. 4.

Americans, who fought in World War II and survived, returned home. They got married, had children, and moved to the suburbs. America was in the prime of an economic boom that flourished on November 22, 1963. When the shots rang out in Dealey Plaza at approximately 12:30 p.m. CST that day, the Deep State decided to go rogue, blasting apart the head of a sitting president in full public view. Lyndon Johnson, who should have been worried this was the first act of a Russian full-scale nuclear attack on the United States, took his time getting out of Dallas. LBJ waited to take off for Washington until JFK's body was secured back in Air Force One, and federal judge Sarah Tilghman Hughes swore LBJ to the oath of office at 2:38 p.m. CST. At 2:47 p.m. CST, the wheels of Air Force One lifted off from Love Field in Dallas, heading back to Andrews Air Force Base in Washington, DC.[164]

On November 26, 1963, one day after JFK's funeral, LBJ signed National Security Action Memorandum 273 (NSAM 273), rescinding and reversing JFK's NSAM 263, signed October 11, 1963, which had ordered a United States military pull-out from the civil war in Vietnam. JFK's NSAM 263 remained hidden from the American public until the publication of the Pentagon Papers in 1971. LBJ hid the true purpose of NSAM 273 by deceptively portraying it as "reaffirming the US commitment to Vietnam and the continuation of Vietnam programs and policies of the Kennedy administration."[165] Had JFK lived, we would never have fought in Vietnam.

The war in Vietnam was the primary impetus for the anti-war demonstrations of the 1960s—demonstrations that mixed a desire to

---

164 Garrett M. Graff, "From the Archives: After JFK's Assassination, His Final Flight from Dallas," *Washingtonian*, Washingtonian.com, November 23, 2023, https://www. washingtonian.com/2023/11/22/from-the-archives-after-jfks-assassination-his-final-flight -from-dallas/.
165 James K. Galbraith, "Exit Strategy: In 1963, JFK ordered a complete withdrawal from Vietnam," *Boston Review*, BostonReview.net, September 1, 2003, https://www .bostonreview.net/articles/galbraith-exit-strategy-vietnam/.

avoid the draft with neo-Marxist ideological views designed to erode the postwar view of the United States as a defender of freedom. The radical left was able to portray the US involvement in Vietnam as an imperialist nation fighting colonial war, just as JFK had feared. As a US Senator, President Kennedy had spoken out loudly opposing de Gualle in Algeria. JFK had already rejected going to war in Laos, and now he did not want to replace the French in Vietnam. In retrospect, Vietnam was a turning point in viewing the United States as having fought for God and freedom—the predominant political perception of our victory over Nazi Germany and Imperial Japan in World War II. Gone forever was the 1950s luster of a nation in postwar prosperity after emerging from World War II as the dominant world superpower. At 12:30 p.m. CST in Dallas on November 22, 1963, the bright promise of JFK's New Frontier died.

The JFK Assassination: A Deep State Coup d'état

Dr. David W. Mantik, armed with a PhD in physics and an MD with a medical practice extending over five decades as a radiation oncologist, has seen the JFK autopsy skull X-rays more than anyone else. Using a densitometer, he measured the light coming through the X-rays millimeter-by-millimeter (with some measurements at a tenth-of-a-millimeter calibration). In a new book that I co-authored with Dr. Mantik, *The Assassination of John F. Kennedy: The Final Analysis*,[166] Dr. Mantik presents his conclusions that all three extant JFK autopsy skull X-rays currently in the National Archives collection are forgeries, not originals—altered copies designed to mask evidence of frontal shots. Dr. Mantik's forensic analysis of the JFK autopsy X-rays also proved JFK received two headshots from the front and one from the rear.

One frontal shot hit JFK in the right forehead at the hairline. The

---

166 Jerome R. Corsi, PhD and David W. Mantik, MD, PhD, *The Assassination of John F. Kennedy: The Final Analysis* (New York: Post Hill Press, 2024).

bullet fragmented within the skull. A bullet fragment trail can be seen on the right lateral JFK autopsy skull X-ray going from the entry wound on the forehead across the top right quadrant of JFK's skull. The largest bullet fragment is in the rear of the head, and the bullet did not exit JFK's skull, providing indisputable evidence of a frontal shot.

The second frontal shot was an oblique shot that hit JFK in the temporal bone to the front of the right ear. This tangential shot blew out the back right occipital region of JFK's skull, blowing out a furrow of cerebral matter from the right temporal bone entry wound to the massive, gaping wound in the right rear of JFK's head.

The one rear headshot was at a low angle, entering JFK's head at the external occipital protuberance (EOP), i.e., the bump at the back of the head. None of the three JFK headshots evident in the three extant JFK autopsy skull X-rays came from the angle required if the shot had come from the sixth floor of the Texas School Book Depository.

Dr. Manulis's forensic evidence proves indisputably that Lee Harvey Oswald was not the "lone gun assassin," as the Warren Commission concluded. The moment the Secret Service parked the JFK limousine at Parkland Hospital, after getting JFK and John Connally into the emergency room, the Secret Service took a pail of water to wash the blood and gore from the limousine's back seat—thus effectively altering a crime scene. When spectators at Parkland Hospital noticed a frontal shot through the limousine windshield that hit JFK in the throat, the Secret Service cordoned off the limousine to prevent bystanders from photographing it. Government officials flew the JFK limousine to Dearborn, Michigan, where at the Ford Motor Company's (FMC) River Rouge Assembly Plant, Building B, where George Whitaker Sr., an FMC employee, supervised the destruction and replacement of the JFK limousine's front windshield on Monday, November 25, 1963, the day of JFK's funeral.

Within minutes of Lee Harvey Oswald's arrest in Dallas, the Dallas

Police told the press that Oswald was the assassin. Almost simultaneously, a press bulletin was distributed worldwide with a full biography of Oswald, identifying him as an ex-Marine who had served at a US base in Japan before defecting to the Soviet Union. The inevitable conclusion is that the JFK assassination was a Deep State coverup that has persisted for over six decades—a coverup designed to mask a government-executed coup d'état.

But the Deep State had a problem. The Secret Service agents at the scene of the shooting knew JFK was shot from the front. Secret Service agent Clint Hill was assigned to Jacqueline Kennedy on November 22, 1963. When the shooting began, Hill jumped from the running board of the Secret Service follow-up car and ran to the rear handhold on the limousine after the first shots. Hill was "the closest reliable witness" to JFK's head wounds.[167]

On November 30, 1963, Hill recalled:

> As I lay over the top of the back seat I noticed a portion of the President's head on the right rear side was missing and he was bleeding profusely. Part of his brain was gone. I saw a part of his skull with hair on it lying in the seat.[168]

At a book signing (available on YouTube), Hill described his run from the follow-up car to the limousine:

> As I approached the vehicle [JFK's limousine] there was a third shot. It hit the President in the head, upper right rear of the right ear, causing a gaping hole in his head, which caused brain matter, blood, and bone fragments to spew forth out over the car, over myself. At that point

167 Ibid., p. 1140.
168 "Statement of Special Agent Clinton J. Hill, dated November 30, 1963," Commission Exhibit 1024, *WCH*, Volume XVIII, pp. 740–745, at p. 742.

Mrs. Kennedy came up out of the back seat onto the trunk of the car. She was trying to retrieve something that had gone off to the right rear. She did not know I was there. At that point I grabbed Mrs. Kennedy, put her in the back seat. The President fell over into her lap, to his left.

Hill continued:

The right side of his head was exposed. I could see his eyes were fixed. There was a hole in the upper right rear portion of his head about the size of my palm. Most of the grey matter in that area had been removed, and was scattered throughout the entire car, including on Mrs. Kennedy. I turned and gave the follow-up car crew the thumbs-down, indicating that we were in a very dire situation. The driver accelerated; he got up to the lead car, which was driven by Chief Curry, the Dallas Chief of Police.[169]

In Trauma Room One at Parkland Hospital, the medical personnel attending Kennedy recognized immediately unmistakable evidence of frontal shots. In his testimony, Dr. Robert McClelland gave the "most detailed description of the Kennedy head wound."[170] McClelland depicted the scene:

As I took the position at the head of the table that I have already described, to help out with the tracheotomy, I was in such a position that I could very closely examine the head wound, and I noticed that

---

169 James H. Fetzer, "Who's telling the truth: Clint Hill or the Zapruder film?" The Education Forum, EducationForum.ipbhost.com, January 12, 2011, https://educationforum.ipbhost.com/topic/17242-whos-telling-the-truth-clint-hill-or-the-zapruder-film/. Also see "Warwick's Books Presents *The Kennedy Detail: JFK's Secret Service Agents*," YouTube, posted 2011, https://www.youtube.com/watch?v=lYpY8zI_wwA&t=1482s.
170 Josiah Thompson, *Six Seconds in Dallas: A Micro-Study of the Kennedy Assassination* (New York: Bernard Geis Associates, 1967), p. 107.

the right posterior portion of the skull had been extremely blasted. It had been shattered, apparently, by the force of the shot so that the parietal bone was protruded up through the scalp and seemed to be fractured almost along its right posterior half, as well as some of the occipital bone being fractured in its lateral half, and this sprung open the bones that I mentioned in such a way that you could actually look down into the skull cavity itself and see that probably a third or so, at least, of the brain tissue, posterior cerebral tissue, and some of the cerebellar tissue had been blasted out. There was a large amount of bleeding which was occurring mainly from the large venous channels in the skull which had been blasted open.[171]

While McClelland did not explicitly describe the head wound as an exit, his use of "blasted out" was even more dramatic. McClelland also concluded that the throat wound was an entrance:

At the moment [in the emergency room], of course, it was our impression before we had any other information from any other source at all, when we were just confronted with the acute emergency, the brief thoughts that ran through our minds were that this was one bullet, that perhaps entered through the front of the neck and then in some peculiar fashion which we really had, as I mentioned the other day, to strain to explain to ourselves, had coursed up from the front of the vertebra and into the base of the skull and out the rear of the skull.[172]

Dr. Charles Crenshaw, another member of the emergency medical team, vividly described his first impression of the wounds:

---

171 "Testimony of Dr. Robert M. McClelland Resumed," *WCH*, op. cit., Volume VI, March 21, 1964, pp. 30–36, resumed pp. 36–39, at p. 33.
172 Ibid., p. 37.

Then I noticed that the entire right hemisphere of his brain was missing, beginning at his hairline and extending all the way behind his right ear. Pieces of skull that hadn't been blown away were hanging by blood-matted hair. Based on my experience with trauma to the head from gunshots, I knew that only a high-velocity bullet from a rifle could dissect a cranium that way. Part of his brain, the cerebellum, was dangling from the back of his head by a single strand of tissue, looking like a piece of dark gray, blood-soaked sponge that would easily fit in the palm of a hand.[173]

Crenshaw added:

Blood was still seeping from the wound onto the gurney, dripping into the kick bucket on the floor. Seeing that, I became even more pessimistic. I also identified a small opening about the diameter of a pencil at the midline of his throat to be an entry bullet hole. I had seen dozens of them in the emergency room. At that point, I knew that he had been shot twice.[174]

At Parkland Hospital, some ninety minutes after the shooting, a struggle arose over JFK's body. British journalist and author Anthony Summers related the incident in his 1980 book *Conspiracy*:

At the hospital as the Secret Service team prepared to take the body to Washington, Dr. Earl Rose, the Dallas County Medical Examiner, backed by a Justice of the Peace, barred their way. The doctor said that, under Texas law, the body of a murder victim may not be removed until

---

173 Charles A. Crenshaw, MD, with Jens Hansen and J. Gary Shaw, *JFK: Conspiracy of Silence* (New York: Signet, paperback edition, 1992), pp. 78–79.
174 Ibid., p. 79.

an autopsy had been performed. And the J.P., Judge Ward, declared, "It's just another homicide as far as I'm concerned.[175]

Unfortunately for history, Rose's argument did not prevail. Summers continued:

> The Secret Service agents put the doctor and the judge up against the wall at gunpoint and swept out of the hospital with the President's body. They were wrong in law, and with hindsight, they denied their president an efficient autopsy.[176]

From the moment the Secret Service seized JFK's casket at gunpoint in the halls of Parkland Hospital until the moment of his burial in Arlington Cemetery on Monday, November 25, 1963, the US government had complete control over his body, which was the best evidence in the case.

But the government conspirators had not anticipated that Associated Press photographer James William "Ike" Altgens would be standing in front of the JFK limousine as it headed down Elm Street toward the triple overpass. Altgens snapped a photograph (known as Altgens 6) as JFK was raising his hands to his throat, with both elbows extended outward, in reaction to a frontal shot through the windshield that created an entry wound in JFK's throat.[177] That photograph showed the Texas School Book Depository (TSBD) behind the JFK limousine when the shooting started. Later, about an hour into the flight of Air Force One, the Dallas Police announced they had arrested Lee Harvey Oswald, an employee of the TSBD. The Dallas Police told the press that Oswald

---

175 Anthony Summers, *Conspiracy* (New York: McGraw-Hill Book Company, 1980), p. 42.

176 Ibid.

177 Richard B. Trask, *Pictures of the Pain: Photography and the Assassination of President Kennedy* (Danvers, MA: Yeoman Press, 1994), pp. 307–324, Altgens 6 photo at p. 314).

was the assassin, insisting he shot the president from the sixth floor of the TSBD. At 2 p.m. CST, The Altgens 6 photograph moved across the AP wire and was published in newspapers nationwide.[178]   If Oswald were the sole assassin, all the shots that day had to have come from the rear. The problem was the Parkland Hospital doctors had already given a press conference announcing to the world their conclusion that JFK had been shot from the front.

JFK's body arrived at the Bethesda Naval Hospital morgue at 6:35 p.m. ET on the night of the assassination, approximately one hour and a half before the official autopsy was to begin before the gallery observers in the Bethesda morgue.[179] The body arrived in a body bag that had been placed in a plain pinkish-gray metal shipping casket—not the ceremonial casket in which JFK's body left Parkland. Numerous Navy corpsmen and Tom Robinson, the mortician from the funeral home assigned to prepare JFK's body for return to the White House, witnessed as Drs. Humes and Boswell, the two Navy pathologists assigned to conduct the autopsy, performed pre-autopsy surgery on JFK's head to transform front entry wounds into rear entry wounds. Humes and Boswell also removed fragments of bullets from JFK's head in their efforts to erase any evidence of frontal shots. If altering the JFK autopsy skull X-rays were not enough evidence that the government altered the medical evidence to make JFK's gunshot wounds match the false public narrative, witnesses observing government doctors altering JFK's head wounds before the official autopsy, in front of the gallery witnesses, should seal the case that the Warren Commission was more interested

---

178 Larry Rivera and Roy Schaeffer, "JFK: The James 'Ike' Altgens Photo Timeline," OpenGovTV.com April 2, 2015, Larry Rivera and Roy Schaeffer: opengovtv.com/index. php/sdvosb/item/4427-jfk-the-james-ike-altgens-photo-timeline

179 Jerome R. Corsi, PhD. and David W. Mantik, MD, PhD, *The Assassination of John F. Kennedy: The Final Analysis*, Chapter 5, "The Medical Coverup: Illicit Bethesda Surgery Before the Official Autopsy," pp. 344–404.

in keeping the government's involvement in the coup d'état secret than in discovering the truth.'

The Dulles Brothers

In the 1930s, much of the financing for Hitler's rise to power came from the United States. Prescott Bush and George Herbert Walker Bush, the grandfathers of President George Herbert Walker Bush, were partners in the Wall Street investment banking W. A. Harriman & Company. The Dulles brothers worked as lawyers at the prominent New York law firm Sullivan & Cromwell.

In his 2004 book entitled *American Dynasty: Aristocracy, Fortune, and the Politics of Deceit in the House of Bush*, political commentator and former Republican Party strategist Kevin Phillips wrote that among the most prominent Wall Street principals turning their attention to Germany in the 1930s were Averell Harriman, George Herbert Walker Bush, and the Dulles Brothers.[180] "In 1941, the *New York Herald Tribune* had featured a front-page story headlined "Hitler's Angel Has $3 Million in US Bank," reporting that steel baron Fritz Thyssen had channeled the money into the Union Banking Corporation, possibly to be held for "'Nazi bigwigs,'" Phillips noted. "UBC was the bank, nominally owned by a Dutch intermediary that Brown Brothers Harriman ran for the German Thyssen steel family. Prescott Bush was a director."[181] Since the 1930s, Brown Brothers Harriman was one the two most notable active investors in a rapidly rearming Germany that came under Nazi control when Hitler became chancellor in 1933. President Franklin D. Roosevelt ordered Union Bank to close after the Japanese attack on Pearl Harbor and the subsequent declaration of war by Nazi Germany on the United States. Going back to the 1930s, one

---

180 Kevin Phillips, *American Dynasty: Aristocracy, Fortune, and the Politics of Deceit in the House of Bush* (New York: Viking, 2004), page 37.
181 Ibid., page 39

of Sullivan & Cromwell's most notorious Nazi connections was the legal work the firm did for the German chemical firm I. G. Farben, the manufacturer during World War II of the Zyklon-B poison gas the Nazis used to kill Jews in the concentration camps of the Holocaust. John Foster Dulles, the chief legal contact at Sullivan & Cromwell for I. G. Farben, signed "Heil Hitler" in his correspondence to the German chemical firm before World War II.

Hitler and the NSDAP in Germany initially called themselves "National Socialists," not "Nazis." Joseph Goebbels first used the term "Nazi" in 1926 in a publication called *Der Nazi-Sozi* [*The Nazi-Sozi*], used as an abbreviation of "National Socialism."[182] In the 1930s, Hitler's rise to power attracted the attention of Wall Street. Hitler's perfect state envisioned a small self-appointed, (i.e., the Nazis) inner circle would align with multinational corporations to form an oligarchical elite whose concentrated wealth would allow them to command for themselves all the natural resources of Germany and, ultimately, the world. When Hitler assumed power in 1933, he was initially happy to extend Otto von Bismarck's government-funded healthcare program to government employees and the elderly to provide socialized health care for the German population. He initiated the construction of the Autobahn in 1933 to offer high-speed roadways to the public at government expense. In 1933, Hitler also launched a "Strength through Joy" program to provide German workers with affordable government-sponsored vacation packages and paid time off.[183] In 1937, he promoted the founding of Volkswagen (in English, "the people's car")

---

182 Joseph Goebbels, *The Nazi-Sozi*, a pamphlet that was one of Goebbels's earliest publications, archived at Research.Calvin.edu, https://research.calvin.edu/german-propaganda-archive/nazi-sozi.htm. The pamphlet is also archived in its original German-language print edition at Archive.org, https://archive.org/details/Goebbels-Joseph-Der-Nazi-Sozi/page/n1/mode/2up.
183 "Strength through Joy," Erenow.com, n.d., https://erenow.net/ww/hitlers-revolution-ideology-social-programs-foreign-affairs/14.php.

to provide cheap manufactured vehicles that German families could afford. Hitler's version of national socialism was that the government should provide a regulatory structure allowing international corporations to develop German businesses while at the same time providing a government-sponsored basic standard of living for the German population.

As we shall see, Hitler's vision of Nazi Germany bears a disturbing similarity to the globalism of Klaus Schwab and the World Economic Forum (WEF). Both shared the idea that the world's resources could greatly support a small ruling oligarchy. This oligarchy would accumulate enormous wealth by controlling multinational corporations through interlocking directorates and common shareholders. Through technological advances in both commercial manufacturing and military weaponry, the ruling Nazi or WEF masters could produce with their machines the material resources needed for the ruling oligarchs to live a life of luxury without the nuisance of having to engage in manual labor. As long as it was useful, the government could control the population through a modicum of state-provided welfare. The government could easily ideologically mold a middle class dependent on government largess for survival. The ultimate aim was a New World Order ruled by a One World Government. Any means necessary to the achievement of these goals were laudable, even if it meant intentionally crafting political messages as mendacious propaganda designed for their psychological manipulation value (i.e., *psyops*).

In his important 2015 book, *The Devil's Chessboard: Allen Dulles, the CIA, and the Rise of America's Secret Government*, David Talbot wrote:

In the view of the Dulles brothers, democracy was an enterprise that had to be carefully managed by the right men, not simply left to elected officials as a public trust. From their earliest days on Wall Street— where they ran Sullivan and Cromwell, the most powerful corporate law firm in the nation—their overriding commitment was always to the circle of accomplished, privileged men whom they saw as the true seat of power in America. Although (John) Foster (Dulles) and Allen (Dulles) did not come from the same wealthy families who dominated this elite club, the brothers' shrewd talents, missionary drive, and powerful connections firmly established them as top executives.[184]

Talbot concluded that "[Allen] Dulles undermined or betrayed every president he served in high office."[185] Talbot stressed: "Mind control experimentation, torture, political assassination, extraordinary rendition, massive surveillance of US citizens and foreign allies—these were all widely used tools of the Dulles reign."[186] In my 2013 book about the JFK assassination, *Who Really Killed Kennedy?* I came to this conclusion: "The day JFK removed Allen Dulles (after the disastrous Bay of Pigs) from directing the CIA was the day JFK signed his death warrant."[187]

In the concluding paragraphs of his 2015 book, *The Devil's Chessboard*, Talbot relates a confession that James Jesus Angleton, the infamous "Ghost" of the CIA, responsible for much of the CIA's nefarious work tracing back to the founding of the CIA, with activities that ranged from spying on antiwar and black ops to playing a role in MK-ULTRA.[188] As Talbot related the story, at the end of his life, Angleton confessed that he "had not been serving God, after all, when he followed Allen Dulles. He had been on a satanic quest."[189]

---

184 David Talbot, *The Devil's Chessboard: Allen Dulles, the CIA, and the Rise of America's Secret Government* (New York: Harper, 2015), pp. 3–4.
185 Ibid., p. 5.
186 Ibid., p. 9.
187 Jerome R. Corsi, Ph.D., *Who Really Killed Kennedy* (Washington, DC: WND Books, 2013), p. 301.
188 Jefferson Morley, *The Ghost: The Secret Life of CIA Spymaster James Jesus Angleton* (New York: St. Martin's Press, 2017).
189 David Talbot, *The Devil's Chessboard: Allen Dulles, the CIA, and the Rise of America's Secret Government*, op. cit., p. 620.

Angleton's dying words, spoken to journalist Joseph Trento, were delivered "between fits of calamitous coughing—lung-scraping seizures that still failed to break him of his cigarette habit—and soothing sips of tea." Angleton admitted that within the CIA, "(t)he better you lied and the more you betrayed, the more likely you would be to be promoted. . . . Outside of their duplicity, the only thing they had in common was a desire for absolute power. I did things that, in looking back on my life, I regret. But I was part of it and loved being in it." Angleton invoked the names of past CIA directors—Allen Dulles, Richard Helms, and Frank Wisner. Angleton insisted these men were "the grand masters." He said, "If you were in a room with them, you were in a room full of people that you had to believe would deservedly end up in hell." Then, after taking a slow sip of steaming tea, he concluded: "I guess I will see them there soon."[190]

Allen Dulles and Martin Bormann[191]

On the morning of November 9, 1942, Henrich Himmler, the Reichsführer of the *Schutzstaffel*, more commonly known as the SS, held a private meeting with Martin Bormann, the head of the *Parteikanzlei*, the Party Chancellery for the National Socialist German Workers' party, more commonly known as Nazis, and the personal secretary to Adolf Hitler, at the Brown House in Munich. The day before, the Allies had launched Operation Torch, an amphibious landing in French North Africa, marking the beginning of the end of the Third Reich. Leaving that meeting, Himmler and Bormann began taking active steps starting in 1943 to prepare for life after Germany lost the war, even if that meant staging their own deaths, and possibly the death

---

190 Ibid.
191 The paragraphs in this section and the next section are drawn heavily from my 2014 book *Hunting Hitler: New Scientific Evidence That Hitler Escaped Nazi Germany* (New York: Skyhorse Publishing, 2014), Chapter 4, "Allen Dulles, the OSS, the Vatican, and the Nazi Ratline," pp. 77–101.

of Hitler, and fleeing Germany to avoid capture. However, in order for going underground to be successful required finding and funding a haven for postwar survival. The two best alternatives in 1942 for the postwar survival of the Nazi party rested with Argentina and, ironically, the United States of America.

On November 11, 1942, two days after Himmler and Bormann met privately in Munich, Allen Dulles, an officer of the Office of Strategic Services, or OSS, the predecessor organization to today's CIA, arrived in Bern, Switzerland, just before the Germans sealed the French borders. In Bern, Dulles set up residence at No. 23 Herrengasse, and began his official appointment to serve as Special Assistant to the American Minister. In reality, Dulles, who spent the duration of World War II in Bern, served as the United States' top spy in Europe. [192]

Beginning in 1943, Bormann implemented an operation code-named *Aktion Adlerflug*, or Project Eagle Flight, with the goal of transferring German funds, whether counterfeit, stolen, or legitimate government funds, to safe havens abroad. Between 1943 and 1945, Bormann funded more than two hundred German companies in Argentina, with other investments in companies in Portugal, Spain, Sweden, and Turkey. Bormann is estimated to have created some 980 front companies outside Germany, with 770 in neutral countries, including 98 in Argentina. Additionally, he acquired shares of foreign companies, especially those listed on North American exchanges in Canada and the United States. These investments were designed to assist prominent Nazis fleeing Germany to resume economically productive lives elsewhere. SS *Oberstrumbanführer* Adolf Eichmann, a principal organizer of the Holocaust, when Israeli intelligence agents captured him

---

192 Dr. Greg Bradsher, "Allen Dulles and No. 23 Herrengasse, Bern, Switzerland, 194201945," National Archives website, Nov. 9, 2012, http://blogs.archives.gov /TextMessage/2012/11/09/allen-dulles-and-no-23-herrengasse-bern-switzerland-1942 -1945/.

in 1960, was working at the time of his capture under the assumed name of Ricardo Klement in the Mercedes Benz factory established by a Bormann investment at González Catán in the suburbs by a Buenos Aires.[193]

In the final days of World War II, Bormann was wrapped up in the dispersal of several billion dollars around the globe. "He dwelled on control of the 750 corporations [established as new German enterprises worldwide]," wrote celebrated CBS correspondent Paul Manning in his 1981 book, *Martin Bormann: Nazi in Exile.* "Bormann had utilized every known legal device to disguise their ownership and their patterns of operation: use of nominees, option agreements, poll agreements, endorsements in blank, escrow deposits, pledges, collateral loans, rights of first refusal, management contracts, service contracts, patent agreements, cartels, and withholding procedures."[194] Allen Dulles, in Bern, Switzerland, had to be aware of Bormann's efforts as German firms in the flight capital program used six Swiss private banks.

As Paul Manning pointed out, "all major Swiss banks were serving the Germans in the massive movement of funds," as Swiss financial agents and Swiss banks were beneficial to Bormann in his massive effort to diversify German capital investments outside Germany, anticipating the war would not come to a favorable end for the Nazis and Hitler's Germany.[195] Manning further commented German economic specialists had successfully penetrated eleven nations and had the economies of each under control; Bormann cultivated a base of several hundred thousand various business relationships outside Germany who felt comfortable working with German economic leadership because it was always profitable. Ultimately, Bormann's web stretched across France,

---

193 Ibid., pp. 56–58.
194 Paul Manning, *Martin Bormann in Exile* (Secaucus, NJ: Lyle Stuart, Inc., 1981), p. 144. Manning used the Anglicized spelling of "Mueller," instead of the German spelling, "Müller."
195 Ibid., p. 139.

Belgium, Holland, Norway, Yugoslavia, Austria, Poland, Spain, Sweden, Switzerland, Turkey, Portugal, Finland, Bulgaria, and Romania, and "reached out to such South American countries as Argentina, among others, that preferred an association with Germany to one with Britain and the United States."[196]

Even though Washington and London knew that Bormann was shifting German capital overseas, the US Treasury could not successfully intervene to block Bormann's efforts. In New York, Bormann used foreign exchange funds from Swiss banks to make large demand deposits in large money center banks, including National City (now Citibank) and Chase (now J. P. Morgan Chase), and several others now defunct such as then Manufacturers and Hanover (known as Manufacturers Hanover Trust before being reorganized out of existence). In return, Manning noted, the New York money center banks provided services such as the purchases of stocks and transfer or payment of money on demand by customers of Deutsche Bank, including representatives of the Bormann business organizations and Bormann himself, who ended up with demand accounts in three different New York City banks.

Allan Dulles went from financing Hitler before the start of World War II to helping the Nazis invest in the global network of stock markets as World War II wound to an end and the world prepared to rebuild. Ironically, Dulles ended up stimulating the US postwar economic boom by capturing the wealth Germany plundered from Europe for the US businesses that defeated Hitler. In the end, for Dulles and the other globalists, it was all about the money, and war ends up being good for you, as long as you worked for the bank.[197]

Dulles and the Gehlen SS

At the end of World War II, Dulles, still operating in Bern, Switzerland,

---

196 Ibid., p. 114.
197 Ibid., p. 139.

rescued Nazi intelligence director Reinhard Gehlen from a prison camp. Under Hitler, Gehlen had been responsible for Nazi military intelligence on the Eastern Front, including the Soviet Union. Gehlen fit perfectly into the plan Dulles had masterminded to use the Nazi SS intelligence operation built by Himmler as a critical element in the plan to evolve the wartime OSS into the peacetime CIA. Key to Dulles's plan was a decision by the United States to hold what eventually became the postwar Allied military tribunals judging Nazi war criminals in what was known as the Nuremberg Trials. Nazi intelligence assets such as Gehlen were much too valuable to future US intelligence to be found guilty of the war crimes they had committed. Gehlen planned to reemploy his network of SS intelligence agents in Eastern Europe as the backbone around which an anti-Soviet, anti-Communist intelligence network could be formed, headquartered in what emerged as Western Germany and tasked with performing undercover work against Communists throughout Eastern Europe.

"By the summer of 1945, Dulles had finished his negotiations with Gehlen," wrote JFK assassination researcher James DiEugenio in his 2012 book *Destiny Betrayed: JFK, Cuba, and the Garrison Case*. DiEugenio reported that by September 1945, Gehlen and six of his aides were flown to Washington by Eisenhower's chief of staff, Gen. Walter Bedell Smith.[198] As a result of high-level discussions in Washington, Gehlen's Nazi intelligence organization was transferred under his control to work in Eastern Europe until Germany was reorganized.

Why Was JFK Assassinated?

Jack Kennedy did not want to go to war. In the 1962 Cuban missile crisis, JFK resisted General Curtis LeMay's insistence that the United States should launch a military invasion of Cuba. JFK refused to go to

---

198 James DiEugenio, *Destiny Betrayed: JFK, Cuba, and the Garrison Case* (New York: Skyhorse Publishing, Second Edition, 2012), pp. 4–5.

war in Laos. As noted previously, JFK had decided to withdraw from Vietnam. In the Cuban missile crisis, JFK implemented a naval blockade and backchanneled with Russia's premier, Nikita Khrushchev. In a compromise deal, JFK agreed to pull US missiles out of Turkey in exchange for Russia pulling the missiles out of Cuba. After the Cuban Missile Crisis, JFK negotiated a nuclear test ban treaty with Russia. In a commencement address at American University in Washington, DC., on June 10, 1963, JFK argued to end the Cold War with Russia, saying:

> In short, both the United States and its allies, and the Soviet Union and its allies, have a mutually deep interest in a just and genuine peace and in halting the arms race. Agreements to this end are in the interests of the Soviet Union as well as ours—and even the most hostile nations can be relied upon to accept and keep those treaty obligations, and only those treaty obligations, which are in their own interest.
>
> So, let us not be blind to our differences—but let us also direct attention to our common interests and to the means by which those differences can be resolved. And if we cannot end now our differences, at least we can help make the world safe for diversity. For, in the final analysis, our most basic common link is that we all inhabit this small planet. We all breathe the same air. We all cherish our children's future. And we are all mortal.[199]

Kennedy's unwillingness to take military action infuriated General LeMay. In his 1992 book *JFK and Vietnam: Deception, Intrigue, and the Struggle for Power*, military intelligence expert John M. Newman noted that LeMay's push to use nuclear weapons spilled over from the

---

199 President John F. Kennedy, "Commencement Address at American University, Washington, D.C., June 10, 1963," John F. Kennedy Presidential Library and Museum, JFKLibrary.org, https://www.jfklibrary.org/archives/other-resources/john-f-kennedy-speeches/american-university-19630610.

Cuban missile crisis to Vietnam. "LeMay was anxious to defeat the communists in Southeast Asia, which in his view was the best place for a showdown," Newman wrote. "He reasoned that 'US military intervention in Southeast Asia, including the use of nuclear weapons, could be followed by many layers of escalation before the ultimate confrontation would occur' [emphasis added]."[200]

Kennedy thought LeMay's willingness to risk thermonuclear war was madness—a mistake the US military and NATO appear to be making once again in Ukraine. However, as General Smedley Butler reminds us, there are billions of dollars to be made in war, and generals typically do not achieve historic and lucrative advancements in their careers in peacetime.

LeMay attended the JFK autopsy, smoking his trademark cigar.[201] The smoke from LeMay's cigar bothered Dr. Humes, who loudly ordered whoever was smoking the cigar to "put the damn thing out." Humes ordered Navy corpsman Paul O'Connor to "see to it" that whoever was smoking the cigar stopped doing so. According to O'Connor, Humes was busy conducting the autopsy, so he had his back to O'Connor when he barked out this order. O'Connor went over to LeMay in the autopsy room gallery only to have LeMay blow smoke in his face. When O'Connor informed Humes that General LeMay was smoking the cigar, Humes turned pale and dropped the issue.[202] At Jim Garrison's 1969 JFK trial in New Orleans, Dr. Pierre Finck, the Army pathologist who joined Drs. Humes and Boswell, testified that military

---

200 John W. Newman, *JFK and Vietnam: Deception, Intrigue, and the Struggle for Power* (New York: Warner Books, 1992), p. 162.

201 Interview with Navy corpsman Paul O'Connor, in William Matson Law, *In the Eye of History: Disclosures in the JFK Assassination Medical Evidence* (Walterville, OR: Trine Day LLC, Second Edition, 2015), pp. 191–218, at p. 195.

202 Douglas Horne, *Inside the Assassinations Records Review Board*, Volume II, p. 487.

brass attending the JFK autopsy gave orders to the pathologists during the autopsy.[203]

In *The Rise of the Fourth Reich*, Jim Marrs enumerates the many enemies JFK had created by 1963:

> By mid-1963, Kennedy was beginning to exert his autonomous influence over the most powerful—and violent—groups in US society. He was threatening to disband the CIA, the homebase of many Nazis; withdraw US troops from South Vietnam; close the tax breaks of the oil depletion allowance; tighten control over the tax-free foreign assets of US multinational corporations, many with connections to the Bormann empire; and decrease the power of both Wall Street and the Federal Reserve System. In June 1963, Kennedy actually ordered the printing and release of $4.2 billion in United States Notes, paper money issued through the Treasury Department without paying interest to the Federal Reserve System, which is composed of twelve regional banks all controlled by private banks whose owners often are non-Americans.[204]

On April 27, 1961, President Kennedy gave a speech to the American Newspaper Publishers Association meeting at the Waldorf-Astoria Hotel in New York City. In that speech, JFK warned about the danger of secret societies. "The very word 'secrecy' is repugnant in a free and open society; and we are as a people inherently and historically opposed to secret societies, to secret oaths and to secret proceedings," Kennedy explained. "Today no war has been declared—and however fierce the struggle may be, it may never be declared in the traditional fashion. Our way of life is under attack. Those who make themselves our enemy

---

203 "Clay Shaw Trial Transcript, 25 Feb 1969 (Testimony of Dr. Finck) Part 3," MaryFarrell.org, transcript p. 6, https://www.maryferrell.org/showDoc. html?docId=1301#relPageId=9.

204 Jim Marrs, *The Rise of the Fourth Reich: The Secret Societies That Threaten to Take Over America*, op. cit., p. 221.

are advancing around the globe. The survival of our friends is in danger. And yet no war has been declared, no borders have been crossed by marching troops, no missiles have been fired."[205]

Why Is the JFK Assassination Relevant Today?

The relevance is that the Deep State—Allen Dulles in the CIA, Curtis LeMay in the Pentagon, J. Edgar Hoover in the FBI—planned a military operation to kill a sitting president—to lie about it by framing Lee Harvey Oswald as the assassin—then to codify their lie with the Warren Commission.

The Deep State has run America ever since—with a series of perpetual wars and an endless string of contrived crises—all done with the complicity of a government-controlled press.

- Why did buildings that were not hit by airplanes collapse on 9/11 (Building 7)?
- Why were no weapons of mass destruction found in Iraq after the 1991 war?
- Why was a bad virus turned into a pandemic?
- Why does a vaccine that did not prevent you from getting the disease end up killing you?

The Deep State killed JFK because he understood—too late—that he was not in control, and he was going to fix that problem.

The JFK assassination is the Rosetta Stone to understanding the CIA-staged revolution in Guatemala in the 1950s, HSBC money

---

205 President John F. Kennedy, "The President and the Press: Address Before the American Newspaper Publishers Association, April 27, 1961," John F. Kennedy Presidential Library and Museum, JFKLibrary.org, https://www.jfklibrary.org/archives/other-resources/john-f-kennedy-speeches/american-newspaper-publishers-association-19610427.

laundering for the Mexican drug cartels (I caught them in 2011) with the Treasury Dept and the CIA turning a blind eye to the wire transfers they had to be monitoring.

Everything changed after JFK was killed because that was the day the CIA quit pretending the president and the Congress ran the country.

Peter Dale Scott was one of the first to catch on with his 1993 book *Deep Politics and the Death of JFK.*[206]

James W. Douglass, in his 2008 book *JFK and the Unspeakable: Why He Died and Why it Matters* probed the spiritual transformation that allowed JFK to bring us back from the brink of apocalypse before the Deep State so brutally ended his pursuit of peace.[207]

In the JFK case, the medical personnel at Parkland Hospital and Secret Service agent Clint Hill all knew JFK was shot from the grassy knoll. So, JFK's wounds, as the best evidence of the crime, had to be altered to make the "evidence" fit the lie.

What about the J6 prisoners,? Why are they the insurrectionists? Why not Antifa or BLM—to whom the DOJ takes a knee?

And what about Ukraine? Do Obama and Biden really want to go to war with Russia? Is NATO even relevant as the geopolitics enters a new phase where the US, Russia, and China compete as superpowers in a new phase of multipolar geopolitics? Could the Deep State possibly be contemplating engaging in a nuclear war? With war also raging in the Middle East, the Deep State seems to be rushing headlong into World War III? Why?

The music stopped the day JFK was assassinated. With his passing, LBJ ramped up the Vietnam war. The Deep State killed Kennedy precisely because they feared he would succeed as a world-historic peacemaker.

---

206 Peter Dale Scott, *Deep Politics and the Death of JFK* (Berkeley and Los Angeles, CA: University of California Press, 1993).

207 James W. Douglass, *JFK and the Unspeakable: Why He Died and Why it Matters* (New York: Maryknoll, 2008).

CHAPTER 4

THE GLOBALIST DEATH CULT: DEPOPULATION HOAXES, TWENTY-FIRST CENTURY STYLE

"If the present growth trends in world population, industrialization, pollution, food production, and resource depletion continue unchanged, the limits to growth on this planet will be reached sometime in the next hundred years. The most probable result will be a rather sudden and uncontrollable decline in both population and industrial capacity."
—Donella H. Meadows, Dennis L. Meadows, Jørgen Randers, William W. Behrens III, *The Limits to Growth: A Report for the Club of Rome on the Predicament of Mankind*[208]

"The declines in carrying capacity already being observed in scattered areas around the world point to a phenomenon that could easily be much more widespread by 2000. In fact, the best evidence now available—even allowing for the many beneficial effects of technological developments and adoptions—suggests that by 2000 the world's human population may be within only a few generations of reaching the entire planet's carrying capacity."
—The Global 2000 Report to the President [Jimmy Carter][209]

---

208 Donella H. Meadows, Dennis L. Meadows, Jørgen Randers, William W. Behrens III, *The Limits to Growth: A Report for the Club of Rome on the Predicament of Mankind* (New York: Universe Books, 1972), p. 23, https://archive.org/details/TheLimitsToGrowth /page/n23/mode/2up.
209 The edition cited here is the following: Gerald O. Barney, *The Global 2000 Report to the President: Entering the Twenty-First Century*, a Report Prepared by the Council on Environmental Quality and the Department of State, *Entering the Twenty-First Century* (New York: Penguin, 1988), p. 41, https://archive.org/details/global2000report0000unse /page/n55/mode/2up?q=declines.

We are in the middle of a globalist planned extinction level event aimed at drastically reducing the world's population from the 2024 total of 8.1 billion to a "more manageable" level of around two billion, or lower.

Conservationist Jane Goodall spoke at the 2020 World Economic Forum in Davos, Switzerland. There she proclaimed, "We cannot hide away from human population growth, because it underlies so many other problems. All these things we talk about wouldn't be a problem if the world was the size of the population that was there 500 years ago."[210] In 1500, there were only 450,000 people in the world.[211]

Dennis Meadows, a prominent member of the Club of Rome, insisted the depopulation of the planet, down to one or two billion people—as much as an 87.5 percent reduction of Earth's current population—can "occur in a civil way." In a video clip, Meadows pontificates, "The planet can support something like a billion people, maybe two billion, depending on how much liberty and how much material consumption you want to have. If you want more liberty, and more consumption, you have to have fewer people. And conversely, you can have more people, I mean, we could even have eight or nine billion, probably if we have a very strong dictatorship."[212]

Energy, Global Warming, and Climate Change Lies[213]

In 1939, at the start of World War II, the population of the world was

---

210 World Economic Forum, "Securing a Sustainable Future for the Amazon, Davos 2020," YouTube, posted in 2020, https://www.youtube.com/watch?v=9XKm0MUIJQs. Sophia Tulp, "Conservationist Jane Goodall's words on population distorted," Associated Press, APNews.com, December 28, 2022, https://apnews.com/article/fact-check-jane -goodall-population-299442560681.

211 "World Population by Year," Worldometer, Worldometers.info, no date, https:// www.worldometers.info/world-population/world-population-by-year/.

212 Wide Awake Media, @wideawake_media on X, posted March 26, 2024, https:// twitter.com/wideawake_media/status/1772552819385540718.

213 Much of this discussion, in a greatly expanded form, is provided in my previous book: Jerome R. Corsi, PhD, *The Truth About Energy, Global Warming, and Climate Change: Exposing Climate Lies in an Age of Disinformation* (New York and Nashville: Post Hill Press, 2022). Here, as throughout the book, paragraphs and passages from my original works are reproduced, sometimes with minimal alteration.

approximately 2 billion people. While precise estimates of the number of people killed between 1939 and 1945 is impossible, a reasonable estimate is that between 75 and 85 million lost their lives, amounting to some 3–3.7 percent of all people living at that time. With the horror of World War II ending with the United States dropping two atomic bombs on Japan, a reasonable assumption would be that the world had tired of killing. But that reasonable assumption is unfortunately false. Today, we are closer to nuclear war than we have ever been.

During World War II, nuclear physicist Harrison Brown was recruited into the Manhattan Project to work at the Metallurgical Laboratory at the University of Chicago, where he conceived and developed the chemical processes required for the isolation of plutonium for the "Fat Man" bomb dropped on Nagasaki. Brown's first book, published in 1945, entitled *Must Destruction be Our Destiny? A Scientist Speaks as a Citizen*,[214] expressed fear over the dangers of nuclear war. Brown concluded the creation of the atomic bomb made the creation of a world government even more urgent. "The atomic bomb did not create the need for world government: the need existed long before uranium fission was discovered," Brown wrote in his 1945 book. "The possibility that technological achievements might ultimately precipitate disaster in the world has become increasingly apparent during the last fifty years. The atomic bomb is but the latest in a series of developments that make political nationalism a senseless concept, and there is every reason to believe that these developments will continue at an ever-increasing pace."[215]

With the publication of his second book in 1954, *The Challenge of Man's Future*,[216] Brown had embraced Malthusian principles that the rapid propagation of humanity would certainly exhaust our natural

---

214 Harrison Brown, *Must Destruction Be Our Destiny? A Scientist Speaks as a Citizen* (New York: Simon & Schuster, 1946).
215 Ibid., pp. 90–91.
216 Harrison Brown, *The Challenge of Man's Future: An Inquiry Concerning the Condition of Man During the Years That Lie Ahead* (New York: Viking Press, 1954).

resources. Regardless of the topic, whether it be vital statistics, food, or natural resources in general, Brown was cautious about how much we could accomplish. He warned there were "fundamental physical limitations to man's future development and of the hazards which will confront him in the years and centuries ahead."[217] Brown insisted that "both Malthus's reasoning and the principles he enunciated were sound."[218] Brown proposed using eugenics to "prevent the long-range degeneration of human stock." He recommended implementing the "science of human genetics" to create the desired characteristics of a "super-race."[219]

Brown doubted humans had the intelligence today needed to breed the desired characteristics of a "super-race."[220] Still, Brown remained concerned that "it does appear that the feeble-minded, the morons, the dull and backward, and the lower-than-average persons in our society are outbreeding the superior ones at the present time. Indeed, it has been estimated that the average intelligence quotient of Western population as a whole is probably decreasing with each succeeding generation."[221] Brown envisioned his world government would impose severe restrictions on human breeding by restricting sexual intercourse, making abortion readily available, imposing sterilization upon inferior races, and perfecting the use of chemicals or devices to prevent conception. [222]

In his 1968 book *The Population Bomb*,[223] Paul Ehrlich embraced the fears expressed by Thomas Malthus in 1789 that population growth would inevitably outstrip the ability to produce food and would be the

---

217 Ibid., p. 7.
218 Ibid., p. 6.
219 Harrison Brown, *The Challenge of Man's Future*, op. cit., p. 105.
220 Ibid., p. 106.
221 Ibid., p. 103.
222 Ibid., pp. 86-87.
223 Paul R. Ehrlich, *The Population Bomb* (New York: a Sierra Club/Ballentine book, 1968).

ultimate undoing of humankind. In a section of chapter 1 subtitled "Too Many People," Ehrlich wrote:

> Americans are beginning to realize that the underdeveloped countries of the world face an inevitable population-food crisis. Each year food production in these countries falls a bit further behind burgeoning population growth, and people go to bed a little bit hungrier. While there are temporary or local reversals of this trend, it now seems inevitable that it will continue to its logical conclusion: mass starvation. The rich may continue to get richer, but the more numerous poor are going to get poorer. Of these poor, a minimum of three and one-half million will starve to death this year, mostly children. But this is a mere handful compared to the numbers that will be starving in a decade or so. And it is now too late to take action to save many of these people.[224]

Ehrlich was serious: his primary conclusion was that there were too many people in the world. "The battle to feed all of humanity is over," Ehrlich explained in *The Population Bomb*. "In the 1970s the world will undergo famines—hundreds of millions of people are going to starve to death in spite of any crash programs embarked upon for now." Nothing could save the world, Ehrlich argued, except population control, defined as "the conscious regulation of the numbers of human beings to meet the needs, not just of individual families, but society as a whole."[225] In the prologue to *The Population Bomb*, Ehrlich signaled that Brown was also his mentor: "The birth rate must be brought into balance with the death rate or mankind will breed itself into oblivion." This sentence appeared lifted almost word-for-word from Brown's conclusion in *The Challenge of Man's Future*, published fifteen years earlier. "We can no longer afford to treat the symptoms of the cancer of population growth;

224 Paul R. Ehrlich, *The Population Bomb*, p. 17.
225 Ibid., "Prologue," *The Population Bomb*, first paragraph, page unnumbered.

the cancer itself must be cut out," Ehrlich continued. "Population control is the only answer."[226]

The decision of plasma physicist John Holdren to enter the depopulation movement was pivotal to the hijacking of the environmental concerns expressed by Harrison Brown morphing into a hysteria that burning hydrocarbon fuels would cause catastrophic global warming. Holdren realized that since burning hydrocarbon fuels releases carbon dioxide (CO_2), a greenhouse gas, into the atmosphere, it could be argued that human activity since the industrial revolution has caused Earth's temperature to rise to dangerously catastrophic levels. If anthropomorphic CO_2 was an existential threat, then industrial society could be induced to stop using coal, oil, and natural gas. The "renewable green energies" of wind and solar do not exhibit CO_2, so the "transition" away from hydrocarbon fuels could be made into an ideological movement that would induce people to utilize less efficient and more costly forms of energy.

The result would be to undermine the modern industrial state by inducing climate hysteria that would deprive the modern industrial state from burning hydrocarbon fuels—the inexpensive energy needed to grow the world's population to the current total of more than 8 billion people. Without the availability of hydrocarbon fuels, millions if not billions of people would die. Thus, with Holdren's evil genius, Paul Ehrlich morphed the population bomb scare into a global warming scare, with the same goal—to depopulate by the millions if not billions. When global temperature readings failed to show the catastrophic increases the global warming theorists predicted, the climate ideology quickly shifted from "global warming" to "climate change." The shift in focus now insisted that using hydrocarbon fuels would produce more hazardous climate events in the form of floods, hurricanes, and tornadoes.

---

226 Ibid., last paragraph, page unnumbered.

Thus, by demonizing hydrocarbon fuels one way or the other, Holdren and Ehrlich hoped to run a psychological operation on those not versed in legitimate climate science by achieving depopulation in the name of saving the planet from an existential climate disaster. Even more demonic, direct discussion of depopulation objectives need never be mentioned in global warming/climate narratives suggesting a future of green, planet-healthier energy for all, once the "transition" from hydrocarbon fuels to wind and solar was complete.

In his 2008 book, *Climate Confusion*, meteorologist Roy Spencer, PhD, made clear that carbon dioxide is not the turning knob of Earth's temperature. Dr. Spencer is a principal research scientist at the University of Alabama in Huntsville, and the US Science Team Leader for the Advanced Microwave Scanning Radiometer on NASA's Aqua satellite.[227] "The current concentration of about 380 ppm means that for every million molecules of air, 380 of them are carbon dioxide," he wrote. "Or alternatively, for every 100,000 molecules of air, 38 of them are carbon dioxide." Spencer concluded: "This small fraction reveals why carbon dioxide is called one of the atmosphere's 'trace gases.' There simply isn't very much."[228] Spencer pointed out that water vapor accounts for between 70 and 90 percent of all greenhouse gases, combined with clouds that have a significant greenhouse effect, even though clouds are not a gas but consist of water droplets and ice crystals. He also pointed out that should we reach a doubling of the preindustrial atmospheric carbon dioxide concentration, projected for later in this, the twenty-first century, "we will have enhanced the Earth's natural greenhouse effect by about 1 percent."[229]

Daniel H. Rothman, a professor at the Department of Earth,

227 Dr. Roy Spencer's website is at https://www.drroyspencer.com.
228 Roy W. Spencer, *Climate Confusion: How Global Warming Hysteria Leads to Bad Science, Pandering Politicians and Misguided Policies That Hurt the Poor* (New York: Encounter Books, 2008), pp., 62–64, at p. 63.
229 Ibid., p. 64.

Atmospheric, and Planetary Sciences at MIT, published an important paper in the *Proceedings of the National Academy of Sciences* in 2002.[230] His research established that over most of the geologic record of the past 500 million years, Earth's CO_2 concentration fluctuated between values two to four times greater than those of today. However, over the past 175 million years, the data shows a long-term decline in the air's CO_2 content. Again, we encounter an inherent problem with time-series analysis. What is the proper period to identify the actual trends the data reflects? Since the inception of the industrial age, CO_2 levels in the atmosphere have risen. Yet, if we look back over the past 175 million years, the trend is different. Over the past 175 million years, the CO_2 levels in the atmosphere have continued to drop, including through today.

In his 2022 book, *Marx in the Anthropocene*, associate professor at the University of Tokyo Kohei Saito reimagined the writings of the "young Marx" to argue Marx was a "degrowth ecological communist." Saito embraces the Net Zero emissions (NZE) movement because he understands that "ecosocialism is the basis for degrowth." He rejects the possibility of sustainable growth under socialism, realizing that only through degrowth ecosocialism can the "anarchy of capitalism" be transcended.[231] After years of the radical eco-left preaching the evil of hydrocarbon fuels, we have higher energy costs caused by the systematic implementation of sun, wind, and batteries (SWB) technology that makes no sense, given the rigors of economic theory, energy dynamics, or climate science. The global warming/climate change ideologues preached green energy, but not because the neo-Marxist left knew we

---

230 Daniel H. Rothman, "Atmospheric carbon dioxide levels for the past 500 million years," *Proceedings of the National Academy of Sciences of the United States of America (PNAS)*, Volume 99, Number 7 (April 2, 2020), pp. 4167–4171, https://www.pnas.org/content/99/7/4167.
231 Kohei Saito, *Marx in the Anthropocene: Towards the Idea of Degrowth Communism* (Cambridge, UK: Cambridge University Press, 2022), pp. 216–217.

had to achieve NZE to save the planet. Today's radical green revolutionaries embrace NZE because they know that capitalism will fail, not because the world's workers will unite, but because advanced industrial economies will collapse without abundant, cheap hydrocarbon fuels. Thus, neo-Marxist "degrowth" quickly translates into yet another ideological twist of the underlying depopulation goal. Terming the current geological era the "Anthropocene" presumes that we human beings will be the cause of our species' demise. After all, we exhale CO_2, so under the global warming hypothesis, eliminating human beings would help "save the planet." The neo-Marxist "degrowth" agenda reveals how self-loathing the depopulation agenda is at its core. The obvious solution is suicide (i.e., voluntary euthanasia), thus obviating the need for Green New Deal zealots to kill us slowly through crippling the productivity of the modern industrial state by demonizing hydrocarbon fuels.

What distinguishes woke ideologies is that their favored solutions become secular religions that mask the underlying reality that their ideas do not work. So, electric vehicles (EVs) are not "net zero emission" vehicles when we take into account the amount of hydrocarbon fuels that must be applied to extract the rare earth minerals needed to create the EV batteries, or the quantity of hydrocarbon fuels needed to produce the electricity needed to recharge the EV. The charging needed infrastructure to support a fleet of automobiles and trucks "transitioned" to EVs, which does not currently exist. The lack of a plentiful national infrastructure of quick-charge electrical units limits the reliable distance an EV can be driven, while risking extraordinarily long recharging times depending on the EV demand to use a particular EV charging station at any given time. EVs do not easily recharge in the bitter cold, with the result that abandoned EVs in wintertime can become a hazard, clogging charging stations and roadways with EVs that are immobile because they are out of juice. The electric grid in the United States works because transformers are allowed to cool off from peak-time use during the down hours of nighttime. If millions of Americans start charging their EVs at night in their garages, transformer life is going to be shortened across the grid, adding millions if not billions in infrastructure upgrades that are not needed as long as cars and trucks operate primarily on combustible hydrocarbon fuels. EV batteries are prone to spontaneous bursting into a fire not easily extinguished by water—adding the risk of burning down the family home to the convenience of charging your EV in the garage overnight.

The use of solar panels is limited in geographical areas receiving little sunlight—the same problem wind turbines suffer in areas that typically receive little wind. Even in favorable geographical areas, the sun does not shine all the time and the wind does not blow all the time. The energy efficiency of combustible hydrocarbon fuels obviates the trouble and expense required to store solar and wind power in batteries. Planned offshore wind turbine farms are being abandoned worldwide. Once government subsidies run out, the private investment funds required to build out and operate offshore wind farms tends to dry up.

Global warming/climate change true believers are unsophisticated in climate science or unknowledgeable in technology that works. True believers are typically intolerant of criticism and incapable of debate because their climate views fall into the category of secular religious ideas in which the terms of the debate are normative, i.e., not fact- or reality-based. Climate hysterics cannot be refuted by climate science, because their beliefs are based on a subjective dislike for hydrocarbon fuels, despite the fact that hydrocarbon fuels actually work. In the final analysis, we must face up to the reality that the evil geniuses who constructed the climate hoax did so knowing that solar, wind, and battery technologies would not work. The elaborate scheme to demonize CO_2 was done to force us to stop using hydrocarbon fuels, leaving us no alternative but to use the less efficient and more problematic solar, wind, and battery technologies. The point is that Holdren and Ehrlich demonized CO_2 *because* solar, wind, and batteries do not work. Now, with the global warming/climate change movement demonizing nitrogen fertilizers, targeting cows for extinction, and making it impossible for small farms to operate, we can begin to understand that the goal of the climate movement was always depopulation—depriving the modern industrial state of the available and affordable hydrocarbons that fueled the industrial revolution, allowing the global population to exceed 8 billion people for the first time in human history

Pandemic Lies

COVID-19 was a psychological warfare operation that hyped a bad flu into a global pandemic. As Robert F. Kennedy Jr. noted in his 2021 book, *The Real Dr. Fauci: Bill Gates, Big Pharma, and the Global War on Democracy and Public Health*, Dr. Fauci's strategy was "to suppress viral spread by mandatory masking, social distancing, quarantining the healthy (also known as lockdowns), while instructing COVID patients to return home and do nothing—receive no treatment whatsoever—until difficulties breathing sent them back to the hospital to submit to intravenous remdesivir and ventilation."[232] Meanwhile, inexpensive but effective treatments like hydroxychloroquine and ivermectin were demonized.

On January 31, 2020, a group of medical scientists from India published an article in the medical journal *BioRXiv* that published an early genome study of COVID-19, showing that the spike glycoprotein in the COVID-19 virus was "not present in other coronaviruses," but "have identity/similarity to amino acid residues in key structural proteins of HIV-1," a characteristic that "is unlikely to be found in nature."[233] The article signaled that COVID-19 was a lab-engineered

---

232 Robert F. Kennedy Jr., *The Real Dr. Fauci: Bill Gates, Big Pharma, and the Global War on Democracy and Public Health* (New York: Skyhorse Publishing, 2021), p. 1.
233 Ashutosh Prashant Pradhan, Ashutosh Kumar Pandey, Akhilesh Mishra,

bioweapon, suggesting that whoever bioengineered COVID-19 sought to combine an HIV attack on the immune system with a SARS attack on the pulmonary system. We must ask: Why does Fauci's name appear on four US patents for a key glycoprotein that appears related to the HIV genome elements inserted in the SARS virus chassis to create the current COVID-19 epidemic? The four patents on which Fauci is named as an inventor are the following:

- Patent Number: 9896509, patent granted August 3, 2016. "Use of antagonists of the interaction between HIV120 and α4β7 integrin."
- Publication Number: 20160333309, patent application filed August 3, 2016. "Use of Antagonists of the Interaction Between HIV GP120 and α4β7 integrin."
- Patent Number: 9441041, patent granted September 13, 2016. "Use of antagonists between HIV GP120 and α4β7 integrin."
- Publication Number 2016007586, patent application filed September 21, 2015. "Use of antagonists of the Interaction Between HIV GP120 and α4β7 integrin."[234]

Again, Robert F. Kennedy Jr. had the answer:

I was astonished to realize that the pervasive web of deep financial entanglements between Pharma and the government health agencies had put regulatory capture on steroids. The CDC (Centers for Disease Control), for example, owns 57 vaccine patents and spends $4.9 of its

---

Parul Gupta, Praveen Kumar. Tripathi, Manoj Balakrishnan Menon, James Gomes, Perumal Vivekanandan, Bishwajit Kundu, "Uncanny similarity of unique inserts in the 2019-n spike protein to HIV-1 gp 120 and Gag," *BioRXiv*, January 31, 2020, https://www.biorxiv.org/content/10.1101/2020.01.30.927871v1.full.
234 "Patents by Inventor Anthony S. Fauci," Justia Patents, no date, Patents.Justia.com, https://patents.justia.com/inventor/anthony-s-fauci.

$12 billion-dollar annual budget (as of 2019) buying and distributing vaccines. NIH owns hundreds of vaccine patents and often profits from the sale of products it supposedly regulates. High level officials, including Dr. Fauci, receive yearly emoluments of up to $150,000 in royalty payments on products that they help develop and then usher through the approval process. The FDA (Food and Drug Administration) receives 45 percent of its budget from the pharmaceutical industry, through what are euphemistically called "user fees." When I learned that extraordinary fact, the disastrous health of the American people was no longer a mystery; I wondered what the environment would look like if the EPA (Environmental Protection Agency) received 45 percent of its budget from the coal industry![235]

In Chapter 45, "A detailed Description of Dr. Fauci's Gain-of-Function Studies in China," of his second book on COVID-19, *The Wuhan Cover-Up and The Terrifying Bioweapons Arms Race*, Robert F. Kennedy Jr. makes clear that Dr. Fauci lied when he testified to the US Senate on May 11, 2021, that the NIH (National Institutes of Health) and the NIAID (National Institute of Allergy and Infectious Diseases) did not fund gain-of-function research at the Wuhan Institute in China.[236] Kennedy detailed how researchers at the Wuhan Institute managed to put "a new spike protein on a laboratory SARS coronavirus," thereby succeeding "in making a novel version of SARS that could both infect mice and attack cells that line the human airway."[237] Kennedy concluded:

235 Robert F. Kennedy Jr., *The Real Dr. Fauci: Bill Gates, Big Pharma, and the Global War on Democracy and Public Health*, op. cit., "Introduction," p. xv.
236 Robert F. Kennedy, Jr., *The Wuhan Cover-Up and The Terrifying Bioweapons Arms Race* (New York: Skyhorse Publishing, 2023), pp. 278-292. See also: "Dr. Fauci, CDC Director Testify Before Senate on COVID-19 Guidelines Transcript," @Rev, Rev.com, May 11, 2023, https://www.rev.com/blog/transcripts/dr-fauci-cdc-director-testify-before-senate-on-covid-19-guidelines-transcript.
237 Ibid., p. 287.

Based upon abundant circumstantial evidence including US intelligence agency assessments, however, the August 2021 Republican congressional investigation concluded that the virus leaked from the Wuhan lab "sometime before September 12, 2019" and that Chinese officials knew that a SARS-like respiratory pneumonia was afoot in Wuhan and were already trying to control both the virus and the narrative by that date.[238]

In April 2020, Li-Meng Yan, MD, PhD, an experienced Chinese virologist at the Hong Kong School of Public Health, escaped to the United States. While she remained in hiding, Li-Meng Yan gave an interview to Tucker Carlson in which she insisted COVID-19 was not a virus that escaped from nature, transmitting from bats to humans, but a bioweapon created in a lab. In a series of three scientific reports, Li-Meng Yang insisted that the Chinese government purposely released SARS-CoV-2 (the medical designation of the virus causing COVID-19) as an "Unrestricted Bioweapon."[239] The term "Unrestricted Bioweapon" refers to the title of a Chinese military tract, "Unrestricted Warfare," which argues the Chinese military in this technological era view the battlefield as extending beyond all boundaries, to include information warfare, cultural warfare, economic warfare, etc., and possibly even medical warfare.[240]

Even today, long after May 5, 2023, the date the World Health Organization (WHO) declared the COVID-19 pandemic as finished,[241] most still fail to realize that the Centers for Disease Control

---

238 Ibid., p. 335.
239 Peter R. Breggin, M.D., and Ginger Ross Breggin, *COVID-19 and the Global Predators: We Are the Prey* (Ithaca, NY: Lake Edge Press, 2021), Chapter 4, "Did China Intentionally Unleash COVID-19 on the World?" pp 61–79, at pp. 73–79.
240 Col. Qiao Liang and Col. Wang Xiangsui, *Unrestricted Warfare* (Brattleboro, VT: Echo Point Books & Media, 2015).
241 Rapty Sarker, et. al., "The WHO has declared the end of pandemic phase of COVID-19: Way to come back to normal life," *Health Science Reports*, September

(CDC, the organization that Dr. Anthony Fauci headed) had declared COVID-19 was survivable, except for those who were extremely old or who suffered morbidity from complicating other diseases. According to the CDC, the COVID-19 survivability rate was 99.997 percent for those aged 0–19 years, 99.98 percent for 20–49 years, 99.5 percent for 50–69, and 94.6 percent for 70-plus years.[242]

It was clearly a global social control measure. By March 2020, more than 3.9 billion people—half the world's population, in ninety countries—was under a health lockdown, confined to their homes.[243] Masks and social distancing became common, even though traditional immunology calls for exposure to strengthen the immune system—not prolonged forced lockdowns, mandatory wearing of masks in public, and social distancing with required separations between people assembled together. Government health officials demonized inexpensive but effective medications like Hydroxychloroquine and Ivermectin, while hospitals killed COVID-19 patients with expensive and dangerous medications like Remdesivir and the use of intubation and mechanical ventilation. Families were not permitted to visit family in nursing homes or hospitals that spread the disease among the elderly and those morbidity impaired. Dr. Vladimir Zelenko, whose COVID-19 protocol calling for the use of Hydroxychloroquine, Zinc, and Azithromycin

2023, e1544, NCBI.NIM.NIH.gov, https://www.ncbi.nlm.nih.gov/pmc/articles/PMC10478644/#:~:text=Therefore%2C%20the%20World%20Health%20Organization,life%20on%20May%205%2C%202023.

242 Centers for Disease Control and Prevention, "COVID-19 Planning Scenarios, Table 1, Scenario 5, "Current Best Estimate," updated March 19, 2021, https://www.cdc.gov/coronavirus/2019-ncov/hcp/planning-scenarios.html. Cited in: Dr. Joseph Mercola and Ronnie Cummins, *The Truth About COVID-19: Exposing the Great Reset, Lockdowns, Vaccine Passports, and the New Normal* (White River Junction, VT: Chelsea Green Publishing, 2021), p. 68.

243 Alasdair Sandford, "Coronavirus: Half of humanity now on lockdown as 90 countries call for confinement," EuroNews, EuroNews.com, updated March 4, 2020, https://www.euronews.com/2020/04/02/coronavirus-in-europe-spain-s-death-toll-hits-10-000-after-record-950-new-deaths-in-24-hour.

saved countless lives, railed against the Big Pharma COVID-19 medical treatments. He wrote: "The mismanagement of the COVID-19 pandemic is akin to mass murder and the genocide of the elderly and infirm. The root cause of this crime is the denial of man's divine origin. Man is made in the 'image of God' and, therefore, his or her life has intrinsic value and natural rights."[244]

Life insurance actuaries continue to be alarmed at excess mortality rates that have persisted well after the WHO declared the COVID-19 epidemic was finished. Industry reports show that life insurers paid record levels of death claims in 2021. The Society of Actuaries projects that mortality rates will continue to remain high, taking until 2030 to reach zero percent excess deaths.[245] A sudden and unexplained death syndrome related to COVID-19 vaccine injections has been documented in the published medical peer-reviewed literature. In particular, COVID-19 vaccines have been linked to myocarditis (an inflammation of the heart muscle) which can be fatal.[246] A survey of embalmers in the US, Canada, the UK, Australia, and New Zealand found that 73 percent reported finding white fibrous blood clots blocking the veins and arteries of the dead. These embalmers reported seeing the white fibrous blood clots in about one in five corpses in 2023. None reported seeing any such anomalies prior to the start of the COVID-19 pandemic and the beginning of mass vaccinations.[247]

A 2024 study led by Nicolas Hulscher of the McCullough

244 Vladimir Zelenko, M.D., "Introduction," in Peter R. Breggin, M.D., and Ginger Ross Breggin, *COVID-19 and the Global Predators: We Are the Prey*, op. cit., pp. xix–xxi, at p. xix.

245 Doug Bailey, "'Excess mortality' continuing surge concerns," Life Insurance News, InsuranceNewsNet.com, October 26, 2023, https://insurancenewsnet.com/innarticle/excess-mortality-continuing-surge-causes-concerns.

246 Nicolas Hulscher, "Autopsy findings in cases of fatal COVID-19 vaccine-induced myocarditis," ESC Heart Fail, January 14, 2024, https://pubmed.ncbi.nlm.nih.gov/38221509/.

247 Full Measure Staff, "COVID Clots," FullMeasure.news, April 7, 2024, https://fullmeasure.news/newest-videos/covid-clots.

Foundation in Dallas, Texas, examined excess cardiopulmonary arrest and mortality after COVID-19 vaccination in King County, Washington. Peter McCullough, MD, MPH, King County notes that Seattle King County is well respected for its elite "Medic One" paramedic units "which led the way on out-of-hospital resuscitation research." McCullough also noted that the Seattle King County cardiac arrest statistics are among the most accurate in the United States."[248]

The Hulscher study reported that approximately 98 percent of the King County population had received at least one dose of COVID-19 vaccine by 2023. "Our analysis revealed a 25.7 percent increase in total cardiopulmonary arrests and a 25.4 percent increase in cardiopulmonary arrest mortality from 2020 to 2023 in King County, WA," the researchers found. The researchers estimated that excess cardiopulmonary arrest deaths increased by 1,236 percent from 2020 to 2023, rising from 11 excess deaths to 147 excess deaths. "A quadratic increase in excess cardiopulmonary arrest mortality was observed with higher COVID-19 vaccination rates," the researchers stressed. They noted the general population of King County sharply declined by 0.94 percent (21,300) in 2021, deviating from the expected population size. "Applying our model from these data to the entire United States yielded 49,240 excess fatal cardiopulmonary arrests from 2021–2023," they concluded.[249] In reporting on the Hulscher study in his Substack, Dr.

248 Peter A. McCullough, M.D., MPH, "BREAKING—Seattle, King County Reports 18.5% Increase in Cardiac Arrests from Pre-Pandemic Years," Courageous Discourse, PeterMcCulloughMD.Substack.com, May 5, 2024, https://petermcculloughmd.substack.com/p/breaking-seattle-king-county reports?r=14jb45&utm_campaign=post&utm_medium=web&triedRedirect=true.
249 Nicolas Hulscher, Michael Cook, Raphael Striker, and Peter A. McCullough, "Excess Cardiopulmonary Arrest and Mortality after COVID-19 Vaccination in King County, Washington," PrePrints.org, posted May 27, 2024, file:///Users/jeromecorsi/Downloads/preprints202405.1665.v1%20(1).pdf. See also: Peter A. McCullough, M.D., MPH, "BREAKING—Excess Cardiopulmonary Arrest and Mortality after COVID-19 Vaccination in King County, Washington, PeterMcCulloughMD.Substack.com, May 28, 2024, https://petermcculloughmd.substack.com/p/breaking-publication-

McCullough referenced Ed Dowd's 2024 book, *"Cause Unknown": The Epidemic of Sudden Deaths in 2021 and 2022 and 2023*.[250] Malone commented that the King County findings "are extremely worrisome given the rise in all cause-mortality observed in the United States that has been thoroughly investigated and reported by analyst Edward Dowd. That book documents the sudden death syndrome in which healthy teenagers and young adults drop dead in the middle of ordinary activities, such as playing a sport.

Dr. Robert Malone, credited with having developed the mRNA vaccines used by Pfizer and Moderna, has widely proclaimed that the mRNA vaccines are gene modification therapy that involve injections of the live COVID-19 spike protein into the body. Malone claims the injections cause the body's RNA to replicate the COVID-19 spike protein into cells throughout the body. Moreover, once the vaccination instructs the RNA to begin replicating the spike protein, there is no mechanism that instructs the RNA to stop doing so. In a post on his Substack page on May 8, 2024, Malone claimed the evidence of mRNA vaccine–related morbidity and pathology are finally being admitted by federal government medical officials, not just doctors willing to tell the truth, even if telling the truth risked losing their licenses to practice medicine.

Malone wrote:

> I have been waiting for this moment for years now. The US Federal government is finally starting to acknowledge that they have forced the citizens (including military personnel) of this country to accept toxic

excess-cardiopulmonary?utm_source=post-email-title&publication_id=1119676&post_id=145024621&utm_campaign=email-post-title&isFreemail=true&r=oh9xa&triedRedirect=true&utm_medium=email.

250 Ed Dowd, *"Cause Unknown": The Epidemic of Sudden Deaths in 2021 and 2022 and 2023* (Franklin Lakes, NJ: Children Health Defense Books, Revised Edition, March 5, 2024).

THE GLOBALIST DEATH CULT

injectable products presented as "vaccines." Products which either contain or cause patients' bodies to produce a known toxin: the engineered
SARS-CoV-2 spike protein. We are now seeing an incremental rollout
of limited hangouts, in which current and former federal officials are
starting to acknowledge deaths and harms attributable to various emergency use authorized COVID-19 "vaccine" products.[251]

A peer-reviewed study led by noted gynecologist James A. Thorp, M.D.
noted the COVID-19 vaccine-related risk of adverse effects were great
for women of reproductive age, and particularly great among pregnant
women. COVID-19 vaccines compared to influenza vaccines caused a
proportional reporting of increased rates of a long list of adverse effects,
including menstrual abnormalities, miscarriage, fetal chromosomal
abnormalities, fetal malformation, fetal cystic hygroma, fetal cardiac
disorders, fetal arrhythmias, fetal cardiac arrest, fetal vascular malperfu-
sion, fetal growth abnormalities, fetal abnormal surveillance, fetal pla-
cental thrombosis, low amniotic fluid, preeclampsia, premature deliv-
ery, preterm premature rupture of membrane, fetal death/stillbirth, and
premature baby death. The study recommended a worldwide morato-
rium on the use of COVID-19 vaccines in pregnancy "until random-
ized prospective trials document safety in pregnancy and long-term
follow-up in offspring."[252]

Particularly egregious were the government health assurances that
the COVID-19 vaccines were "safe and effective" for children, even
though the rates of COVID-19 in children ages five to eleven were so
low that in Pfizer tests there were zero cases of COVID-19 and zero

---

251 Robert W. Malone, M.D., "Update on COVID mRNA Vaccine Harms,"
RWMaloneMD.substack.com, May 8, 2024, https://rwmalonemd.substack.com/p/
update-on-covid-mrna-vaccine-harms?utm_source=profile&utm_medium=reader2.
252 James A. Thorp, M.D., "COVID-19 Vaccines: The Impact on Pregnancy Outcomes
and Menstrual Function," *Journal of American Physicians and Surgeons*, Volume 28,
Number 1, Spring 2023, https://www.jpands.org/vol28no1/thorp.pdf.

cases of death from COVID-19. Pfizer also found no statistically significant evidence of vaccine efficacy using a three-dose vaccine in 992
children between the ages six months and five years. Of the 73 million
children in the US, only 453 between the ages of zero to five years old
have died with COVID-19, and only 846 between the ages five and
eighteen have died from COVID-19 during the pandemic. Yet, during
the pandemic, the CDC continued to push pregnant women and children to get vaccinated.[253]

Public Health and Medical Professionals for Transparent Documents
(https://phmpt.org) successfully sued the FDA, obtaining the release
of Pfizer COVID-19 vaccine clinical trial results—a document Pfizer
petitioned the court to keep secret for fifty-five years.[254] The Pfizer
report showed that in the ninety days following the emergency use
authorization release of the Pfizer COVID-19 mRNA vaccine, Pfizer
recorded 1,223 deaths, and 158,000 adverse reactions, including fetal
deaths, spontaneous abortions, and cardiac disorders (tachycardia). The
study also indicated that 1,927 cases (4.6 percent) reported contract-
ing COVID-19 after receiving the Pfizer COVID-19 vaccination. In
other words, the Pfizer COVID-19 "vaccine" produced serious adverse
effects, including death, but did not prevent the patient from contract-
ing the disease.[255]

The truth is that both Pfizer and Moderna rushed forward under
CDC emergency use authorization, suppressing pre-release trials that

---

253 Uncensored Vaccine Injury, "They've come for the babies: Know the facts
before you vax!" UncensoredVaccineInjured.Substack.com, July 17, 2022, https://
uncensoredvaccineinjured.substack.com/p/theyve-come-for-the-babies-know-facts.
254 Celia Farber, "Court-Ordered Pfizer Documents They Tried to Have Sealed for 55
Years Show 1223 Deaths, 158,000 Adverse Events in 90 Days Post EUA Release," at The
Truth Barrier, CeliaFarber.Substack.com, December 5, 2021, https://celiafarber.substack.
com/p/court-ordered-pfizer-documents-they.
255 Pfizer, "5.3.6 Cumulative Analysis of Post-Authorization Adverse Effect Reports of
PF-07302048 (BNT162B2) Received Through 28-Feb-2021," released by Public Health
and Medical Professionals for Transparent Documents, https://phmpt.org/wp-content/
uploads/2021/11/5.3.6-postmarketing-experience.pdf.

were giving flashing red alarm signals that severe adverse effects, including death, were being experienced among those taking mRNA vaccines. Protected by the Public Readiness and Emergency Prepared Act (PREP Act) passed by Congress in 2005 from lawsuits from those experiencing adverse effects from mRNA vaccinations, Pfizer and Moderna allowed the opportunity for windfall profits to put moral blinders on their concern for those patients they might injure, permanently impair, or murder.[256]

COVID-19 hit hardest with the elderly population and those with comorbidity (i.e., other health complications). One could argue that the mRNA "vaccines" were to eliminate the cost of health care for these two groups, in which the cost of medical care could be expected to be among the highest. But the mRNA "vaccines" were most effective in getting the body to reproduce the SARS-CoV-19 spike protein to propagate throughout the body. We do not know if the SARS-CoV-19 spike protein will be like a ticking time bomb in certain bodies, capable of developing illnesses and causing death over different intervals of time based on the age and health of each vaccinated person. But we can confirm today that the risks for pregnant women are exceptionally high. If we judge the mRNA medical technology by the results produced, the depopulation objective is clear. The more babies that can be killed in the womb, the fewer abortions have to be performed, provided your goal is to kill life at the onset. Again, we return to the globalist attack on women. If women are incapable of producing offspring, the reduction in world population seems inevitable. Judging COVID-19 by the results, the globalists ran a successful test of locking down society with a bad flu hyped to pandemic hysteria, setting the conditions to do mass

---

256 MacKenzie Sigalos, "You can't sue Pfizer or Moderna if you have severe Covid vaccine side effects. The government likely won't compensate you for damages either," CNBC.com, December 17, 2020, https://www.cnbc.com/2020/12/16/covid-vaccine-side-effects-compensation-lawsuit.html.

inoculation of a gene treatment therapy that injects the disease patho-
gen to replicate inside their bodies, working to advance their deaths.

Global Depopulation: The Official US Government National Security Policy

Proof that the globalism is a death cult is apparent once we realize that
global depopulation is the official US government national security
policy.

On April 24, 1974, US National Security Advisor and Secretary of
State Henry Kissinger issued on behalf of the National Security Council
a confidential memorandum, numbered National Security Study
Memorandum 200 (NSSM200). The subject of the memorandum was
the following: Implications of Worldwide Population Growth for US
Security and Overseas Interests.[257] NSSM200 resulted in a classified
study that became known as the "Kissinger Report," submitted to the
White House on December 10, 1974.[258] The Kissinger Report called
for taking steps to limit global population to the current 8 billion, by
"not permitting" global population to reach 10 billion, 13 billion, or
more. The theme of the Kissinger Report was that education and family
planning should be the main thrust of encouraging people worldwide
not to have as many children.

Yet throughout the report, the underlying concern was that the
Earth's resources were limited, thus the need to cap global population
growth at 8 billion was an imperative national security goal. Now that
we have already reached the 8 billion maximum target, globalists appear
determined to take more aggressive steps to preserve Earth's resources

---

257 National Security Study Memorandum 200, "Implications of Worldwide
Population Growth for US Security and Overseas Interests," April 24, 1974, https://www.
nixonlibrary.gov/sites/default/files/virtuallibrary/documents/nssm/nssm_200.pdf.
258 National Security Study Memorandum 200, "Implications of Worldwide Population
Growth for US Security and Overseas Interests," The Kissinger Report, December 10,
1974, https://pdf.usaid.gov/pdf_docs/pcaab500.pdf.

for themselves. That intelligence agencies are manufacturing twenty-first-century global warming/climate change natural science hoaxes, along with the COVID-19 pandemic health sciences hoax, is alarming. If efforts since 1974 have been unsuccessful in stopping an exponential population growth, depopulation objectives appear to be conscious globalist efforts to reduce populations by killing people.

Mattias Desmet, a professor of clinical psychology at Ghent University in Belgium, points out in his 2022 book *The Psychology of Totalitarianism* a process of "mass formation" acting as a form of mass hypnosis, resulting in "behaviors of a 'totalitarized' population, including an exaggerated willingness of individuals to sacrifice their own personal interests out of solidarity with the collective (i.e., the masses), a profound intolerance of dissident voices, and pronounced susceptibility to pseudo-scientific indoctrination and propaganda."[259] Thus, twenty-first-century hoaxes like the global warming/climate change movement and the COVID-19 pandemic are intelligence agency psychological operations aimed at creating zombie "true believer" fanatics who adhere to the government's manufactured narrative as a secular religion. A population uneducated in the principles of natural science and human health are subject to fearmongering as effective today as was the witch hoax that propelled the Salem Witch Trials of 1692.

The most effective form of depopulation is suicidal in nature, engineered (as we will see in the next chapter) by making life so miserable for the middle class that voluntary euthanasia becomes an attractive alternative. A population induced to kill itself will save the government the trouble of having to depopulate at public expense. The ultimate irony of the globalist war on humanity is that the Satanic monsters who desire the world's resources for themselves, are willing to offer us voluntary euthanasia as a government-paid "welfare program" final solution.

---

259 Mattias Desmet, *The Psychology of Totalitarianism* (White River Junction, VT: Chelsea Green Publishing, 2022), "Introduction," p. 2.

As Mattias Desmet notes: "To put it in the words of Yuval Noah Harari: Most people wouldn't even notice the shift toward a totalitarian regime. We associate totalitarianism mainly with labor, concentration, and extermination camps, but these are merely the final, bewildering stage of a long process."[260]

---

260 Ibid.

CHAPTER 5

TRANSHUMANISM, ARTIFICIAL INTELLIGENCE, AND PERMANENT LIFE EXTENSION

"The core question of our technological age is whether or not we will remain human at all, and if so, to what degree?. . . Humanity 2.0 will be transnational, transcultural, transgender, transracial, transspecies, and at its extreme edge, transhuman—the final merger of man with the Machine. . . . Fearing the black void of death, transhumanists want to achieve immortality in this world. Whether they achieve bio-longevity through genetic engineering, digital immortality by uploading the mind, or a gradual transition from meat brains to silicon, they demand to live forever by any means necessary."

—Joe Allen, *Dark Aeon*[261]

"Transhumanism is simply the transitional stage between humanism and post-humanism. Make no mistake, the final goal is to eradicate humanity as we know it. Once you understand the final destination, it becomes much easier to look back and identify the psychological conditioning, the biological tampering, the cultural grooming, and the educational prepping, that we have been subjected to for decades, in preparation to making us accept a post-human future. It takes a lot of physical and psychological abuse to get an intelligent species like ours to agree to its own extinction. Most, if not all, that has transcended in the last 60 years was designed to get us closer to accepting such a dystopian reality. Whether you care to accept it or not, we live in a hyper-controlled matrix where

---

261 Joe Allen, *Dark Aeon: Transhumanism and the War Against Humanity* (New York: Skyhorse Publishing, 2023), p. 4, 5, and 7.

our perception of reality is meticulously planned, managed, and executed, in order to control and steer us in whichever direction they wish,
and the direction is a post-human world."

—Laura Aboli, The World Council for Health, 2023[262]

A self-appointed globalist elite have decided they deserve to transcend
the earthly bound realities that dictate the lives of everyone else. While
the battle is truly being fought on a spiritual plane, we begin with the
realization that the middle class in the United States is being intentionally devastated economically.

The Decline of the Middle Class

Since President Biden took office in 2021, the cumulative effect of
persistent inflation has decreased Americans' purchasing power by 19
percent. Groceries are up 21 percent, gasoline up 47 percent, the cost
of shelter 20 percent, and electricity up almost 30 percent. But under
Bidenomics, the average hourly earnings after inflation have fallen 2.5
percent, which means the typical American family must pay $12,000
more just to maintain the standard of living that same family enjoyed
when Biden took office. Given that the purchasing power of the dollar has declined 19 percent under Biden, the value of the dollar today
is only 81 percent of what it was on Inauguration Day, January 20,
2021.[263]

According to the Pew Research Center, the share of adults who live
in middle-class households fell from 61 percent in 1971 to 50 percent
in 2021.[264] The top 1 percent of American earners now control more

---

262 Laura Aboli, "Transhumanism: The End Game," The Better Way Conference
2023 in Bath, UK, June 3–5, 2023, hosted by the World Council for Health,
TheThinkingConservative.com, posted November 19, 2023, https://www.
thethinkingconservative.com/transhumanism-the-end-game/.
263 J. Kennerly Davis, "Inflation Isn't a Bug in the System, It's a Feature," Real Clear
Wire, RealClearWire.com, May 17, 2024, https://realclearwire.com/articles/2024/05/17/
inflation_isnt_a_bug_in_the_system_its_a_feature_1032282.html.
264 Rakesh Kochhar and Stella Sechopoulos, "How the American middle class has

wealth than the entire middle class.[265] A RAND study showed that the three decades following World War II were a period of economic growth where wealth was shared equitably across income distributions.[266] But over the next five decades, since 1971, inequality in taxable income has increased substantially, as capital skimmed $50 trillion from labor from 1975 to 2018. Since 1975, globalization has had a major effect transferring US jobs to cheaper labor oversees. As noted by Charles Hugh Smith, capital has a fundamental advantage over labor in that "capital is globally mobile" but "labor is grounded in a particular place."[267]

Average Americans are struggling to meet monthly expenses. In August 2023, for the first time, credit card debt levels have surpassed $1 trillion, according to data released by the Federal Reserve Bank of New York. Rising credit card debt and auto loan balances drove overall household debt up to a record $17.06 trillion—a spike of $2.9 trillion since the end of 2019, before the pandemic.[268] Amid the high interest rates and the spiking home costs experienced during the Biden administration, middle-class households are being priced out of the housing market. According to the National Association of Realtors,

---

changed in the past five decades," Pew Research Center, PewResearch.org, April 20, 2022, https://www.pewresearch.org/short-reads/2022/04/20/how-the-american-middle-class-has-changed-in-the-past-five-decades/.

265 Daniel de Visé, "The top 1% of American earners now earn more wealth than the entire middle class," USA Today, USAToday.com, December 6, 2023, https://www.usatoday.com/story/money/2023/12/06/top-1-american-earners-more-wealth-middle-class/71769832007/.

266 Carter C. Price, Kathryn A. Edwards, "Trends in Income from 1975 to 2018," RAND, Rand.org, September 14, 2020, https://www.rand.org/pubs/working_papers/WRA516-1.html.

267 Charles Hugh Smith, "Labor Rising: Will Class Identity Finally Matter Again?" OfTwoMinds.com, May 1, 2024, https://www.oftwominds.com/blogmay24/class-identity5-24.html.

268 Alicia Wallace, "Americans' credit card debt hits a record $1 trillion," CNN Business, CNN.com updated August 8, 2023, https://www.cnn.com/2023/08/08/economy/us-household-credit-card-debt/index.html.

approximately 75 percent of the homes on the market in 2023 were out of the reach for those in the middle class.[269]

America's major cities under the grip of Democratic Party control are in serious danger of economic collapse, unable to manage increasing homelessness compounded by out-of-control drug usage, a declining tax base due to increasingly vacant office buildings, rampant crime compounded by "defund the police" budget cuts and Soros-funded prosecutors who see criminals as the victims, and thousands of immigrants crossing an open southern border only to be put in urban hotels at public expense. Law-abiding citizens and countless businesses are fleeing the country's largest urban areas, as once flourishing cities like New York, Los Angeles, and Chicago "are in the early stages of a full-blown societal 'collapse,' and things just keep getting worse with each passing day."[270]

The US Treasury's financial statements as of December 29, 2023, revealed that at the end of the year, the total US debt was over $34 trillion for the first time ever. In January 2009, the total US debt was only $10.4 trillion. In January 2024, the Congressional Budget Office reported the rate of increase of the US debt was growing exponentially, increasing by:

- $1 trillion in the past 3 months
- $2 trillion in the past 6 months
- $4 trillion in the past 2 years
- $11 trillion in the past 4 years.

269 Omar Mohammed, "Housing Crisis Could Be the Death Knell of the Middle Class," *Newsweek*, Newsweek.com, December 12, 2023, https://www.newsweek.com/housing-crisis-could-death-knell-americas-middle-class-1848936.
270 Michael Snyder, "Which Major City Will Completely Collapse First—Los Angeles, Chicago, or New York," EndOfTheAmericanDream.com, April 21, 2024, https://endoftheamericandream.com/which-major-city-will-completely-collapse-first-los-angeles-chicago-or-new-york-city/.

The annual interest in the national debt now exceeds $1 trillion annually. In the third quarter of 2023, when the economy supposedly grew at a healthy 4.9 percent rate, US growth domestic product (GDP) grew $547 billion, but the US budget deficit increased by an even bigger amount, $622 billion.[271] Professor D. W. MacKenzie ridiculed the basic premise of the Modern Monetary Theory in an article he wrote on the Mises Institute's website. "The idea that the government can print its way out of any fiscal deficit is a path to the dark side of hyperinflation."[272]

Not only is the American taxpayer getting saddled with a national debt we will never pay off, the inflationary rate at which the Biden administration has created dollars out of nothing dramatically reduces the purchasing power of the middle-class household. The US postwar middle class was the strongest and most politically stable middle class the world had ever seen. The elite self-designated masters who aspire to anoint themselves to transhuman status have no use for homo sapiens, as we shall next see. A middle class buried in debt is easily extinguished. For those falling out of the middle class, there is an available descent from abuse of alcohol, tranquilizers, and opioids to the homeless' use of fentanyl in the streets. Then, there is always voluntary euthanasia and assisted suicide, which is already legal in Hawaii, Oregon, Washington, California, Colorado, Washington, DC, Vermont, and Maine.[273]

No less an authority than Aristotle warned us that the destruction of the middle class is a certain way to destabilize a political community. In the Politics, Book IV, Aristotle wrote:

---

271 Tyler Durden, "US Debt Hits a Record $34 Trillion," ZeroHedge.com, January 3, 2024, https://www.zerohedge.com/markets/us-debt-hits-record-34001-trillion.

272 D. W. MacKenzie, "Both of Biden's Key Economic Advisers Get Basic Econ Wrong," Mises Institute, Mises.org, May 16, 2024, https://mises.org/power-market/both-bidens-key-economic-advisers-get-basic-econ-wrong.

273 "Voluntary and involuntary euthanasia," *Medical News Today*, MedicalNewsToday.com, no date, https://www.medicalnewstoday.com/articles/182951.

It is therefore also that the political community administered by the middle class is the best, and that it is possible for those states to be well governed that are of the kind in which the middle class is numerous, and preferably stronger than both the other two classes, or at all events than one of them, for by throwing in its weight it sways the balance and prevents the opposite extremes from coming into existence.[274]

Aristotle explained his reasoning as follows:

Hence it is the greatest good fortune if the men that have political power possess a moderate and sufficient substance, since where some own a very great deal of property and others none there comes about either an extreme democracy or an unmixed oligarchy, or a tyranny may result from both of the two extremes, for tyranny springs from both democracy and oligarchy of the most unbridled kind, but much less often from the middle forms of constitution and those near to them.[275]

Political theorist Leslie Rubin, in his 2018 book *America, Aristotle, and the Politics of a Middle Class*, stressed the impact Aristotle's views had on our Founding Fathers regarding the strength of a constitutional republic designed with a balance of power between the legislative, judicial, and executive functions, created with principles of limited government that were aimed at fostering a strong middle class. The decline of the middle class in the United States today threatens us with economic, social, and political decline precisely because the collapse of the middle class inevitably results in "political polarization, economic stagnation,

---

274 Aristotle, H. Rakham, trans., *Politics* (Cambridge, MA: Loeb Classic Library, Harvard University Press, first published 1932, reprinted with corrections, 1944), Book IV, ix, 6–8 at 8, 1295b, p. 331.
275 Ibid., 1296a, pp. 332–332.

and government dysfunction."[276] What we are forced to realize is that the evil masters of the New World Order view the destruction of the middle class and the collapse of the American constitutional republic as a necessary condition to their creation of a transhuman globalist one-world government.

Enter Yuval Noah Harari

Yuval Noah Harari, a professor at the Department of History at the Hebrew University in Jerusalem, has played a prominent role in articulating the philosophical base of the transhuman futurist movement. With a series of bestselling books and speeches on international forums, including appearances at the World Economic Forum in Davos, Switzerland in 2018 and 2020, Harari has both entertained and shocked millions with outrageous statements, including the claim that artificial intelligence (AI) will supersede human intelligence both in creativity and task achievement, with the result that most human beings will become members of the "useless class" of people who have no skills the new AI economy needs.[277] As AI machines become better than humans at most tasks, Harari believes the question of the twenty-first century will become this: "What do we need humans for, or at least, what do we need so many humans for?"[278] Harari has argued that the final solution for a world of useless people is "a combination of drugs and computer games."[279]

276 The quotation is from the following source: Lee Trepanier, "America, Aristotle, and the Politics of a Middle Class," Book Review published in *Voegelin View*, VoegelinView. com, July 24, 2018, https://voegelinview.com/america-aristotle-and-the-politics-of-a-middle-class/#:~:text=Finally%2C%20the%20middling%20will%20exact,regime%20 because%20it%20promotes%20stability. See: Leslie G. Rubin, *America, Aristotle, and the Politics of a Middle Class* (Waco, TX: Baylor University Press, 2018).
277 Yuval Noah Harari, "AI and Useless Class," posted by Great Minds Official, YouTube, 2023, https://www.youtube.com/watch?v=94o-9zR2bew.
278 Yuval Noah Harari, "Useless People," posted by Wednesday Warriors, YouTube, 2023, https://www.youtube.com/watch?v=94o-9zR2bew.
279 Yuval Noah Harari, "On Yuval Noah Harari's final solutions for a world of useless

In his 2011 book, *Sapiens: A Brief History of Humankind*, Harari makes clear that his intellectual background stems from post-modernism. More precisely, Harari fits in the intellectual tradition that French philosopher Jean Baudrillard established. Baudrillard believed all experience was subjective. Even more important, he believed all experience consisted of language constructs, the narratives we construct to give meaning to otherwise meaningless experiences. As I explained in my 2023 book, *Neo-Marxism, Cultural Maoism, and Anarchy*,[280] Baudrillard's 1981 book *Simulacra and Simulation*[281] set out the proposition that reality itself is nothing more than the images we create such that the images become the reality. When discussing the transition in how people perceive images in history, Baudrillard explained that the view of images are accurate reflections of a profound external reality that led to the mistaken beliefs in God, theology, and natural law. Now that technology allows us to appreciate that there is no objective reality to perceive, we can finally perceive that there never was God. We also understand that theology implying the necessity of a Last Judgment to impose natural law rulings on the morality of human lives was, as Freud maintained, an illusion we created for social control purposes.

In his 2011 book *Sapiens: A Brief History of Humanity*,[282] Harari focuses on the last seventy thousand years of Earth's approximately four-billion-year history—a time period in which Harari asserts "organisms belonging to the species Homo sapiens started to form even more elaborate structures called cultures." He continues to note: "The

---

people," posted by Decrevi Determined Be Catholic, YouTube, 2022, https://www.youtube.com/watch?v=6ObBQ3os2YQ.

280 Jerome R. Corsi, *Neo-Marxism, Cultural Maoism, and Anarchy*, op. cit., pp. 303-312.

281 Jean Baudrillard, *Simulacra and Simulation*, trans. Sheila Faria Glaser (Ann Arbor: University of Michigan Press, 1994). Originally published in French as: Jean Baudrillard, *Simulacres et Simulation* (Paris: Éditions Galilée, 1981).

282 Yuval Noah Harari, *Sapiens: A Brief History of Humanity* (London, UK: Vintage, 2015). First published in Hebrew in Israel in 2011 by Kinneret, Zmora-Bitain, Dvir. Page references are to the Vintage edition.

subsequent development of these human cultures is called culture."[283] Harari acknowledges that humans are distinguished from other life forms on Earth in that we are conscious, self-reflective, thinking beings capable of cognition. Harari ponders what caused the "Cognitive Revolution," but here he has no explanation.

What caused it [the Cognitive Revolution]? We're not sure. The most commonly believed theory argues that accidental genetic mutations changed the inner wiring of the brains of Sapiens, enabling them to think in unprecedented ways and to communicate using an altogether new type of language. We might call it the Tree of Knowledge mutation. Why did it occur in Sapiens DNA rather than in that of Neanderthals? It was a matter of pure chance, as far as we can tell. But it's more important to understand the consequences of the Tree of Knowledge mutation than its causes. What was so special about the new Sapiens language that it enabled us to conquer the world?[284]

Harari answered his question by positing that what made humans powerful was our ability to use language to create myths. He explained with regard to what he terms the "Agricultural Revolution":

Myth, it transpired, are stronger than anyone could have imagined. When the Agricultural Revolution opened opportunities for the creation of crowded cities and mighty empires, people invented stories about great gods, motherlands and joint stock companies to provide the needed social links. While human evolution was crawling at its usual snail pace, the human imagination was building astounding networks of mass cooperation unlike any other ever seen on earth.

---

283 Ibid., p. 3.
284 Ibid., pp. 23–24.

Harari rejects all concepts of God or human rights as myths. He ridicules Thomas Jefferson's opening statement in the Declaration of Independence.

> And what are the characteristics that evolved in humans? 'Life', certainly. But 'liberty'? There is no such thing in biology. Just like equality, rights, and limited liability companies, liberty too is a political ideal rather than a biological phenomenon. From a purely biological viewpoint, there is little difference between the citizens of a republic and the subjects of a king. And what about 'happiness'? So far biological research has failed to come up with a clear definition of happiness or a way to measure it objectively. Most biological studies acknowledge only the existence of pleasure, which is more easily defined and measured. So, 'life, liberty, and the pursuit of happiness' should be translated into 'life and the pursuit of pleasure.'[285]

He rewrote Jefferson's sentence as follows: "We hold these truths to be self-evident, that all men evolved differently, that they are born with certain mutable characteristics, and that among these are life and the pursuit of pleasure."[286]

For Harari, the concept of God and human rights are just subjective constructs—narratives we choose to believe—but in the final analysis when you cut into a person, you find bone, blood, and guts, but no soul, no God, and no human rights. Like Baudrillard, Harari is a nihilist who truly believes in nothing—an atheist because a world devoid of meaning must also be a world devoid of God. Harari ends his book *Sapiens* by projecting that scientific advances including genetic engineering and the ability to create life in the laboratory will soon spell the end of Homo sapiens as a species. Harari finds little to celebrate in

285 Ibid., p. 123.
286 Ibid.

the history of humans. "Time and again, massive increases in human power did not necessarily improve the well-being of individual Sapiens, and usually caused immense misery to other animals," he laments.[287] Harari ends *Sapiens* with an afterword that he titles, "The Animal That Became God."[288]

Predictably, in 2015, Harari wrote a sequel titled *Homo Deus: A Brief History of Tomorrow*.[289] Here, Harari lays out his proposition explaining how Homo sapiens (wise humans) become Homo Deus (human gods). Our evolution, Harari projects, is not to achieve a more self-conscious fulfillment, but as Homo Deus progresses, Harari reduces conscious-ness to brain activity, insisting that intelligent machines are capable of "thinking" at advanced levels the human brain cannot reach.

He wrote:

> For thousands of years people believed that all our actions and deci-sions emanate from our souls. Yet in the absence of any supporting evidence, and given the existence of much more detailed alternative theories, the life sciences have ditched the soul. As private individuals, many biologists and doctors may go on believing in souls. Yet they never write about them in serious scientific journals.[290]

Harari reduces intelligence to the operation of algorithms—a process that does not involve conscious thinking. He argues that machines can process non-organic algorithms more effectively than humans. "Today facial-recognition programs are able to identify people far

---

287 Ibid., p. 465.
288 Ibid., pp. 465–466.
289 Yuval Noah Harari, *Homo Deus: A Brief History of Tomorrow* (London: UK: Vintage, 2017). This revised edition was first published with the title *The History of Tomorrow* in Hebrew in Israel in 2015 by Kinneret, Zmora-Bitain, Dvir. Page references are to the Vintage edition.
290 Ibid., p. 134.

more efficiently and quickly than humans can," he notes.[291] Observing that AI computer intelligence, problem solving, and creativity already exceeds the capabilities of Homo sapiens, intelligence decouples and increases the gap with consciousness. Harari envisions a world run by algorithms—algorithms that replace the gods that once ruled the world:

> If the algorithm makes the right decision, it could accumulate a fortune, which it could then invest as it sees fit, perhaps buying your house and becoming your landlord. If you infringe on the algorithm's legal rights—say, by not paying rent—the algorithm could hire lawyers and sue you in court. If such algorithms consistently outperform human capitalists, we might end up with an algorithmic upper class owning most of the planet. This may sound impossible, but before dismissing the idea, remember that most of our planet is already owned legally by non-human intersubjective entities, namely nations and corporations. Indeed, 5,000 years ago much of Sumer was owned by imaginary gods such as Enki and Inanna. If gods can possess land and employ people, why not algorithms?[292]

Harari concludes that Homo sapiens equipped with "twenty-first century techno-humanism hopes to reach that goal [creating the transhuman Homo Deus] with the help of genetic engineering, nanotechnology, and brain-computer technologies."[293]

Permanent Life Extension

Russian anarchist Mikhail Bakunin (1814–1876) wrote in *God and State*, an unfinished manuscript that remained unpublished in Bakunin's

---

291 Ibid., p. 372.
292 Ibid., p. 377.
293 Ibid., p. 411.

lifetime, made his admiration of Satan clear. In his chapter 1 discussion of Adam and Eve in the biblical Garden of Eden, Bakunin portrayed Satan's role in tempting Eve to taste the forbidden fruit as follows:

> But here steps in Satan, the eternal rebel, the first freethinker and the emancipator of worlds. He makes man ashamed of his bestial ignorance and obedience; he emancipates him, stamps upon his brow the seal of liberty and humanity, in urging him to disobey and eat of the fruit of knowledge.[294]

Bakunin prefigured Friedrich Nietzsche's 1886 book *Beyond Good and Evil*. Like Bakunin, Nietzsche believed "good" and "evil" are simply conventions, artifacts of a Christian religion designed to enslave believers. In Part Four of *Beyond Good and Evil*, epigram 129 reads: "The devil has the broadest perspective on God, which is why he keeps so far away from God:—the devil, that is, as the oldest friend of knowledge."[295] So too, Bakunin concluded: "Christianity is precisely the religion *par excellence*, because it exhibits and manifests, to the fullest extent, the very nature and essence of every religious system, which is *the imprisonment, enslavement, and annihilation of humanity for the benefit of divinity*."[296] Bakunin reversed Voltaire's famous saying on God. In the *Epistle to the Author of "The Three Imposters"* published in 1769, Voltaire proclaimed: "If God did not exist, it would be necessary to invent him."[297]

---

294 Mikhail Bakunin, *God and State* (New York: Dover Publications, 1970), p. 10.
295 Friedrich Nietzsche, *Beyond Good and Evil: Prelude to a Philosophy of Future*, eds. Rolf-Peter Hortsmann and Judith Norman, trans. Judith Norman (Cambridge: Cambridge University Press, 2001), 66.
296 Bakunin, *God and State*, op. cit., p. 24.
297 Voltaire, "Epître à l'auteur de livre *des Trois imposteurs*" ["Epistle to the author of the book of the *The Three Impostors*"], ed. Louis Moland, *Oeuvres completes de Voltaire* [*Complete Works of Voltaire*] (Paris: Garnier, 1877–1885), vol. 10, pp. 402–405. See also: The Voltaire Society, "If God did not exist, it would be necessary to invent him," Whitman.edu, n.d., https://www.whitman.edu/VSA/trois.imposteurs.html.

Bakunin's version read: "If God really existed, it would be necessary to abolish him."[298] Bakunin's point is that true knowledge is only available to those who acknowledge that Satan rules on earth. For Marx and Bakunin, God exists, but for them God is the great deceiver.[299]

Today's transhumanists are a technologically sophisticated redo of Nietzsche's *Übermensch* [Superhumans]. The postmodern critique of the Enlightenment rails against reason and science because world wars ravaged the twentieth century. There is no doubt that reason and science since the Enlightenment have produced a world of increasing technological wonders—cellphones, personal computers, transportation of millions of people across continents via advanced commercial aviation, and so on. Yet, by presuming that the Enlightenment would also advance human nature to produce a race of Nietzschean *Übermensch*, we make a mistake assuming advances in technology would necessarily result in advanced human morality. What we are ending up producing is a postmodernist world of technological wonders populated by a woke generation that cannot tell us what a woman or a man is.[300]

In 1988, Carnegie Mellon roboticist Hans Moravec foresaw a "post-biological" future in which the human species would break free of the chains of the exponential production of useless prodigy to experience the creation of a new artificial prodigy of machines, i.e., "Mind Children," that will witness a "Great Replacement" of biological Homo sapiens with a new race that Harari views as Homo Deus.[301] Thus, the New World Order views global depopulation as a necessary transitional that must be taken if the postmodernist Nietzschean *Übermensch* are to

---

298 Bakunin, *God and State*, op. cit., p. 28.
299 These first two paragraphs of this section are drawn from my book *Neo-Marxism, Cultural Maoism, and Anarchy: Exposing Woke Insanity in an Age of Disinformation*, op. cit., "Marx and Satan: How Marx Weaponized Hegel," pp. 136-150, at pp. 143–144.
300 Ibid., p. 176.
301 Hans Moravec, *Mind Children* (New York, Viking: 1988), p. 9. Cited by Joe Allen, *Dark Aeon: Transhumanism and the War Against Humanity*, op. cit., p. 16.

rule. Ray Kurzweil, a computer scientist and futurist who is a research and development star at Google, in his 2005 book *The New Singularity is Near*[302] envisions "an inflection point "where the converging fields of genomics, nanotech, and robotics will yield a material apocalypse,"[303] in which Homo Deus merges Homo sapiens' limited intelligence into the AI-assisted and infinitely more advanced technology empowered by quantum computing. Kurzweil adopts the mathematical concept of singularity, which he defines as "a value that transcends any finite limitation, such as the explosion of magnitude that results when dividing a constant by a number that gets closer and closer to zero. Consider, for example, the simple function $y = 1/x$. As the value of x approaches zero, the value of the function (y) explodes to larger and larger values."[304] Kurzweil sets the date for the Singularity to occur in 2045; he declares the "nonbiological intelligence created in that year will be one billion times more powerful than all human intelligence today."[305]

Kurzweil envisions a future in which Homo Deus will so merge into silicon-assisted AI-enhanced transhuman capabilities that those self-appointed New Age techno-oligarchs will achieve the ability to award themselves digital immortality. In *Singularity*, Kurzweil explains:

Currently, when our human hardware crashes, the software of our lives—our personal "mind file"—dies with it. However, this will not continue to be the case when we have the means to store and restore the thousands of trillions of bytes of information represented in the pattern that we call our brains (together with the rest of our nervous system, endocrine system, and other structures that our mind file comprises).[306]

---

302 Ray Kurzweil, *The Singularity Is Near* (New York: Viking, 2005).
303 Joe Allen, Dark Aeon: Transhumanism and the War Against Humanity, op. cit., p. 17.
304 Ray Kurzweil, *The Singularity Is Near*, op. cit., p. 22.
305 Ibid., p. 136.
306 Ibid., p. 325

Kurzweil celebrates this daunting concept of digital immortality:

> At that point the longevity of one's mind file will not depend on the continued viability of any particular hardware medium (for example, the survival of a biological body and brain). Ultimately software-based humans will be vastly extended beyond the severe limitations of humans as we know them today. They will live out on the Web, projecting bodies whenever they need or want them, including virtual bodies in diverse realms of virtual reality, holographically projected bodies, foglet-projected bodies, and physical bodies comprising nanobot swarms and other forms of nanotechnology.[307]

"Foglet" is a reference to collections of nanobots that can manifest in virtual reality to produce the illusion of real objects—typically swamplands, mountains, even human phantasms. The transhuman future not only merges Homo sapiens with AI-assisted machines, the transhuman future merges reality into the metaverse. No longer needing to live a world that British philosopher Thomas Hobbes in his famous 1651 book *Leviathan* calls "solitary, poor, nasty, brutish, and short."[308] Transhumans today envision a science fiction utopia in which the privileged techno-oligarchs transition their physical bodies into computer code that experiences digital immortality surfing metaverses they find pleasurable. Whether the experience of digital immortality includes personal consciousness is irrelevant to thinkers like Harari, who fail to appreciate self-reflection as distinct from intelligence in action. There is no need for God to appear anywhere in this new reality, for there are no consequences beyond experiencing pleasure and avoiding pain. Digital immortality transcends good and evil, as Nietzsche imagined. The

---

307 Ibid.
308 Thomas Hobbes, *Leviathan* (Oxford: Oxford University Press: reprint of the 1651 edition, 1929), Chapter 13, Part 1, p. 99.

transhuman techno-oligarchs have, as Homo Deus, become gods, each achieving salvation for themselves in their self-experienced metaverses. As Harari replaces us mortal Homo sapiens with Homo Deus, Satan with transhumanism has imagined the most seductively evil Gardens of Eden ever imagined on this all too temporal-bound planet.

The question Harari and his transhuman acolytes fail to answer is this: Once Homo Deus achieves digital immortality, how do they keep the plug from being pulled on their digital version of Heaven? Transhumans fail to escape Macbeth's despair, as articulated in Act 5 of the Shakespeare play. Macbeth says:

> Out, out brief candle
> Life's but a walking shadow, a poor player
> That struts and frets his hour upon the stage.
> And then is heard no more. It is a tale
> Told by an idiot, full of sound and fury,
> Signifying Nothing. [309]

Dogs have only two types of cones in their retinas. Thus, the range of colors dogs can see is limited compared to humans, who standardly come equipped with three types of cones in their retinas. An atheist is typically similarly limited in that the atheist lacks a moral perception of a spiritual experience that arguably has been part of human experience since prehistoric periods. Ultimately, there may be no logical or empirical proof of God's existence. Yet, we humans come hard wired with a God awareness. The atheist cannot explain their disbelief in God without first positing the concept of God. In ancient Greek, the opposite of τηεοσ [theos] is ατηεοσ [atheos] (in ancient Greek, "God" or "non-God").[310]

---

309 William Shakespeare, *Macbeth*, act 5, scene 5, lines 16–27.
310 See the expanded discussion of atheism in my book *Neo-Marxism, Cultural Maoism,*

Like Karl Marx, Bakunin was not an atheist. He knew God existed, but he hated God—like Satan himself, Bakunin hated God because he wasn't God. Bakunin concluded his rendition of the Genesis story, insisting he had discerned the true understanding of Adam and Eve's actions:

> Let us disregard now the fabulous portion of this myth and consider its true meaning, which is very clear. Man has emancipated himself; he has separated himself from animality and constituted himself a man; he has begun his distinctively human history and development by an act of disobedience and science—that is, by *rebellion* and by *thought*.[311]

In a similar vein, Saul Alinsky dedicated his seminal 1971 book *Rules for Radicals* with an acknowledgment to Lucifer:

> Lest we forget at least an over-the-shoulder acknowledgment to the very first radical: from all our legends, mythology, and history (and who is to know where mythology leaves off and history begins—or which is which), the first radical known to man who rebelled against the establishment and did it so effectively that he at least won his own kingdom
> —Lucifer. [312]

With his identification of Lucifer as a rebel, we can assume Alinsky intended for us to catch his obvious wink to Bakunin. Alinsky embraced the dark side, modeling himself after the Prince of Darkness as if to say that fulfillment of his destiny demands rebelling against the established

---

and Anarchy, op. cit., "The Logic and Grammar of Atheism," pp. 287–291.
311 Bakunin, *God and State*, op. cit., p. 12. Italics in original.
312 Saul Alinsky, *Rules for Radicals: A Pragmatic Primer for Realistic Radicals* (New York: Vintage, 1971), ix.

powers in the United States. In his rebellion, he bows down to Satan, identifying himself with Lucifer's goal in the biblical revolution— namely, to grab power from the hands of God to place himself on the heavenly throne. So too, in imagining Homo Deus, transhumanists have the same hatred of God—fury at being subject to God's will and God's law.[313]

We have formed the Anti-globalist Alliance to fight this spiritual battle. Part II of this book proceeds with the articulation of the Anti-globalist Alliance Manifesto—a more comprehensive statement of the evil we are battling and the methods by which we the people can wrest the future from the grasp of these dystopian totalitarians who mask themselves as globalists in their evil determination to bring Satan's rule over Earth to fruition, merging themselves into a digital cyberspace to launch themselves into eternity.

---

313 See the expanded discussion of Saul Alinsky in my book *Neo-Marxism, Cultural Maoism, and Anarchy,* op. cit., "Marx and Satan: How Marx Weaponized Hegel," pp. 136–150, at pp. 144–146.

PART II:
ENDING THE WAR ON HUMANITY

MANIFESTO OF THE
ANTI-GLOBALIST ALLIANCE

Premise

In the first part of this essay, we saw on which fronts elite attacks target, ranging from the deep-state assassination of a sitting president in the streets of Dallas to the staging of a global pandemic as a pretext to vaccinate millions of people with a potentially lethal mRNA gene modification serum.

I will propose possible solutions to oppose this attack in this second part. Still, it is first necessary to understand an essential element that will enable us to make our resistance effective. We start from the premise that the elite uses systems of mass manipulation and social engineering to induce the population to accept the implementation of the "reforms" it has already decided on: the fact that the elite present their "reforms" as fictitious solutions to false problems is part of this deception. We need to dwell on this point before analyzing the possible answers we can give. That is why we will try to "dismantle" each of the points addressed in the first part without allowing ourselves to be confused by the excuses and the pretexts that the elite use to legitimize their fraud.

The premise on which the globalist fraud is based is the lie, of which Satan is the father: *Ye are of your father, the devil, and the lusts of your father ye will do. He was a murderer from the beginning, and abode not in the truth because there is no truth in him. When he speaketh a lie, he speaketh of his own: for he is a liar, and the father of the lie.* (John 8:44). To believe that goodwill animates the exponents of the elite, that they are as philanthropic as they claim, or that they have the good of humanity at heart, is utterly foolish and foolhardy: We know well—and we have seen it in the previous chapters—that they refer to a philosophical and pseudo-theological approach totally opposed to the Christian view, based therefore on hatred of God and consequently hatred of his Creation on the one hand and of Redemption on the other. They aim to erase the perfections of Creation by replacing them with a substitute, with a grotesque counterfeit that wants to appear as such, precisely so that those who accept it are aware that they are being cheated.

We might ask why those who intend to deceive people would want to make the deception obvious. Still, we must understand that this kind of shameless and paradoxical "honesty" is part of Luciferian thinking, which in accomplishing evil, believes it can avoid its implications by manifesting evil. And this, on closer inspection, is what the devil has been doing all along: even the temptation of Adam and Eve in the earthly paradise was clearly based on a contract that was entirely disadvantageous to our progenitors. The serpent proposes to them—who were already *sicut dii*, i.e., similar to gods (Genesis 3:5), in that they had not yet fallen as a result of the consequences of original sin—to break God's command and suffer the punishment they knew was inevitable, in exchange for the knowledge of what is good and what is evil. Adam and Eve thus agreed to subscribe to their own condemnation in order to have the death of soul and body in exchange for eternal bliss. Quite a bargain, no doubt.

Yet, this is what each of us chooses to do when faced with the proof—with temptation—we accept as our interlocutor none other than the father of lies, knowing that he will lie—since he knows how to do nothing else—and that his deception will inevitably be to our detriment. He who is homicidal from the beginning is capable of nothing but killing, yet we listen to him and, at the moment when we have to choose whether to obey God or Satan, we agree to antagonize the Almighty, knowing that this will entail consequences for us and for the society in which we live. We decide to pander to the evil will of Satan, who we know is undoubtedly our enemy and who envies our chance of salvation that is denied to him. This decision may appear to be folly, and in fact, it is, but therein lies the ultimate meaning of sin: we freely choose to do evil, knowing that it is evil, knowing who urges us to so decide intends us to do evil. If this were not the case—i.e., if we were simply deceived by the devil and believed in good faith that we were doing something morally permissible or at least not particularly serious—we would not be making a moral choice, and therefore would not be imputable for an action that is not totally conscious.

Those who read these remarks of mine should not think that this theological view of the devil's way of acting is limited to a Christian sphere. It permeates the action of the enemy and his adherents, who believe in the existence of an all-powerful and triune God no less than Christians do, but who, at the same time, in a maddening blindness of reason, want to delude themselves that Evil can overcome Good; that a creature—albeit fallen—can overcome the Creator; that a damned spirit can defeat the Savior. It is the folly of the ὕβρις [hubris, i.e., pride] of the Classics, that pride that usurps God of His absolute supremacy, going to inexorable νέμεσις [nemesis, i.e., punishment]. We need to understand not whether this view is true, but that this is nevertheless the view from which the action of people devoted to Evil starts. And we know that they are dedicated to Evil by their own admission, by their cultural and philosophical references, by their dealings with undeniably anti-Christian entities and movements, and by their ostentatious aversion to everything that constitutes the foundations of our Civilization, which is undeniably Christian in origin.

Let me give an example. In Nazi Germany, the Reich leadership belonged to movements that theorized the existence of a superior race and the elimination or domination of inferior races. In their political and social action, the Nazis were starting from an approach that none of us would share— a view that is repugnant to our culture, our Religion, and our very membership in the human family; but this is entirely irrelevant if what motivates Nazism is its insane conviction that it is an instrument of power for the Aryan race. That is why we must understand that we cannot look at the effects of Nazism without identifying and understanding its ideological matrix. Likewise, we cannot look at the impact of the globalist coup as if it were the result of pure coincidence or mere lust for power and not rather—as it actually is— the logical and consistent consequence of a specific *forma mentis.*

Those who serve Evil do not just want to deceive us: they want us to recognize and accept the deception, taking part in the Revolution; that is, in that reversal of the divine order—the κόσμος [*cosmos,* i.e., the universe rightly ordered] —which is ontologically impossible precisely because the κόσμος is based on God. Those who serve Evil want us to become accomplices in the subversion, knowing that our free and conscious choice will only bring us ruin.

This way of acting not only touches our existence when we are personally confronted with a moral choice, but we also find it at the social level, when the fraud is aimed at making the masses accept as inevitable that which we more or less consciously consider most likely to be harmful to us, to our Nation and all humanity. The choice, in this case, is similar but not identical, for in manipulating the masses, there is a need for the concurrence of a multiplicity of individuals who do not necessarily realize the ultimate goal and the ideas that determine it but who, in their cooperation in the subversive plan, know that they must obey people who are certainly not animated by good intentions. And it is incredibly revealing that this collaboration of subordinates is always obtained either through bribery or through blackmail: through bribery, by offering money and power in exchange for uncritical obedience; through blackmail, by threatening to bring to light crimes or scandals of subordinates if they do not comply. Then, if these crimes were committed with the logistical cooperation of members of the elite, as with Epstein's island or his apartment on Avenue Foch in Paris, the evidence for blackmail is already in the hands of the blackmailer. No wonder, then, that the elite relies primarily on these two levers—the economic and the blackmail levers—which are often complementary.

Just to give an example of the level of corruption that reigns unchallenged at the top of governments and institutions, consider that former Prime Minister Rishi Sunak—not elected by the British people—increased his personal wealth from 120 million pounds at the beginning of his term to 651 million pounds at the end of his term, refusing to specify whether this exorbitant wealth was due to speculative investments in Moderna vaccines. When a criminal investigation verifies the origin of the money accumulated by these politicians, we will have proof of their total corruption. [314]

Let us not forget that the techniques of social engineering—also studied in American circles since the early twentieth century and developed through academic confrontation with exponents of German National Socialism—serve to apply to social groups the rules that apply to individuals, according to a mentality that looks at human behavior as being traceable to the dynamics of laboratory guinea pigs or a termite mound.

---

314 Juliette Garside, "Rishi Sunak refuses to say if he will profit from Moderna Covid vaccine," *The Guardian*, November 17, 2020, https://www.theguardian.com/politics/2020/nov/17/rishi-sunak-refuses-to-say-if-he-will-profit-from-moderna-covid-vaccine

On the other hand, the pseudoscientific approach of Malthusianism—which starts from a totally false premise, such as world overpopulation and the progressive reduction of available resources—shows itself as a pretext exactly as are, for example, the theory of anthropogenic global warming, gender theory, the alleged need for global health governance to cope with threatening pandemics, etc.

The Goals of the 2030 Agenda

The so-called *Sustainable Development Goals* (SDGs) of Agenda 2030 are part of a project proposed by the United Nations World Organization and endorsed in 2015 by its 193 member countries. The wording of the goals and their vague description conceals, like all projects spawned by the globalist elite, unmentionable but easily identifiable purposes.

Here is a summary table of them:

Declared Goals	Real Targets
1. No poverty	Population reduction
2. Zero hunger	Monopoly of the food industry
3. Good health and well-being	Abortion, euthanasia, vaccination
4. Quality education	Indoctrination, woke ideology
5. Gender equality	Feminization and division of society
6. Clean water and sanitation	Privization of the Planet's water.
7. Affordable and clean energy	Energy speculation and green taxation
8. Decent work and economy growth	Labor exploitation and tax slavery
9. Industry, innovaton. and infrstructure	IV Industrial Revolution (transhumanism)
10. Reduced inequalities	Unique law for all nations
11. Sustainable cities and communities	Supervision and totalitarian control
12. Responsible consumption and production	Transgenic, synthetic and manipulated foods

Declared Goals	Real Targets
13. Climate action	Climate geoengineering and sun dimming
14. Life below water	Total control of fisheries and marine resources
15. Life on land	Total control of natural resources
16. Peace, justice, and strong institutions	Police state and end of freedom
17. Partnerships for the goals	Global Government and the New World Order (NWO)

A False Solution for a False Problem

And here we come to the crux of the matter: **How do we behave in our dual capacity as individuals and as members of a social body at a time when an entity that is so powerful in means and resources is forcing us to change our lives, our daily routines, our work, the way we look at our own and our children's futures, and everything that constitutes our identity from a material and spiritual point of view?**

Thus, when we see that the reasons given as justifications for a measure are not decisive and indeed appear inconsistent with the results they achieve, we need to understand that those reasons are specious and conceal fraud. Having understood this, we will be able to reverse, so to speak, the distorted point of view and know that **the fraud consists precisely in artificially creating a false problem in order to make us believe that what we are forced to do or suffer is the only solution to cope with it.**

The difficulty we encounter in being confronted with the inconsistency between the alleged problem and the proposed solution lies in the logical inversion operated by those who offer themselves as determined solvers of emergencies for which they are actually the first and only responsible. We find a similar mechanism in the cases analyzed by psychiatry: the mother who makes her son sick so that she can then cure him and thus keep him under control, or the fireman who starts a fire so that he can promptly intervene and receive public commendations. These instances show us that the psychopath's purpose is not to cure or solve a problem, because if that were the case, that mother would never have poisoned her son and that fireman would not have started the fire.

When we are told that a vaccine is needed to cope with a pandemic—which is very accurate, in the abstract—we have to make an effort of will to understand that this sharable principle is flawed in its premises since it is the pandemic that was planned in the laboratory *for the purpose of* making us believe that a vaccine (and "vaccine" it is not) had to be rushed into production to prevent millions from dying from the disease. What we got was a "vaccine" that not only does not serve to contain the virus or avoid complications for those infected with it, but also does not prevent you from getting the disease the "vaccine" was touted to prevent. Thus, the vaccine was not created to cure the disease. The vaccine was created to cause illness and death. And that is precisely the primary purpose: to exterminate the population, to create chronically ill people, to make the inoculated sterile so that they do not reproduce. Thus, some of the inoculated are forced to treat themselves—with therapies prepared by those responsible for the diseases—and others are left to resort to surrogacy or artificial insemination, offered as a solution to what would have otherwise been a nonexistent problem. What we previously had naturally and freely—or at any rate, as our choice among multiple options—is in fact replaced by its surrogate, which we most likely would have ruled out if we had been left with alternatives.

The Modus Operandi

Multinational corporations, observed from a psychopathological point of view, give evidence of acting like criminally insane people. The corporate pathology of placing profits ahead of morals is the theme of Joel Bakan's 2004 book, *The Corporation: The Pathological Pursuit of*

Profit and Power.[315] Bakan, a law professor at the University of British Columbia, notes that in recent years, managers of some large corporations have given capitalism a whole new face and language. As income inequality increased, wages stagnated, and the climate crisis escalated, these corporate managers realized they needed to make social values and environmental protection the core of their identity and communication. The problem is that corporations are still, first and foremost, concerned about their profits.

In a lucid and uncompromising investigation, Joel Bakan unveils the deception: in reality, corporations are increasingly aggressive toward personal freedom and threatening to democracy because they are capable of bringing ESG [environmental, social, and governance] rules into the boardroom, seeking to increase profits through politically correct social positioning. Bakan speaks with top managers and their harshest and most biting critics to demonstrate the unscrupulousness and destructive force of the rules that now govern our world. Unbridled privatization is crumbling the welfare state and the public good, governments are neglecting their duty to protect the environment, and every aspect of daily life is capitalized. At the same time, each of us experiences a condition of increasing alienation. And the profound injustice of an increasingly corporate-governed society has been definitively laid bare by the pandemic.

However, this behavior finds empirical confirmation if we analyze the rules of the so-called "free market" commercial strategies. The fraudulent modus operandi is to proceed in successive steps.

- The first step places a paid product or service alongside a good we already enjoy, making us believe that we can choose whether

---

315 Joel Bakan, *The Corporation: The Pathological Pursuit of Profit and Power* (Free Press, 2004).

or not to avail ourselves of it and that no one will deprive us of the preexisting alternative.

- The second step aims to incentivize the use of the new product while simultaneously discouraging the one we already had available.
- The third step makes it difficult or impossible to have the pre-existing good and forces us to buy only the one proposed.

This methodology applies to the green transition and the forced shift to "transitioning" to electric cars and renewable energy—particularly wind turbines, solar panels, and battery technology—and away from internal combustion engines burning hydrocarbon fuel; to the lucrative business of surrogacy pregnancy, away from natural motherhood within a traditional family; and, last but not least, to the illusion of health to be achieved through pharmaceutical drugs, away from a healthy life with a natural immune system.

Where simple marketing operations cannot induce this shift, the external action of the seller intervenes, forcing the choice of his product and making it the only one available at the price he has predetermined—a price that no one can now prevent him from increasing. The multinational corporation acts no differently when it offers a low-level product to the masses in competition with a small company that provides a high-level product as an alternative. Initially, the multinational corporation places its low-level product alongside its own high-level product to push the small company out of the market. Finally, the multinational corporation eliminates its high-level product, forcing customers who want to buy a high-level product to purchase the only product on the market, namely its low-level product. This modus operandi is an application of the Hegelian dialectic: one creates the problem to get the desired reaction so that the masses passively accept it or, under the psychological pressure of emergencies and crises, even come to desire it.

We have further confirmation of this in the words of Mariana Mazzucato, an economist with dual Italian-US citizenship who is an economics professor at University College London and a member of the World Economic Forum (WEF). Pope Francis appointed Mazzucato to be a member of the Pontifical Academy for Life, despite her being a staunch abortionist. At an international panel, Mazzucato explained the following:

> Whether it was the digital divide, the vaccine rollout, what Dr. Tedros called vaccine apartheid because the mission was not eight vaccines, it was global vaccination, and we failed to do that. Again, what have we learned? And this is really what the council set out to do, to make sure that we actually are learning from these interlinked crises: climate, biodiversity, health.[316]

Attending a WEF conference, Mazzuccato made clear that an easily comprehended global crisis was necessary to create the conditions where the global population would agree to be "vaccinated," i.e., controlled:

> Our attempt to vaccinate the entire planet failed, and "climate change" is "too abstract" for people to understand, but the coming water crisis is something that everyone will get on board with. [317]

So let's be prepared for a water emergency, planned and announced by the same actors responsible for the previous crises.

---

316 A video clip of Mazzucato speaking at an international meeting, posted by Camus on X, dated June 2, 2024, https://x.com/newstart_2024/status/1797215135078945136.
317 A video clip of Mazzucato speaking at a World Economic Forum meeting, posted by Kelly DNP Functional/Integrative Medicine, June 3, 2024, https://x.com/kacdnp91/status/1797605437757358430.

Total Commodification

The mercantile mentality underlying this process of market manipulation is the same because the actors involved are the same. And no wonder: this mentality is peculiar to those who neither know how (nor want to know how) to observe reality, except according to a materialist vision peculiar to economic Liberalism, from which every sphere of human life must necessarily be traced back to a commercial transaction. Fundamental to the mercantile mentality is monetization—the possibility of translating not only material goods into money but also the immaterial, including even the most sacred and inviolable aspects of our lives.

The globalist merchant asks himself: **How do I turn what is currently free or obtained at a reasonable expense and does not enrich me into my own income?** The answer is before our eyes: eliminating what is free or offered by others and replacing it with something that must be paid for. **The result is that we transform everything into a commodity.** At that point, since profit is the primary purpose and the resulting centralization of power, the quality of the "product" may be minimal or void since the market has been distorted by the absence of rules and the elimination of "competition."

One of the reasons why the elite literally hates Christianity is that it robs it of the profits from all those charitable—therefore free—initiatives that a host of lay people, religious, and nuns carried out in the service of the poor, the sick, children, young people, the elderly, and families: hospitals, orphanages, institutions for the disabled, kindergartens, schools, and charities that in the name of the Gospel constituted indispensable help for society. These were seen as competitors to be eliminated in order to create a new market to be exploited, where those without means no longer have someone to help them selflessly, and now find in their place a company run by McKinsey and Company. The suppression of these

charities began in Europe in the nineteenth century at the urging of Freemasonry.

Major pharmaceutical companies, all owned by large investment funds, have succeeded in turning national healthcare systems into passive purchasers of drugs. In many nations, the privatization of healthcare—often forced through the imposition of spending cuts in the name of balanced budgets—has led to the drastic reduction of beds and treatment, eliminating treatments that are too expensive and unprofitable for the healthcare company. This profit-driven approach has gone so far as to deny treatments for severe diseases, pushing instead for the more profitable types of treatments, such as those needed for so-called "gender transition."

But we do not believe that what has happened is the result of an unfortunate coincidence: it has long been the case that Big Pharma has literally taken control of global health care—through the World Health Organization and its offshoots—to the point that in 2018, Goldman Sachs asked: "Is curing patients a sustainable business model?"[318] The pharmaceutical companies answer this seemingly rhetorical question: "No." Profit comes before patient care. Thus, it makes no sense for a company to give up profit, and the healthcare business, being almost entirely in the hands of private economic interests, cannot take on unproductive expenses. Some time ago, Bill Gates lamented the "very, very high medical costs" of patient care by health services. He, therefore, suggested the establishment of "death commissions" to induce the seriously ill to die. Gates insisted that "the money used to keep poor and sick people alive for a few extra months could be better spent on teachers."[319]

---

318 Tae Kim, "Goldman Sachs asks in biotech research report: 'Is curing patients a sustainable business model," CNBC, CNBC.com, April 11, 2018, https://www.cnbc.com/2018/04/11/goldman-asks-is-curing-patients-a-sustainable-business-model.html.
319 A video clip of Bill Gates giving a speech, posted on X by "Sudden and Unexpected," May 27, 2024,

Here, then, citizens are turned into the chronically ill, and the chronically ill into chronic clients until their commercial uselessness makes them worthy of being killed by euthanasia.

To enable the transformation of healthy people into sick people, so-called predictive medicine has also been invented, i.e., the adoption of therapies to be administered to healthy people whom an algorithm indicates are statistically likely to develop a specific disease in the future. Italian journalist Antonio Amorosi recently wrote about this. Amorosi cited two recent British studies published in the "prestigious scientific journal *Nature* that discussed a protein in the blood capable of signaling a tumor seven years before it developed. Amorosi asked: "If they told you: in seven years you will get cancer, take this drug to avoid it, would you do so?" [320]

Exactly what we were saying: so-called predictive medicine. **You are predicted to get sick because an index reports it at x percentage.**

It sounds like the Steven Spielberg movie *Minority Report*, where a person's murders were predicted before they came true, arresting the potential perpetrator before the crime was committed. The film chronicles precisely the distortion of a system that was created to prevent crimes but instead arrests innocents by responding to the creators' seat of power and money.

Healthy people of all ages are a considerably larger percentage of sick people. **Think what a massive business it can become for pharmaceutical companies to treat healthy people who are diagnosed with a potential illness in the future? And if you are then suggestible and are yourself afraid of dying, the business is as good as done. Pandemic management has shown how easy it is.**

---

https://x.com/toobaffled/status/1795029524754940143

320 Antonio Amorosi, "Curare i sani, il nuovo business della medicina che passa dai tumori," AntonioAmorosi.it, May 22, 2024, https://www.antonioamorosi.it/2024/05/22/curare-i-sani-il-nuovo-business-della-medicina-che-passa-dai-tumori/.

The model that regards public health as a right envisions that the government has a duty to guarantee to provide the health care needed to citizens by drawing on the inexhaustible coffers of the treasury. However, when this concept became an obstacle to developing a healthcare market promising enormous profits, that obstacle had to be removed, and health care moved from a government-provided human right to a private enterprise healthcare model based on the principle of maximizing profit. How do we get to the point of privatizing health care if not by imposing such government budget cuts that make it impossible for the state to provide these services? Of course, the transition to a for-profit healthcare model could only be achieved by indoctrinating physicians as early as the universities—where they learn to meekly follow the protocols laid out by Big Pharma, seduced by the prospect of receiving colossal bonuses and sponsorships.

Most hospitals and physicians today choose treatments for their patients not based on their efficacy, but on the money given to them by the companies in the industry. The more expensive a treatment is— regardless of whether it is harmful or useless—the more the profit margin allows to generously remunerate those who advertise it in "scientific" journals or in the media, as well as those who prescribe it without scruples. Meanwhile, the medical personnel who do not submit to its "vaccines" and who denounce its dangerousness are suspended from their jobs.

The billions spent by pharmaceutical companies in lobbying health agencies, governments, and supranational bodies have demonstrated total dependence on Big Pharma, which becomes complicit in a crime against humanity because the corrupters and corrupt knew from the beginning that they were causing harm and death.

If we apply this mercantile principle to the actions of the elite, we will find plenty of illustrative cases. According to this approach, the presence of grandparents in the family is considered a loss of income for the nursing homes. Nursing homes have multiplied after destroying the patriarchal family and forcing both parents to work. A healthy life in the country is a loss of income for the pharmaceutical companies, as well as for clinics that profit from medicine and disease. Sexuality within a conjugal love and dedication to the family is a loss of "opportunity" for the markets of pornography, prostitution, sex tourism, and the exploitation of women and minors.

We are plagued today with a thriving sex trade market, born as a necessary consequence of deliberate tampering with the morals of the masses, which were once religious and therefore vehemently opposed to lifestyles incompatible with the belief that sex is a sacred gift from God that allows human beings to engage in bringing forth life on Earth. Gone is the special reverence for women that results from the realization that all of us here enter life through the womb of a mother. The billion-dollar business of gender transition clinics, as we saw in the first part of this essay, was possible only after gender theory was artificially imposed without any scientific basis to validate it. Indeed, the prospering of gender transition clinics involved government health authorities concealing all the evidence that demonstrated its absolute invalidity and the dangerousness of implementing and normalizing gender transitioning healthcare into the social fabric.

Laura Aboli understands why the globalist cabal focuses on trangenderism to set the stage for the post-human transhumanism they have in mind as their ultimate godless dystopian future:

> The transgender movement is not a grassroots movement, it comes from the top. It has nothing to do with free speech, sexuality or civil rights. It's an evil psychological operation with a clear agenda to bring us closer to transhumanism by making us question the most fundamental notion of human identity, our gender. If you don't know who

you are, if you already identify yourself as a hybrid between a man and a woman, you'll easily be convinced to become a hybrid between human and machine.[321]

But even before we get to these aberrations by which so many young people are maimed and perpetually rendered infertile, we cannot forget the guilt-ridden work undertaken by governments, non-governmental organizations (NGOs), and religious leaders regarding the migration phenomenon. A huge business has developed to give assistance to a mass of illegal immigrants at the expense of the treasury and for the profit of the receiving agencies and the exploiters of underpaid labor.

The same phenomenon occurs in the agri-business sector: the systematic destruction of small farms has as its sole purpose—beyond the ridiculous excuses about the methane emissions of cows or the environmental impact of field cultivation methods—the elimination of competition to favor the production of synthetic meat and genetically modified organism (GMO) foods by multinationals linked to Bill Gates and his delusions. It escapes no one that the monopoly of this sector allows the imposition of contaminated and toxic food on the masses as a means of eliminating people or making them chronically ill. Mainstream media censorship of the burning of farms and food establishments serves to conceal the systematic attack on agriculture and animal husbandry. At the same time, governments and banks fund bankrupt startups of companies experimenting with food-borne injection of drugs and mRNA "vaccines."

Another example of the monetization of activities is about to materialize with the adoption of credits based on carbon footprints that the System arbitrarily—and quite questionably—imposes in the name of the Net Zero goals of Agenda 2030. Many multinational corporations

---

321 Laura Aboli, "Transhumanism: The End Game," op. cit.

have already implemented carbon exchange principles, selling their untapped share of "polluting" carbon dioxide emissions to other companies that continue to exude carbon dioxide. The obvious result is that it does not reduce the quantity of carbon dioxide emissions. The goal instead is to monetize carbon dioxide for the profit of a few.

The monetization of the air we breathe is inherently self-hating since we humans exhale carbon dioxide with every breath we take. Moreover, far from being a harmful, polluting molecule, carbon dioxide is a necessary component of the carbon cycle without which life on Earth would cease to exist. Carbon dioxide is a trace molecule in the atmosphere (0.04 percent), but photosynthesis depends on plants absorbing carbon dioxide. However, the monetization of the air through imposing a new carbon exchange tax was never designed to prevent global warming, as the elite insist, but to get human beings to submit to totalitarian government surveillance and control voluntarily. Dutch political commentator Eva Vlaardingerbroek rightly points out that the World Economic Forum's plan to assign a CO_2 output threshold to every citizen to establish for each of us a digital identity allows unseen government controllers to monitor in the name of climate change. She explained:

> The CEO of one of the largest Dutch banks said, if everyone gets individual personal carbon credits, why don't we make it so that rich people, who for example want to go on holiday a little too often, can buy personal carbon credits from people who can't afford buying plane tickets or eating meat too often? [...] So what will happen is the rich will get richer, the poor will get poorer, and they're saying it openly as if it's not a controversial thing at all. It's neo-feudalism. That's what it is.[322]

---

322 A video clip of an Eva Vlaardingerbroek interview conducted by Mark Steyn and broadcast on CBN News in the UK, posted by Wide Awake media on X, May 17, 2024, https://x.com/wideawake_media/status/1791365837061750874.

By implementing these principles, the merchant fails to offer a good quality product at an honest price and prevents others from doing so, defrauding customers by offering the worst. The customer has no benefit from this; on the contrary, the quality of his life decreases. The supplier of good-quality raw materials is excluded from the market and put out of business so that he cannot supply other competitors. The only one who profits from this fraud is the unscrupulous merchant who knows he is selling a poor product. The fact that the product placed is counterfeit, poisoned, or harmful is an incentive to distribute it as much as possible because the primary purpose of this fraudulent operation is the physical and spiritual death of humanity. Indeed, this applies not only to tangible goods—food, clothing, furniture, etc.—but especially to intangible ones, such as spirituality, culture, art, literature, and entertainment. In the latter sphere, the globalist fraud shows itself in all its horror and demands from its subjects their adherence to the nihilist woke cult.

The mercantile mentality has appropriated spaces that were once exempt from commodification: religion and politics, because religion and politics have always been "sacred" spheres of human activity since the faith of a people cannot fail to direct its civil and governmental action as well, as has always been the case throughout history. Those who serve religion as clerics or politics as state officials are precisely called "ministers," from the Latin minister meaning "servant." Even in not-too-remote times, all those who held institutional roles in civil or religious spheres had a strong moral sense and understood the responsibility of their vocation and the need to be an example of integrity for others.

Until the early 1960s, it would have been unthinkable to consider religion or politics as a "product" to be traded, and it would have been even more inconceivable to want to place an embarrassing substitute alongside the "original product" already available. Yet this has happened before our eyes in the Catholic Church—a process that has also spread through the Protestant Church as denomination after denomination goes "woke. " In the 1960s, Pope John XXIII convened the Second Vatican Council— a tragically secular conclave that decreed the bankrupt liquidation of two thousand years of Catholicism, and replaced it with an outlet religion;that is, a shoddy doctrinal creed. This destroyed the Latin liturgy with the ersatz "modernization" that undermined the sacred foundations upon which the Catholic Church had for centuries persisted. And when in 2007, Benedict XVI liberalized the Latin rite in "limited edition" with Motu Proprio *Summorum Pontificum*, its success threatened the *deep church* because Benedict appeared determined to persist on a path that would make the fraud of the Second Vatican Council blatantly apparent to all.

In the political sphere, a political party's platform, which was a consistent, practical application of the ideas and principles that the party espoused, has turned into a rhetorical balancing act by which candidates try to foist on voters a simulacrum of good governance that in reality responds to the orders of international lobbies. The resulting globalist-contrived political statement of ends and means has proven to have no moral value, to be scientifically inconsistent, and to cause enormous damage to the health, economy, and welfare of the community. Politics is no longer a public service dedicated to the common good but a cowardly display of power by its courtiers.

For the Deep State, we no longer are patriotic citizens. For the deep church, we no longer are loyal believers. We have become customers of a Deep State and deep church driven to bankruptcy by corrupt managers who are about to flee after emptying its safe. **We are in the frantic phase of total liquidation before the disastrous budgets come to light**: We must keep quiet and buy the only product put on the market since everything not produced or sold by the System has been put out of business, banned, prohibited, declared illegal, or destroyed. In this sense, the persecution of President Trump is symbolic because it shows the hostility of the elite toward a way of doing politics that high ideals animate. President Trump is anathema to the Deep State precisely because he chooses to do the will of the common goal. President Trump dares to call out in colorful detail the cynicism of those who speak after reading polls or receiving orders (and transfers of funds) from Davos. Even in the Roman Church, the deep church persecutes honest, God-serving prelates because they are not blackmailable and are not for sale for twenty pieces of silver.

Each of us has plenty of opportunities in our daily lives to counter these fairground barkers with resistance and boycotts. Because everything the System accomplishes revolves around money, the first way to jam the mechanism is not to buy its products, watch its programs and movies, or use its political platforms. The more we penalize the globalists on the economic front, the stronger the signal we give, which helps coalesce the Resistance. And if, as we have seen, it is possible to use the "Overton window" to influence the masses to accept evil progressively, **perhaps we should also begin to "overtonize" being good Christians, courageous patriots, faithful spouses, wise parents, and honest workers.**

We know very well that the woke ideology has seduced many of our friends and acquaintances. Too many have simply resigned themselves to acquiesce in the face of the most atrocious criminal lies. Too many have donned the mask of political correctness—in the real meaning of the term, i.e., correct for political purposes—even though they know very well that they are dealing with dangerous Satanist fanatics. These friends and acquaintances of ours will decide to abandon the globalist psycho-cult **as soon as it begins to become normal, indeed even "fashionable," to be proudly anti-globalist.** In this collective consciousness-raising, not only individuals and families will openly take sides against the woke, but also companies, local administrators, politicians, journalists, and celebrities.

And when we learn to see those young people who believe that CO_2 is a poison as "losers," you will see that multinational corporations will stop proclaiming themselves eco-friendly. When we reject those who consider abortion and sodomy a "human right," you will see the same multinational corporations stop using transgender people as testimonials. Merchants are already doing this in the Muslim Middle East, where commercial enterprises are as careful not to put the rainbow flag in their logo as they are to eschew all models of sexual behavior contrary to the Koran. The rejection of LGBTQ+ throughout the Muslim world confirms what we already know to be consistent with God's natural law, in which sex must be attached to procreation to achieve the sacred status God proclaimed. **We Christians must also make our voices heard before some homegrown Trudeau comes up with the idea of banning the Bible and outlawing Christianity as incompatible with globalist secular religion.** The truth is that economic leverage is closely linked to ideological leverage, not only at the top of global finance and banking—which manages almost all of the planet's money—but also in the intermediate ranks, those of collaborators throughout the global economy who have sold out to the woke.

Let us keep firmly in mind the two parallel tracks on which the World Economic Forum's dictatorial project advances. The first track, ideologically motivated, pursues unmentionable and criminal aims disguised under flimsy pretexts. The economically motivated second track takes advantage of the cooperation of those who seek to profit, which justifies everything. But the elderly pensioner or the father of a family, to be forced to sell their carbon share to others, must be induced into poverty, a necessary condition to cause them to give up what was hitherto not subject to limitation or counting. If families had a decent standard of living, they would not have to sell their right to go on vacation to someone richer who decided to do it for them.

Here, we encounter an even more sinister aspect of the mercantile mentality of the elite, which is determined to create the preconditions for making the enjoyment of otherwise unavailable goods effectively impossible. And let's not forget that along with the monetization of CO_2 credits, the substitute of virtual travel and virtual vacations is already being prepared for the masses, obviously for a fee, which the elite will offer to the poor, along with a network-connected metaverse visor. From the tiny "housing unit" in the "fifteen-minute city," any location on the planet is accessible through virtual reality—but only the "reality" that our globalist masters allow us to view. In our metaverse vacation, we will be allowed to see the Grand Canal and St. Mark's Square in Venice, Italy. But the interior of Saint Mark's Basilica will be off-limits. Yet, we must buy a virtual ticket with real money to enter virtual museums.

And what then of all those who work in tourism, restaurants, hotels, and all related vacation industries? The globalists will simply fire employees who work in the tourist industries, especially putting out of business artisans and entrepreneurs who make vacations enjoyable. Here then, is the universal income—ready, in perpetual indebtedness to the state, to give the minimum means of subsistence to the chronically unemployed forced to stay in their mini-apartment in their smart city, ordering food to go.

Here we are again at the logical inversion by which the elite obtains an inauthentic outcome designed to advance the elite agenda by presenting "solutions" to "problems" the elite themselves have created— euthanasia for the terminally ill; abortion for the rape victim; same-sex marriage for the LGBTQ+ community; surrogacy for the infertile couple; sex change for those who feel "imprisoned in a body that is not their own"; the refuge in virtual reality for those whose lives are aimless and hopeless; and AI computer-generated answers for those who don't feel like thinking for themselves. Subtly, the self-appointed globalist elite has created the necessary preconditions for those experiencing "problems" experienced only in their bizarre psyop "matrix" reality—"solutions" to "problems" to meet the demand of a "clientele" that no one until now could have imagined existing, not in a reality where God and traditional values prevailed.

Who would imagine killing an old or sick person because the cost of medical care was too expensive? What type of monster would chop to pieces a fetus in the womb, planning to sell the body parts to the highest bidder? Until the age of woke, it was an absurdity to think that one could give legitimacy to homosexual unions or bless the use of a woman as a paid broodmare to birth a child for those who, by nature, could not birth one of their own. But it was also cruel to think of relegating grandparents to nursing homes when multigenerational families respected the elderly as repositories of wisdom. Until the advent of the internet, it was unimaginable to call friendship the ticking off of a name on a social platform or to attribute any attractiveness to the grotesque fiction of the virtual world instead of the reality surrounding us.

But reality ontologically refers back to its Creator and directs creatures toward their first principle, as imprinted by God in our hearts. Reality spurs us on and challenges us, while virtuality deceives us and keeps us locked up in our illusion of self-sufficiency. Reality, above all, is made up of an infinity of things as marvelous as they are *gratuitous*, the result of God's infinite generosity and equally marvelous wonders, the gift of Grace, which is precisely *gratis data* [i.e., freely given]. Just the air we breathe is free, and the sunlight that illuminates us carries no utility bill. So, too, the water of the springs, the fruits of the earth, the smile of a loved one, the harmony of a piece of music, and the beauty of a landscape are gifts of reality the Divine Presence graces.

Something is disturbing about the elite's envy of this magnificence, before which it does not bow gratefully. The globalist elite despises the grace and bounty of God's gifts. Instead, the globalist elite seeks to obliterate reality with the same cynicism with which the dishonest merchant envies and aims to destroy the beautiful creations of the craftsman or artist. And what is this, if not Satan's envy of God and of everything that calls forth from us creative action—which is inherently divine? With a hateful vengeance, the globalist elite feels compelled to destroy redemptive action through Jesus Christ.

When we read in the writings of the medieval saints that money was considered Satan's dung, we are tempted to disagree because we believe that money is very much needed today, especially at a time when the Great Reset–induced economic crisis is forcing vast swaths of the population into poverty. Sometimes, we confuse money with its value—that piece of paper with what it represents in terms of work and experience, physical or intellectual labor, and the passion and expertise of someone whose effort has created value. Satan's dung is precisely represented by the colossal debt money fraud, with each of us indebted to a private bank that calls itself a Central Bank even though it is not a state-owned entity. Satan's dung is the indebtedness of the sovereign people to private bankers who demand that we pay interest on the money we guarantee them in government bonds. Under the thumb of Central Bank–created money, we find ourselves economically dependent on a potent lobby that for for centuries has crafted the economic policy of nations for decline, domestic policy to destroy the nuclear family, and the foreign policy of governments to engage in perpetual war.

Now, the globalist elite wants to see us subjugated when we agree to believe its supreme lie: that the physical and intellectual, the moral and cultural, and the political and religious energies of a people can be controlled by means of a virtual currency, a digital currency that physically resides on a server and to which nothing

corresponds but an infinite series of 0s and 1s. With our labor, we create the good that gives us a living: not those who connect us to a (social) credit card and decide if, what, and when we can buy, where we can go, and if we can eat. The Chinese dictatorship has done in a short time what takes longer with us because of the "too little tyrannical" systems of Western countries and because of the partial failure of the psycho-pandemic operation. The admiration of Schwab, Soros, and other mad technocrats for Beijing shows that the Nazi blood of their fathers, unscrupulous speculators, and collaborators with Hitler still runs in their veins. That must be why so many World Economic Forum members are so indulgent of the Ukrainian regime, in which the neo-Nazi component is dangerously dominant.

The evidence of the data and the dynamics of criminal management of mass "vaccination" in all the countries that locked down their economies under pressure from the World Health Organization (beyond inoculating us with an often deadly, always harmful, sterilizing serum and graphene nanocomponents) was to get us used to the idea of abandoning cash for a 100 percent digital currency. Under a near-global pandemic lockdown, the world of necessity began living in the metaverse of the internet. For the globalist elite, in a lockdown metaverse, the allure of digital money would become overwhelming. We were to forget that digital bank accounts could also be locked if a government official took offense at our political beliefs. Yet, the reality is that in a world where identity and money were 100 percent virtual, a low social credit score could make you an instant non-person. In the world of Central Bank Digital Currency, you have no constitutional rights if your social credit score is deemed politically unacceptable.

Some banks have already begun to limit cash transactions, and digital IDs will soon link to health records. And when we hear about banks on the verge of bankruptcy or the impending financial crisis, we should ask ourselves whether the nonchalance with which globalist leaders squander state coffers and put their citizens in debt is not precisely because a total collapse of the Western financial system is the only way to cover up vast corruption at all levels. With the imminent collapse of fiat currencies backed only by the "full faith and credit" of a bankrupt nation, our globalist masters will insist the only solution is to impose a new electronic currency wholly owned by the System. We will live in fear that a post on social media will be deemed "hate speech" or that government law enforcement units will put us under surveillance because we purchased a Rosary or a Bible on the internet. **There is no freedom, no human rights, for those forced to live in a digital, virtual reality metaverse. How can we escape electronic transactions and continue using paper money, or, if possible, can we barter? How can we circumvent the System's control?**

In a digital, virtual reality metaverse prison, will we conceive of a small community where it is possible to pool one's skills and belongings, as the Vendeans took refuge in the woods during the French Revolution, or will we become too accustomed to our comforts? We must learn to think outside the box because before long, a loaf of natural wheat or a basket of non-GMO apples could be the subject of an exchange with those who, instead of virtual money, pay you with wheels of cheese or a chemistry lesson for your child, or repair the roof of your house.

When Italy was a land of barbarian raids, and Rome was a heap of ruins, monastic communities arose of men and women who had their fill of the violence, wars, and carnage they had witnessed. They lived communal lives, and each pooled their skills in the garden, the vineyard, the stables, the fields, the workshop, the library, the kitchen, the infirmary, and the herbalist shop. They lived and prayed together, and like the monks of the East—who had arisen earlier—together they formed a small autonomous and self-sufficient community, capable even of defending themselves from the assaults of marauders, bands of thieves, and Saracens.

Thanks to St. Benedict, Europe could be reborn spiritually and materially because villages sprang up around the monasteries, universities developed, art flourished again, and it was possible to build that Christendom whose cathedrals we still admire. And looking at the wonder of those architectures, the composure of the frescoes or painted panels, we read there the projection of the creature toward the Creator, and we see God's children proclaiming the glory of God.

What is globalist ideology capable of producing besides pandemics, abortions, sexual confusion, and race hatred? What are the globalists' hopes and dreams? Globalist monstrous monuments are gloomy and gray, obscene representations of violence and rape, grotesque celebrations of evil, horror, and pain. If we did not know that they worship Lucifer, their buildings, their concerts, their Spirit cooking installations, the esoteric symbols they flaunt, and their very looks would be enough to expose them. The Christ-centric world built a Christian society on the rubble of the Roman Empire. The contemporary world, which is founded on the globalist cult, builds a Satanic killing field on the rubble of Christendom. We must create new communities and networks that restore God to his rightful place at the center of creation. I think that feeling of excitement that takes each of us in knowing that we can do something useful to save our future, that rekindling of hope and, with it, the will to fight evil, is at the heart of what it means to be human. The human spirit inevitably rejuvenates with the need to finally feel free to breathe deeply, especially after an interminable time when an oppressive weight prevented us from doing so.

Thirty Pieces of Silver

The elite can understand nothing but the language of corruption and is convinced that each of us has a price. For the globalists, the question is not whether we will allow ourselves to be corrupted but at what price we will do so. We have seen this with politicians, doctors, "experts," and journalists during the psycho-pandemic. Almost all sold out to the globalists—literally prostituted themselves in doing so—to those who paid for their courtesies. As a result, the globalists financed and published falsified medical studies in compromised peer-reviewed journals, which they then broadcast internationally in the echo chamber of globalists' bought-and-paid-for media.

The whole sad sell-out reminded me of John 12:4-6. After raising Lazarus from the dead, Jesus sat at a dinner Mary served, at which also sat Lazarus. At the dinner, Mary took a costly ointment to anoint the feet of Jesus. Judas Iscariot objected: "Why was this ointment not sold for three hundred pence and given to the poor?" He said that not because he cared about the poor; Judas, who held the Apostles' money bag, could steal the coin from the Apostles' meager treasury. How easily the Sanhedrin bribed Judas, simply by offering him thirty pieces of silver to hand over Jesus to the Romans for crucifixion.

Take note of how Judas acts: He does not want Magdalene to "waste" the perfumed balm to anoint Jesus's feet and resorts to an excuse—helping the poor—to appropriate the money, just as today the new "Judas" talks about using money from the treasury (and thus taxpayers' taxes) to deal with all those emergencies the globalists have created. "Judas" is now able to appropriate taxpayer to pay for the Deep State's fraudulent vaccines, a green transition intended to deprive us of affordable energy, the opening of the border to encourage a flood of immigrants without screening for criminal or terrorists, and sending billions of dollars to fund weapons of war in an endless Ukraine war with Russia that the Deep State seems willing to have go nuclear—all policies whose real goal is mass depopulation of Earth's billions of souls—while harvesting as many souls as possible for Satan.

The corrupt are indispensable in advancing a subversive plan because they are willing to sell out, and the elite knows this well. Look at the flood of money used to pay doctors who vaccinated their patients during the psycho-pandemic, even though they knew the danger of the serum they were inoculating. Count the millions that the World Bank and the International Monetary Fund (IMF) give to politicians and rulers who promote Agenda 2030 in their countries.

But precisely because the System is built on corruption, an anti-System action must necessarily be based on honesty and incorruptibility. There are honest people who do not accept that they need to sell out, to prostitute themselves, to barter the principles they believe in for privileges, power, money, and sex. There are people—and there are still many—who know how to be generous, who give freely, who do not expect to be paid for a good deed, for an hour of companionship, for a good word, for a smile. For these people, gratuitousness lights up life's dreariness, especially when the recipient understands and reciprocates that small gift. There are people who are not corruptible and therefore do not have to fear that they can be blackmailed: they are the most fearsome because the System chooses as collaborators and servants only corruptible and blackmailable people so that it is certain to control them. A person who is honest, has faith in God, and has high and noble ideals does not sell out. Why? Because those who put their trust in God do not evaluate everything in terms of a financial transaction. A person who believes in God and knows that he will be judged by God does not allow himself to be bought or seduced by anyone. **Will we be able to make goodness, righteousness, chivalry, and keeping our word go viral?**

The woke ideology would like to accustom us to consider everything relative to deprive us of the values that define our identity. The woke ideology wants to deny us the right to pass on our values to our children so that these values may spread and be shared. The responsibility of parents to raise their children with a moral education is what has made it possible to build civilization over previous centuries. We are heirs to an ethical world that the globalist elite wants to destroy. In order to do so, the globalist elite buys us off, rewarding our resistance, our laissez-faire, and our complicity to the narrative of the moment with small rewards, like you give a cookie to an obedient dog. Yet, the globalist elite exposes its true intentions when it allows us to go to a restaurant only if we have a green pass, to shop if we buy online, to award us social credit points if we buy an electric vehicle, and so on. In turn, the globalist elite punishes us, ghettoizes us, marginalizes itself, and criminalizes us if we do not obey. Churchill said that if in the presence of a no-smoking sign, one person smokes, you assess them fines. If ten smoke, you ask them to move. If they all smoke, you remove the sign. **Perhaps it is time to understand that obedience to our rulers is not without conditions and that the control to which they want to subject us should instead be used so that we are the ones who control them.**

In a world that cannot comprehend anything but money, those who cannot be bought become a fearsome enemy, and that is what each of us must aspire to become if we are to endure in the current crisis, to be able tomorrow to rebuild what has been destroyed, and to restore what has been abandoned. And this non-corruptibility, this pride of those who do not see themselves as commodities for sale, must be based on the realization that **we do not live on this earth to accumulate power and money, but to glorify and love God, thus deserving eternal reward.**

Let us turn to Matthew 6: 19-21: Lay not up for yourselves treasures upon earth, where moth and rust doth corrupt, and where thieves break through and steal: but lay up for yourselves treasures in heaven, where neither moth nor rust doth corrupt, and where thieves do not break through nor steal. For where your treasure is, there will your heart be also.

The Great Chimera of Virtual Reality

The advent of artificial intelligence and the refinement of virtual reality are tools of control and manipulation in which the globalist elite are investing exorbitant sums. The metaverse becomes the normal place where we can take refuge to escape an unbearable reality: where we can be what we are not, where we can choose which society to live in and which rules to obey. In the metaverse, we can vent our instincts, our morbidities, our most unmentionable inclinations, or even just legitimate desires and unfulfilled aspirations. In the metaverse, we meet virtual friends, find virtual lovers, mate with virtual spouses, and give birth to virtual children. All this is for a fee, of course. And in that "virtual reality,"—i.e., in that "non-reality" that we know to be so and whose fiction we accept—we come to experience what we are no longer allowed to do or no longer have the means to afford. On the other hand, we will also be accustomed to the metaverse at work, with the use of meeting simulators that will allow us to "virtually meet" our colleagues working on the other side of the globe or talk to the clerk at a store below our home who works online from Albania or the Philippines.

It will cost us less to have a virtual family at $99.99 a month than to support a real wife and children, and with the virtual family, we have the advantage of being able to change them if they do not satisfy us. And it will also be convenient to have a virtual lover whom we can tear to pieces or torture if we feel like it. The instinctive horror that ordinary people feel at this disturbing prospect should not, however, distract us from another important aspect, which is given by the vast, colossal business of virtual eternity. Let us make a premise: Klaus Schwab and his followers already theorize the creation of a digital eternity, achieved by transferring our minds (or souls) to the cloud. But like everything that is proposed to us by the globalist elite, this dream of immortality (always represented as a nearly imminent possibility) is also a total lie. This colossal fraud offers an annihilated and dehumanized humanity that famous eternity of drugs and video games that Yuval Noah Harari likes to promise us on Earth, but now extended to eternity.

Globalist religion will offer a digital alternative to the genuine eternity of heaven and hell, making us believe that we can choose—for a fee, of course, since we can always assume without saying that the globalist elite will make us pay for the privilege—the kind of heaven we desire simply by uploading our faculties to a server. It will be our inheritance in the name of the company running this service (or the renewal payments we assume that our living relatives will pay to the globalist elite) that will guarantee us a blissful eternal life in an all too obvious counterfeit of a genuinely spiritual reality. **But the truth is that this virtual eternity will not exist, and no one from the afterlife will be able to warn us of the deception.** An AI-constructed hologram of our deceased loved ones will probably reassure us of how happy they are in their virtual paradise. The virtual eternity will be an illusion. But our future digital paradise will be the supreme illusion—the methodology these criminal psychopaths will utilize to turn our hope for a blissful virtual eternity into money in their pockets. Just wait until the globalist elites induce religious leaders to champion this digital paradise in the metaverse in return for a share of the revenues of that lucrative business.

When we hear Bergoglio (a.k.a. Pope Francis) propagating the climate emergency and calling for "conversion" to the green agenda, we understand that the complicity of the leadership of the Catholic Hierarchy and other religious denominations was necessary for the fulfillment of the subversive plan to compromise religious authority, just as the globalist elite has compromised civil authority.

Our response to this folly must begin with the realization—

philosophical even before theological—that the human soul is immortal and that it is the substance of our body. There can be no physical place to house our soul except in our body, which, as Christians, we know will be resurrected at the end of time, to which we will be reunited for eternity. A soul can have no other "support" than that together with the body with which it was conceived. Humans do not have the power to change the ontological characteristics of the human soul. Transhumanists want to believe that the electromagnetic waves of our brain are replicable by an electronic circuit. Yet, transhumanists deny the spiritual reality of the human soul, which is the only inviolable sanctuary where only the voice of the Lord can enter. **There is no virtual reality. If it is reality, it is not virtual, and if it is virtual, it is not reality. And there is no such thing as artificial intelligence. If it is intelligence, it is not artificial, and if it is artificial, it is not intelligence.**

To fall into this deception is an unforgivable folly. An innate revulsion makes us realize, once again, that the purpose the globalist elite wants to achieve is to subjugate us not only in this life, but also in the next. For once we have signed the contract with those who promise us an eternity-for-a-fee, we will have literally sold our souls to Satan and will have lost forever the true God, whose salvation is gratuitous and the fruit of generosity as infinite is His love. Let us think well of the paradox to which we expose ourselves. Our executioner asks us to pay him to be his slave in life and even in eternity.

Another element worth drawing attention to is **the virtualization of knowledge** through digitizing paper books and their publication in electronic format. Recently, the heirs to the rights of Agatha Christie have agreed that the English writer's famous novels should be revised (and thus manipulated) to expunge anything that is not politically correct and may contain "potentially offensive" material.[323] Suppose this operation were to be extended to other works, as is foreseeable in the cancel culture projects of publishers. In that case, we might soon find the Bible, the *Iliad*, the *Divine Comedy*, or *King Lear* censored in the woke sense without knowing it: not least because the file of a book is located in the cloud from which the original copy would be removed.

Aldous Huxley wrote in 1943:

> I saw newspaper reports which did not bear any relation to the facts, not even the relationship which is implied in an ordinary lie. I saw great battles reported where there had been no fighting, and complete silence where hundreds of men had been killed. I saw troops who had fought bravely denounced as cowards and traitors, and others who had never seen a shot fired hailed as the heroes of imaginary victories; and I saw newspapers in London retailing these lies and eager intellectuals building emotional superstructures over events that had never happened. I saw, in fact, history being written not in terms of what happened but of what ought to have happened according to various "party lines."[324]

As long as we have libraries this manipulation would be partial; but what will happen when books are published only in electronic format? Who will be able to know whether the copy they are reading on the tablet is intact or censored? And what incalculable harm to culture would it be to destroy classic authors just because they do not conform to the globalist mindset? Here is the usual pattern: put the paper books side-by-side with the digital ones, then push on the digital ones and eliminate the paper ones under a pretext. Finally, make the

---

323 Rachel Hall, "Agatha Christie novels reworked to remove potentially offensive language," *The Guardian*, March 26, 2023, https://www.theguardian.com/books/2023/mar/26/agatha-christie-novels-reworked-to-remove-potentially-offensive-language.
324 Aldous Huxley, *Homage to Catalonia*

digital books the only ones available so that they can control the content. And those who will believe that they can independently save their files on the cloud will have the bitter surprise of having them deleted for violating the terms of service of Google Drive, or its cloud successor.

War on Humanity

This unprecedented attack in history, this war on humanity, is conducted outside the normal dynamics of a conflict and is articulated through the treacherous and cowardly means of a coup d'état. We are considered enemies of the governments that are supposed to protect and defend us. Instead, we are the object of unceasing hammering propaganda by the System, which considers us parasites of the planet and, as such, seeks to exterminate us by any means: wars, social conflicts, ethnic replacement, pandemics, famines, and economic crises. And if we dare to rebel or even protest against our executioners, we are mocked, marginalized, ostracized, criminalized, and made the object of outright persecution. Our guilt is to want to continue to be what we have been for millennia, to want to preserve the humanity that makes us capable of choosing, of wanting, of loving, of hoping—a humanity that in two thousand years of Christianity has been able to build a civilization whose vestiges remain even today, despite two centuries of unremitting war.

But who, for God's sake, established that a lobby of technocrats had the right to decide the fate of the world and humanity? Who has given these tyrants the power to use the full might and power of the System against us, demanding that we allow ourselves to be killed, harmed, corrupted, and marginalized without protest?

We are living in a logical short circuit: we have had democracy imposed on us—a concept unknown until the end of the eighteenth century, at least in the form in which it is understood today. Democracy today reduces to DEI—diversity, equity, and inclusion—a standard under which race and gender diversity are declared equal rights by the System—a standard that ignores the fundamental understanding that human rights are inalienable, given to all freely and equally by God. The rights of "life, liberty, and happiness" are not the enhanced sexual rights of LGBTQ+ and the diminished racial rights of "white privilege." We were under the illusion that if we declared ourselves repositories of national sovereignty, we would have been able to free ourselves from the absolutism of the monarchies of divine right. But today, we discover that republican regimes—as was already the case in ancient history—have been the pretext by which the elite usurped the authority of the rulers by appropriating it with our forced consent. We have lost all freedoms when the System ignores all election abnormalities once corrupted election board officials certify rigged voting without honest scrutiny or investigation.

This usurped authority managed to evade all personal responsibility—which a king had before God and his subjects—by dissolving it in the *popular will*, an ectoplasm that answers to no power and which no revolt can challenge. This "depersonalization" of the responsibility of rulers has not only not freed us from tyranny but the assertion of government tyranny, on the contrary, has made the loss of our inalienable human rights under God almost irreversible. The alibi of the *will of the people* and the anonymity of collegial bodies allowed blatant violations of fundamental rights without anyone being held accountable. *Europe demands it of us*, European leaders say to citizens forced into new taxes, continuous sacrifices, and new limitations rained down from above. The standard of ESG—environmental, social, and governance—determines energy policy *is to save the planet*, or at least, so claim the proponents of the Green Deal. It is to protect the frail, the vaccine hawkers claim. But there is not a single one of them who takes responsibility before the people for their statements, for the decisions they make, or for the adverse consequences their wrongly-premised decisions have on individuals and society.

Another element that none of the advocates of the republic point out is that in a monarchical regime high finance certainly has less power than it has been able to achieve in republican regimes. Rousseau wrote this to Dalembert:

> *Jamais dans une Monarchie l'opulence d'un particulier ne peut le mettre au-dessus du Prince; mais dans une République elle peut aisément le mettre au-dessus des lois. Alors le gouvernement n'a plus de force, et le riche est toujours le vrai souverain. Sur ces maximes incontestables, il reste à considérer si l'inégalité n'a pas atteint parmi nous le dernier terme où elle peut parvenir sans ébranler la République.*

> In a monarchy the opulence of an individual can never put him above the Prince; but in a Republic it can easily put him above the laws. Then the government has no more force and the rich man is always the true ruler. On the basis of these indisputable maxims, it remains to consider whether inequality has not reached among us the end point it can reach without undermining the Republic.[325]

If we look at the secretive Bank of International Settlements in Switzerland that sits at the top of the banking empire and gigantic international investment funds—BlackRock, Vanguard, State Street, and Geode Capital Management, to name just a few—we realize how the financial lobby has monopolized power, coming to use political leaders and rulers as servants, for its own exclusive benefit and to the detriment of citizens and nations. Never in history have we witnessed such a concentration of trillions of dollars of wealth in the hands of a

---

325 Jean-Jacque Rousseau, Lettre de J.J. Rouseau à M. D'Alembert, 1758, in Édition de François Poudevigne 2014, Obvil.sorbonne-universite.fr, https://obvil.sorbonne-universite.fr/corpus/haine-theatre/rousseau_lettre-a-d-alembert_1758.

few private families who consider the resources of the planet as their own private domain.

Everything that until yesterday was considered a freely available good—air, sun, and water—must be privatized, that is, come under the control of those who can profit from goods, even though nobody should pay for the enjoyment of these traditionally free resources. For these merchants, life is a commodity for which payment is due. Every child who comes into the world is already burdened with debts contracted by a state that has abdicated its sovereignty—including monetary sovereignty—in order to perpetually indebt itself to central banks, which, as we know, are private corporations.

But what freedom can the individual have when a lobby of private individuals can twist natural law by making us pay for the air we breathe? How should we react before a Moloch that considers us as useless eaters and dangerous producers of CO_2? How should we regard a System that theorizes social credit systems worthy of communist regimes, favors the elimination of the elderly and sick by euthanasia, and discourages births through abortion, mass sterilization, homosexualization of society, and the sexual disfigurement inherent to the gender transition surgery?

Our problem is that we do not want to open our eyes to a disturbing reality: **those in authority in Western governments claim to represent the people and to legislate in their name—and for this, they keep up the charade of elections, which they shamelessly manipulate—but at the same time, they answer not to the people, but to international high finance, that is, to a few families of immoral usurers such as the Rockefellers, the Rothschilds, the DuPonts, the Harrimans, and the Warburgs.** On the other hand, one of the first crimes to be erased from European penal codes after the French Revolution was usury, while Mounts of Mercy and pawnbrokers were suppressed and converted into private banks.

We are led to believe that under Klaus Schwab's "Reset," we will obtain freedom—"You will be like gods," Yuval Noah Harari proclaims in *Homo Deus*—but in reality, we have never been so dominated and controlled as we are today. If we contemplate how our ancestors, or even our great-grandparents, lived, we realize that we have been deceived again. Because democracy, freedom, inalienable human rights, and all revolutionary rhetoric were and are a colossal sham—yet another lie behind which the globalist elite hide their lust for power and money. And we wanted to believe this fraud, with the same wretched folly with which Adam and Eve succumbed to the temptation of the Serpent.

Let us not kid ourselves: if democracy really worked, these globalist criminals would never have allowed us to benefit from it. Not long ago, after the dissolution of the British Parliament and the calling of elections for July 4, 2024, Labour Party leader Keir Starmer said that if he had to choose between Westminster and Davos, he would choose Davos.[326] Starmer, who is a member of the World Economic Forum, admits with impunity that he has Schwab as his master and that he is a traitor to the nation without raising the slightest scandal.

Democracy is a broken toy, a jammed mechanism that has no chance of working because it was designed to enslave us just when we thought we were shaking off the yoke of Monarchies that legitimized them. But again, what the globalist elite presented to us as a solution to a false problem was part of a subversive plan: anti-Christian and anti-monarchist propaganda has filled pages and pages of history books with lies and historical falsehoods to delude us into thinking we have made progress, while we have regressed to barbarism. The rhetoric that until yesterday formed the basis of liberal or Marxist propaganda has today been obliterated and replaced by woke rhetoric and propaganda, in all its declinations—an application of "Newspeak" George Orwell would

326 A video clip on X of a Keir Starmer interview, posted by James Melville, May 23, 2004, https://x.com/jamesmelville/status/1793760309989024094

appreciate. The result is a form of propaganda that combines the worst of liberal thought with the worst of communist ideology.

Archbishop Carlo Maria Viganò astutely called attention to this phenomenon in a foreword he wrote to a recent book I co-authored with David W. Mantik, MD, PhD, *The Assassination of President John F. Kennedy: The Final Analysis*. In that foreword His Excellency wrote the following regarding a recent essay of mine on the assassination of President Kennedy:

> *The Final Analysis* has the merit of directly confronting the reality of the *coup d'état* that was perpetrated by the *Deep State* through the assassination of President Kennedy, who was considered an obstacle to the achievement of objectives that today we understand were achieved in any case, with or without the approval of the "sovereign" people. A coup that has led the institutions of the United States of America—not unlike those of other nations and of the Catholic Church herself—to be the unique and totalitarian expression of a subversive power that dangerously combines the individualistic interests of capital with the tyrannical methods of communist collectivism. This *privatization* of the State is mirrored in the chronic and irreversible indebtedness of the citizens, who are called upon to pay the bankruptcy costs of the speculations of the very powerful international financial lobby. And it should not escape our notice that there is a parallel with the *privatization* of the Catholic Church, which has now been taken over by an elite no less subversive than that of the *Deep State,* in which positions of power have been infiltrated by heretical and corrupt prelates who use the authority of Christ to guarantee obedience from the faithful.[327]

---

327 Archbishop Carlo Maria Viganò, "Foreword" to: David W. Mantik, MD, PhD. and Jerome R. Corsi, PhD., *The Assassination of President John F. Kennedy: The Final Analysis,* op. cit.

A coup d'état that has transformed the institutions of the United States of America— not unlike the institutions of the United Nations, Western Europe and the European Union, as well the Catholic Church herself—to be the unique and totalitarian expressions of a subversive power that dangerously combines the individualistic interests of capital with the tyrannical methods of communist collectivism. This privatization of the State is mirrored in the chronic and irreversible indebtedness of the citizens, who are called upon to pay the bankruptcy costs of the speculations of the very powerful international financial lobby.

The former Apostolic Nuncio to the United States expressed the same concept, elaborating on it, in another speech on January 27, 2024:

> The "masterstroke" of the New World Order consists in having brought together, in an infernal alliance, Liberalism and Communism (two sides of the same Masonic coin) to its advantage. On the one hand, by restricting the positive intervention of the state, which offers citizens free of charge or at non-market rates those services that the elite wants to privatize in order to make a profit; on the other hand, by using the coercive force of a supranational socialist regime to distort competition with small and medium-sized enterprises and to reduce labour costs. In a sense, the elite has succeeded in ousting the state from its natural role in favor of a super-state that acts not in the interests of the collective, but of the elite itself. This, ultimately, is the role of the European Union and the US federal government, both in the hands of the Deep State.[328]

This disturbing combination of liberalism and communism should come as no surprise when we consider the subservience of many politicians not only to the World Economic Forum—an expression of

---

328 Archbishop Carlo Maria Viganò, "Messagio a partecipanti al Congresso Nazionale di Democrazia Sovarana e Popolare, Roma 27–28, Gennaio 27, 2024, https://exsurgedomine.it/240127-congresso/

the most brutal and ruthless liberalism—but also to the Chinese dictatorship and with the tyrannic power of the WHO, whose General Director Tedros Adhanom Ghebreyesus has had relations with the Tigray People's Liberation Front (TPLF), Ethiopia's communist-based terrorist organization[329]

Premeditation and Criminal Intent

The globalist elite, to carry out the coup d'état we are witnessing, has strategically planned an attack on multiple fronts, seemingly disconnected from each other. Still, all fronts are perfectly consistent with the ultimate subversive purpose. This diversity of fronts serves two purposes. First, to keep us constantly under media siege with emergencies and catastrophic alarms. Second, to keep a variety of seemingly unrelated emergencies and catastrophic alarms in play to confuse and disorient us.

The coup d'état can only succeed if all the besieged fortresses collapse. If too many people catch onto the game and begin to see a pattern in perpetual wars, constant economic crises, and never-ending bizarre cultural confusion, the globalist elite risk losing in their race to the finish line. Let me explain further. Those planning a global coup must be able to control rulers, parliamentarians, opposition, judiciary, law enforcement, military, banks, education, media, and religious leaders of every state involved—while keeping the general public disoriented and demoralized—otherwise they lose. The transhumanists have been planning their global post-human takeover for a long time.

When some intellectuals brought to light, in the early 1800s, the documents of lodges and secret sects related to this subversive project (with details on how to organize, where to infiltrate, and which

---

329 Reuters, "Ethiopia says WHO chief has links to rebellious Tigrayan forces," Reuters. com, January 15, 2022, https://www.reuters.com/world/africa/ethiopia-accuses-who-chief -links-rebellious-tigrayan-forces-2022-01-14/.

accomplices to choose), most of the public dismissed these as fake news, abetted by the press that was already under their control. But we are baffled to reread today the many previous meticulous descriptions of the planned corruption of youth, the homosexualization of society, the attack on women, and the promotion of abortion, euthanasia, immigration, and indebtedness were supposed to destroy the social fabric each of us is—baffling, to say the least.

If the police break into a den of burglars and discover plans to carry out an armed bank robbery, any legitimate trial or magistrate would convict the burglars of a conspiracy to commit armed robbery. But if the Club of Rome, the United Nations's World Health Organization, the World Economic Forum, the Trilateral Group, the Bilderberg Group, Bill Gates, George Soros, and a thousand others explicitly explain that they want to exterminate us and how they intend to do it, no magistrate moves.

Speaking at a conference in Rome, Italy, in May 2024, Archbishop Carlo Maria Viganò captured the heart of the problem with great lucidity by suggesting that we should take a forensic approach to documenting the abundant evidence the globalist elite's ultimate goal involves the criminal scheme to achieve mass global depopulation through the creation of a health holocaust. He explained:

> The reason for this instinctive refusal of the masses to recognize themselves as victims of a real crime against humanity, however, does not detract from the evidence of the intentions of the perpetrators of this crime. These intentions, which have been declared for decades on the basis of a grotesque falsification of reality, take the form of a systematic action aimed at fostering the depopulation of the Planet through pandemics, famines, wars and clashes between different segments of the population, impoverishment of the weaker classes and drastic reduction of those public services—including Health, Social Security

and Safety—that the State should guarantee to its citizens. The Bill & Melinda Gates Institute for Population and Reproductive Health is among the principal architects of a population reduction plan that starts from the neo-Malthusian assumption that the Earth's population must be drastically reduced, and that its food and energy resources must be the subject of interventions that promote this reduction. **The statements confirming this plan of extermination are not even disguised any longer; on the contrary, they are explicitly reiterated in the conferences and studies produced by the network of bodies and institutes funded by self-proclaimed philanthropists.**[330]

And that is precisely the crux of the issue.

But if a lobby of very rich people claims to want to reduce the world's population through mass vaccinations that cause sterility, disease, and death; and if these vaccinations actually cause sterility, disease, and death in millions of inoculated people, I think we should all—and I address my appeal to distinguished jurists and intellectuals, as well as physicians and scientists—look up and not limit ourselves to an investigation that has as its sole object the adverse and deadly effects of the experimental serum.[331]

And, more importantly:

If we do not frame the handling of the psycho-pandemic in the broader context of the criminal plan that engineered it, we preclude ourselves from not only understanding the premeditation of the crime, but also from seeing on what other fronts we are or will be subject to new attacks, which, however, have in common with this

---

330 Archbishop Carlo Maria Viganò, "Guardare Oltre: Un approccio 'forense' al crimine psicopandemico," ExSurgeDomine.it, May 13, 2024, https://exsurgedomine.it/2405120-guardare-oltre/.
331 Ibid.

one the ultimate goal, which is the physical elimination of billions of people.[332]

Climatologist Bill McGuire, an Emeritus Professor of Geophysical and Climate Hazards at University College London, called for using a deadly pandemic as a tool to solve the global warming problem. On May 14, 2024, McGuire posted the following on X:

> If I am brutally honest, the only realistic way I see emissions falling as fast as they need to, to avoid catastrophic climate breakdown, is the culling of the human population by a pandemic with a very high fatality rate.[333]

With this, we have confirmation that self-styled "experts"—as reliable as the virology experts who appeared like mushrooms during the psycho-pandemic —consider it acceptable to "cull the human population" in order to avoid a phantom and unproven climate collapse, and to achieve this they believe a pandemic with a very high fatality rate can be used, as globalist psychopaths could theorize.

The Obligation to Resist

We must, inevitably, realize that the psycho-pandemic—as well as the climate emergency, the woke ideologies, the endless wars, and the destruction of the middle class, plus all the other pseudo-catastrophes that can be contrived for intimidation purposes—are critical pieces in the framework of a larger global coup d'état that must be opposed. It becomes imperative to denounce these evil, criminal perpetrators at the top of these subversive organizations in governments, public institutions, and even within our churches. The transhuman monsters

---

332 Ibid.
333 Bill McGuire, post on X, May 14, 2024, https://x.com/therabbithole84/status/1790392079874723852.

seeking to self-elevate themselves to Homo Deus status in their imagined post-human utopia will inevitably have to be tried and convicted for high treason and crimes against humanity.

But while we wait to see the perpetrators of this transhumanist coup d'état brought before an international tribunal, we must organize a tangible form of resistance to the globalist agenda. I speak of resistance advisedly because we must realistically understand that our strength at the moment is in the ever-growing number of those who are no longer willing to passively witness the elimination of themselves and their loved ones, along with all the principles we hold dear, including our abiding faith that God is sovereign in Heaven as on Earth, not Satan.

German politician Christine Anderson, a member of the European Parliament, has openly proclaimed the need to resist these evil woke governments. In a statement to the European Parliament, she said the following:

I am really imploring the people and all peoples around the world. For God's sake, stop giving your "democratically-elected" governments the benefit of the doubt. They are not deserving of that. They are not. Stop rationalizing whatever your government is doing. Stop rationalizing and come up with some good intentions. They have no good intentions. Never. As I said before, in the entire history of mankind, there has never been a political elite concerned about the well-being of regular people. And it isn't any different now. Why should it? Stop giving them the benefit of the doubt. Because I can tell you, you cannot comply your way out of a tyranny. Trying to do so, you will only feed a gigantic alligator in the hopes of being eaten last. But guess what? Your turn will come. And then you will be the one swallowed up.[334]

---

334 A video clip of comments by Christine Anderson, a member of the European Parliament, addressed to the European Parliament. Posted on X by James Melville, January 11, 2024, https://x.com/JamesMelville/status/1745385090627056083.

She continued:

> I also have to ask the people—end your silence. Speak up! For God's
> sense, stop complying, start rebelling. They are out to get you if you
> do not resist. I would also urge you to stop voting for those who inflict
> this psychological abuse on you, who mock you for their own good. In
> order to deal with this unfree world, to defy this unfree world, I have
> decided to become so absolutely free that my very existence is an act of
> rebellion. And that's what we all need to do.[335]

We are here to tell you, the globalization misanthropists, that you
picked this fight. You wanted this fight. Well, guess what? Let's fight.
You are the small fringe minority. You do not have the right to dictate
to the people.

We find ourselves having to disobey the representatives of authority
precisely because we recognize how you abuse that authority. We understand what your actual purposes are and know how evil and corrupt—
how ungodly and Satanic—your true purposes are. Our Declaration of
Independence was born from just such a time, from just such a recognition. Natural law universally recognizes the right and duty of a people
to change or suppress a government that acts against its common interests or threatens the security of the people without just cause:

Thus, the Declaration of Independence starts with one of the most
articulate statements ever written explaining the right of a sovereign
people to resist:

> We hold these truths to be self-evident: That all men are created equal;
> that they are endowed by their Creator with certain unalienable rights;
> that among these are life, liberty, and the pursuit of happiness; that, to

---

335 Ibid.

secure these rights, governments are instituted among men, deriving their just powers from the consent of the governed; **that whenever any form of government becomes destructive of these ends, it is the right of the people to alter or to abolish it, and to institute new government**, laying its foundation on such principles, and organizing its powers in such form, as to them shall seem most likely to effect their safety and happiness. [336]

Imagine systematically boycotting globalist brands in all countries of the world at the same time. What if we all decided to take our children out of public schools? Imagine if we could have our own financial circuits, our own banks, our own broadcasters, our own schools, our own stores.

If those entrepreneurs willing to fight with foresight and courage would begin to address a traditional and avowedly anti-globalist target audience, vast sums of money could be shifted from the monopoly of the elite to be circulated among the people, families, artisans, farms, and small businesses throughout the world. Mel Gibson launched a no-woke film production company. **What stops a supermarket chain, a banking circuit, an insurance company, an energy consortium, a publishing house, or a university campus from being proudly anti-globalist? Why are bookstore shelves full of gender smut and children's woke books while traditional children's literature is primarily removed?** While it is relatively easy to boycott woke companies, we must help those who oppose globalist dictatorship, starting with farmers, ranchers, fishermen, trade workers of all kinds—the list goes on. And let's not forget that these forms of solidarity create social groups—especially at the local level—that can exercise forms of lobbying on public administrators, mayors, governors, labor associations,

---

336 Declaration of Independence, July 4, 1776.

school board administrators, and city council members. Those who want our vote must earn it with an openly anti-globalist commitment and program.

British commentator and pundit James Melville recently wrote: "We should be focusing on genuine old school environmentalism that protects farming, natural ecosystems and sustainable environments, rather than the corporatist con-trick and asset grab of net zero. Let's have a national referendum on Net Zero."[337]

The idea of holding a referendum of the sovereign people does not touch those who govern and administer public policy—who all too often have been paid to follow the dictates of their globalist elite masters. Resistance itself is a form of referendum—as Churchill understood, if enough people just say, "No!," pretty soon the rules and regulations change, or the people change those in charge of making the rules and regulations.

Laying the Foundation for Resistance

Awareness of our momentary disorganization should spur us to remedy it immediately. Still, we must do so by having a few guidelines in mind and then knowing how to adapt them to specific cases, depending on where we are, what the laws of our country are, whether we have a possible political backbone of real opposition still present in the Congress, or in Parliament, etc. Doing resistance in Trudeau's Canada or Macron's France is not the same as organizing a form of political pressing in Italy or Sweden. Having relations with other resistance groups abroad does not exclude establishing exchanges and contacts with countries not subject to Agenda 2030 or World Health Organization health dictates. Indeed, one could create the basis for "diplomatic" relations with

---

337 A video clip of a podcast interviewing James Melville, posted by James Melville on X, June 5, 2024,
 https://x.com/JamesMelville/status/1798297616884912374.

avowedly anti-globalist nations, especially between various states in the United States and EU member states in Europe. Hungary shows that it is possible to put the defense of one's sovereignty and the welfare of citizens before the criminal interests of the European Commission, and this can be an excellent encouragement for an awakening in other countries as well.

Let us not confuse our disorganization with a lack of real power: **The fact that we do not have the economic, media, and institutional resources the globalist elite have is an element of weakness only when we decide to compete and fight the enemy by standing by its rules and using its weapons**—rules and weapons that are designed to ensure that they win and we inevitably lose. But it is not necessarily the enemy who can decide on which field to challenge us. We can and should be the ones to choose where to attack them and how to fight them, not least because we can avail ourselves of the only absolute and indisputable advantage we have: numerical superiority. **We are infinitely more numerous than the conventicle of subversives that claims to domesticate us and keep us in chains**. And I am not talking about the inert and unformed masses who passively endure daily humiliation by the System, but about that ever-growing phalanx of those "awakened" from the ideological narcosis of modern thought, that people—in the Latin meaning of the term populus—made up of millions of honest, upright, uncorrupted moral people who love God and thus also love their homeland and family. I am talking about those who do not want to pervert their children by dressing boys up as women or amputating their sexual attributes—those who do not tolerate woke indoctrination, who are proud of their identity and traditions, who honor their parents and elders, who work to the point of breaking their backs to ensure that they and their loved ones have the means of livelihood for a dignified life.

It is against these people of goodwill that the globalist attack is unleashed because it is their very existence that is a threat to the survival of the System. The mother who educates her daughters to respect marriage; the father who teaches his sons values such as honesty and honor; the grandparents who pass on unwritten knowledge to their grandchildren; the husband who loves and defends his spouse by recognizing her indispensable role in the moral formation of her offspring; the wife who honors her husband by feeling with him that she is one flesh (Genesis 2:24) are dangerous continuers of that model of society and civilization against which the demonic globalist elite has waged unrestricted war.

The rhetoric of cancel culture imposed in schools and universities can be demolished by a few words heard at home, by the tale of the grandfather who fought in the war, by the memory of family history handed down through generations, the simplicity of truth can overcome all the lies of those who want us without historical roots that ground us with hope projected into the future. The follies of gender theory and LGBTQ+ perversions can be dismantled by the presence and example of a manly father figure and a feminine mother figure, without the grotesque caricatures of those who celebrated their psychologically bizarre behavior that defies all nature and civilization have shown to be praiseworthy and virtuous. The widespread mentality of corruption in the workplace based on the exaltation of cunning and unscrupulousness in dealings with one's neighbor must be rejected—even in small things. Colleagues and clients must find a counterbalance in uncompromising models of honesty and integrity.

In short, we need to rediscover the pride of being decent people and good Christians and the ability not to be intimidated by those who exalt and promote all that is false, bad, and ugly. We must also have the courage to stand firm against any attempt to normalize what is not normal, to legitimize what reason shows us to be a sin and a crime. We must resist the temptation to pervert the concept of freedom into libertinism. Let us not forget that all great civilizations have sunk inexorably into oblivion as soon as moral corruption—especially of legitimate law and righteous authority—became the rule. On the rubble of those civilizations, new ones have arisen, not in the destructive erasure of the past, but in having been able to combine what was good in the previous civilizations with the impetus of new constructive energies and in having been able to reject the deviations that had been the leading cause of that decadence.

Where Were We?

Before waging war on globalism, we should do a sincere examination to understand the mistakes made in the past so we can avoid them in the future. This self-examination must begin with recognizing that **the globalist elite has progressively invaded all institutions and infiltrated all structures of education, training, and information in complete silence on our part.** We have allowed ourselves to be sidelined *as if* our marginalization were somehow justified and due, *as if* we had to accept suffering social stigma for our ideas, our culture, our education, and our beliefs. In short, we have allowed ourselves to be labeled as second-class citizens (and believers), on the wave of an ideological indoctrination that has been successful, first and foremost, *because of our unwillingness to fight and assert our rights.*

We have witnessed the invasion of schools of all ranks, where the System has placed teachers imbued with a destructive mix of liberalism and socialism that they have used to indoctrinate our children. We have let the publishing houses, the press, the media, the cinema, and the internet—the whole ideological propaganda machine—become the exclusive preserve of the Radical Neo-Marxist Left. We have seen cultural centers, think tanks of intellectuals, institutes, and foundations of conservative orientation disappear, thus condemning ourselves to social and political irrelevance. We have allowed our politicians, rulers, and shepherds to betray the principles and values for which we recognize them as our representatives and guides. And why? Out of a sense of inferiority that was imposed on us and that we at first endured with resignation: being Christians and patriots. We bound ourselves to a family and cultural tradition that cautioned us not to rebel. But with the passage of time, our restraint and patience widened the gap between us—survivors of a world doomed to extinction—and monsters vowed to create a post-human utopia for themselves, while proceeding under a deceitful banner of progress, freedom, equality, and fraternity designed to keep us asleep.

While our opponents were organizing and giving training and careers to their scions, whom we see today at the top of institutions, many of us were doing all we could to chase the chimeras of progress and single-mindedness while denying ourselves, our faith, our civilization, our traditions. Our politicians, tired repeaters of abstract and unlived "values," have been primarily responsible in the past decades for this advance of globalist tyranny, first and foremost for failing to look far into the future by creating a coherent and determined ruling class. We found ourselves with the ideological wreckage of 1968, which we should have rejected with disdain. Yet we tolerated what was, in reality, a Maoist cultural revolution, thinking we were still a nation while conspirators undermined its foundations. We have allowed ourselves to be convinced of moral and social inferiority as neo-Marxist youths in the streets accused us of racism and imperialism—the chants and slogans common today to all anarchists. On that inferiority complex, we have watched the demolition of our homeland impassively by those who, swearing by the Constitution, used lawfare to wage war against the rule of law they should have protected to make it stronger and more prosperous.

We cannot fail to recognize that this systematic demolition of traditional society—that we understand today was just a prelude to woke critical theory—was largely predictable. An army cannot hope to fight and win after surrendering its fortresses, strongholds, and weapons to the enemy. That is why, along with immediate and short-term action, it is necessary to plan forward-looking and long-term action to reappropriate all those bastions of power that the globalist elite have taken from us. We need to think about the education of our children. Who will teach in our schools? Who will pass on our principles and constitute the future ruling and middle classes? The inevitable extinction of globalism must find us prepared to take back the reins of society with well-trained professionals who adhere to high ideals and are willing to give their lives for their honor. You read that correctly: giving one's life for one's honor. The contemporary world has robbed us of hope because it has made us ashamed of our faith, history, and civilization—a civilization that our forefathers built on those common ideals for which they were ready to fight and die. Who would die today to defend religion, country, or family? Yet without ideals, life is just a succession of meaningless and purposeless events decided by faceless entities whose decisions we cannot criticize.

If we are to fight and resist, we must also have the wisdom to prepare the ground for the years to come, knowing that our children are ultimately the enemy's primary target. The globalist elite most insistently unleashes their ideological indoctrination on our children. Once our children are taught to internalize globalist principles, all their future choices will be set in place. Indoctrinated as globalists, our children will pass on globalism to their children—setting in place the mentality with which generation after generation will vote for their rulers to be globalists like themselves. That is why we must closely watch school curricula and everything related to the education and entertainment intended for the young. At the same time, we must organize alternatives, such as schools, universities, books, programs, and activities consistent with traditional values.

We will also have to think about establishing cultural institutes and centers where intellectuals and personalities of high academic profiles contribute to the knowledge and protection of our culture. **In a sense, we must act like the World Economic Forum, but with opposite purposes—a kind of lobby of the good** that can enhance deserving minds, intellectual abilities, artistic talent, and craftsmanship. Let us not allow the immeasurable heritage of knowledge and thought which is the foundation of our civilization to be erased, , for without roots in the past, we cannot lean toward the future. The best way to prevent this erasure is to defend it, to promote it, and to promote its dissemination. We must dismantle with the force of arguments the lies and forgeries on which the globalist elite have built their success, starting with the scandalous neo-Marxist rewriting of modern and contemporary history texts.

And when someone, from the height of his usurped woke privilege, believes that he can silence us by pointing at us as rigid, fanatical, traditionalist, retrograde, fascist, nationalist, white supremacists, and toxic masculinity supporters of patriarchy, we should simply challenge that person's right to decide to assert the supremacy of their "value judgments." **We must in no way accept being treated as second-class citizens just because we have not agreed to be lobotomized**: that is why it is most important to build the foundation for tomorrow now, before everything we are and everything we think is removed by the System.

In a speech last May to Poland, Archbishop Viganò urged: "If you are few now, you will be in increasing numbers, and you will be able to create widespread communities in which to Christianly educate your children and pass on to them what will make them strong and determined. If you are mocked today, tomorrow you will be honored. If you are marginalized, tomorrow they will come knocking on your door."[338]

---

338 Archbishop Carlo Maria Viganò, "Resistite Fortes," Message to the Catholic Resistance in Poland, ExSurgeDomine.it, May 31, 2024, https://exsurgedomine. it/240531-resistite-eng/

As part of this action to counter and resist the globalist coup d'état, **we cannot overlook the importance of creating the future anti-globalist ruling class**. This training must begin immediately, enhancing the most promising young minds with training courses, conferences, conventions, sports, and cultural activities. An annual cruise could welcome high school or university students to take them on a Mediterranean itinerary to retrace the routes of the Venetians or the French. The same could be done by tour operators choosing a proposal to defend and promote the different European and American cultures. Anti-globalist entrepreneurs and philanthropists must fund foundations and projects, including those in the scientific sphere, that are oriented toward the common good and genuine progress in the various disciplines and not subject to the blackmail of the elite.

Knowing the Adversary's Plans

Given we know the adversary's plans, we can expose, obstruct, or sabotage them. The enemy also acts in precisely the same way when he has to plan a pandemic, a color revolution, a proxy war, or a climate emergency. Those who plan a coup d'état know full well that there will be opponents. So, the coup planners organize in advance to discredit or censor them. We have all seen how the media collaborated in the farce of the J6 Capitol Hill protest of the presidential election on January 6, 2021. We have witnessed how the government medical authorities stubbornly denied adverse vaccine effects during the COVID-19 pandemic. We have witnessed the arson fires set by the climate cult to force the public to accept their fraudulent global warming/climate change narrative.

But when Elon Musk unexpectedly bought Twitter and removed its censorship algorithms, the whole castle of lies and cover-ups collapsed. Today we can report on X on AstraZeneca's and Pfizer's serum adverse health effects without fear of being banned. We now know that on the other side of the globe, many other people think like us, not only on so-called vaccines, but also on the Ukrainian crisis, on the woke ideology, on bizarre gender critical theory, on the criminal pedophile network that unites the members of the elite in a blood act, on climate-driven geoengineering schemes, and a dozen other "conspiracy theories" that today are confirmed by the same media that stubbornly denied them.

So-called "conspiracy theorists" turned out to be *pattern recognitionists* and truth-tellers who were not fooled by government lies and denials. And when the British government, a servant of the World Economic Forum, activated thousands of ULEZ [Ultra Low Emission Zone] cameras for surveillance of its citizens, an anonymous hand began to cut them down with a hose, leading in some cases to suspension of the installations. And we know there are a thousand ways of resistance in which the inventiveness of so many people can be engaged once we understand what and where the weak points are in the machinery.

Tucker Carlson explained: "It's weak men and women who are instruments of evil. The weaker the leader, the more evil that leader will be. So, it's unfortunate that we've reached a time in American history where every leader is either a woman or a weak man, pretty much." [339]

But already, nearly fifty years ago, the French writer Jean Raspail wrote: "The world is controlled, so it seems, not by a single specific conductor, but by a new apocalyptic beast, and one that in some primordial time, must have vowed to destroy the Western World." [340]

Writing a *Resistance Handbook for Dummies* is therefore, useless, as

---

339 A video clip of Tucker Carlson being interviewed, posted on X by Wall Street Apes, June 1, 2024,
  https://x.com/ThrillaRilla369/status/1797035894890738055
340 Jean Raspail, *The Camp of the Saints*, (New York: Charles Scribner's Sons, First English Printing edition, January 1, 1975), p. 38. It's a dystopian fiction novel depicting the destruction of Western civilization through Third World mass immigration to France and the Western world.

well as counterproductive. What we need is to understand the fragilities of the System and act accordingly, like spoilers, and, if possible, also avail ourselves of existing regulations in the country or at the federal or community level. It is also possible that in states whose government is avowedly subservient to the globalist agenda, there are anti-globalist or simply honest local or regional community administrators with whom forms of collaboration and institutional support for citizen initiatives might be possible: let us not forget that many mayors and governors are more attentive to the will of their constituents than many members of Congress or national Parliaments.

Therefore, this second part of this Manifesto is not to propose a single, all-encompassing solution but to provide some concrete proposals focused on five themes: food, health, energy, finance, and education. Each thematic area—which corresponds broadly with the eight themes covered in Part I—will aim to indicate possible forms of resistance and boycott that in each state can be adapted or even just taken as a starting point for possible anti-globalist action. I would like any proposals, amendments, and even criticisms to be shared and included in a future edition of this Manifesto and on the official website of the Anti-Globalist Alliance because we are persuaded that among those who share our vision of the global coup d'état, there are enormous and valuable resources that we have not yet tapped.

The Resistance Networks

The idea of creating networks is not new, but given that we must defeat the globalist elite, building networks is the strategy most likely to succeed. But what is a network? It is simply a way to connect several people who share a specific approach to life or a particular social or political agenda. A network creates a connection by which people who are distant or unknown to each other can encounter each other, share experiences, and experiment with solutions in a world that knows only how to isolate individuals. **Let us not forget that isolation is a psychological technique the System utilizes to destroy any possible mass uprising.** Thus, during the pandemic farce, governments around the world engaged in "lockdowns"—a term not coincidentally borrowed from the prison lexicon. According to many psychologists, the pandemic lockdowns had a devastating impact, especially on minors and the elderly, helping to weaken their immune systems and thus making them more susceptible to the disease.

Lockdowns and confinements have been instrumental in exacerbating an artfully provoked situation for the purpose of raising the level of alarm and social panic so that further compressions of people's inalienable rights can be justified. Still, the lockdowns have mainly served the purpose of being a *ballon d'essai* (a "trial balloon"), designed to test the degree to which the masses would willingly accept these restrictions to communal living—restrictions that could easily be applied again, for instance, if the World Economic Forum were to proclaim the global warming/climate change hoax to be a "global health emergency." The psycho-pandemic was deliberately and maliciously provoked for the sole purpose of forcing us to accept the deprivation of fundamental freedoms in view of the coming imposition of social credits, digital currency, and climate lockdowns.

Having seen what the globalist elite is capable of doing, appreciating the precision with which they plan and carry out their "scenarios," and anticipating what they are planning for the future, we must prepare ourselves to confront this concrete threat with all possible means. The survival of our species, our lives, and the lives of our children and our future depend upon our willingness to preserve, and protect, our inalienable God-bestowed human rights in the here and now.

We do not currently have the means to confront the global coup on equal terms; we can, however, take practical steps to thwart and boycott their plans. When we are inside the System's mechanisms where we can discern its weaknesses, our action can be most effective. Conducting opposition from within the System is a topic we will address in the chapter devoted to the "Mouth of Truth," a project that the Anti-Globalist Alliance intends to launch soon. The Mouth of Truth project will be aimed at physicians and health administrative personnel in hospitals. However, similar operations can be conducted in other areas as well, keeping in mind that what our enemy fears most is the truth. The globalist coup d'état we are witnessing is based on lies and deception. The infallible weapon with which to combat this evil is to bring these falsehoods to light, exposing that the lies of the global elite are instrumental in the fulfillment of their criminal plan.

The pandemic farce and continued attacks on individual freedoms throughout Western countries in the name of false emergencies have prompted many people to come together in groups and movements of Resistance and Denunciation. Associations have sprung up to gather victims of the adverse effects of gene serums. We see networks forming on many fronts: organizations of doctors who respect the Hippocratic Oath and do not submit to the dictates of Big Pharma; committees that protect farmers and ranchers ("No Farmers, No Food"); coordination of military and professionals suspended from work and salary because they were not vaccinated; coordination of parents who reject the LGBTQ+ indoctrination and gender perversions to which their children are subjected in schools and campuses; and political parties that demand the defense of national sovereignty and oppose ethnic substitution imposed through illegal immigration. **All these forces can cooperate with the Resistance without losing their autonomy, making a valuable contribution to countering the subversive plan of the elite.** Membership in these movements within the Anti-Globalist Alliance would enable us to have some sort of representation and coordination at the international level so that our voices will be amplified and heard by those pursuing similar aims in other nations.

If we get around a table and start sharing what we have experienced in our countries, we will discover that there is **one script under one direction**. We will be able to set the stage not only for common resistance action but also for the creation of an independent Criminal Court that can try those responsible for the global coup and the greatest crime against humanity.

This Manifesto is the first step in articulating the establishment of a response that is unique in the principles that will make it invincible yet diverse in the ways our resistance is applied at the local level. The Anti-Globalist Forum to be organized in the next few months will allow all these groups to meet, to get to know each other, and to work together for the achievement of a common goal—to restore God to be the rightful sovereign over Earth, and to restore to each of us the dignity our Creator has bestowed us.

The Health Network

One of the primary forms of opposition and resistance to the globalist coup has spontaneously organized around the psycho-pandemic farce. Since 2019, thousands of scientists, doctors, and healthcare professionals have begun questioning the mainstream narrative, suffering from decertification, salary suspension, and media pillorying. But the persecution did not stop them; on the contrary, it allowed for the assembly of increasingly numerous and widespread "no-vax" movements and groups. All over the world, associations and committees denouncing the adverse effects of serums and the irregularities committed by health authorities in dealing with COVID-19 succeeded in raising awareness among the public and some opposition parliamentarians in many nations. In May 2023, the member states rejected the World Health Organization's Pandemic Treaty, and rejected it a second time in May 2024. In 2024, Director-General Tedros Ghebreyesus expressed wrath at these setbacks. He said:

You know the serious challenge that's posed by anti-vaxxers, and I think we need to strategize to really push back because vaccines work, and we have the science and evidence on our side. [...] I think the time has come to react more aggressively toward anti-vaxers who exploit the Covid situation to sow havoc. [341]

What exactly does Tedros Ghebreyesus mean when he talks about a "more aggressive reaction against anti-vaxxers"? How does he plan to force the world's population to submit to his insane blackmail when the entire history of the WHO is riddled with false pandemics to administer false vaccines?

In May 2024, Tedros sounded more determined to press forward with the WHO international power grab with the global "One Health" policy. "Of course, we all wish we had been able to reach a consensus on the agreement in time for this health assembly, and cross the finish line," he said. "I remain confident that you still will, because where there is a will, there is a way. I know that there remains among you a common will to get this done."[342]

Tedros and the World Health Organization globalists typically will continue pressing forward, determined to get a WHO member state agreement to cede health sovereignty to the WHO. Such a pandemic treaty would allow the WHO extraordinary powers to dictate lockdowns, vaccine treatments, and whatever population control measures the WHO determines to dictate—for whatever health emergency the WHO decides to proclaim (including a health threat from climate

---

341 "WHO director Tedros: 'It's time. to be more aggressive in pushing back on anti-vaxxers," Life Site News, LifeSiteNews.com, June 2, 2024, https://www.lifesitenews.com/news/who-director-tedros-its-time-to-be-more-aggressive-in-pushing-back-on-anti-vaxxers/.
342 Emma Farge and Gabrielle Tétrault-Farber, "WHO chief Tedros 'confident' of eventual pandemic treaty deal," Reuters, May 27, 2024, https://www.reuters.com/world/who-chief-tedros-confident-eventual-pandemic-treaty-deal-2024-05-27/.

change, or simply from overpopulation) —and to force member states internationally to comply.

The obsessive repetition of a scandalous lie, such as the efficacy of experimental gene therapy passed off as a vaccine, will not save the top leadership of the World Health Organization and other health agencies from prosecution and conviction—that much is certain. But in the meantime, the citizens of Western countries must continue their action of denouncing the crimes committed and opposing the dictates they still try to impose on us.

Suppose physicians, nurses, healthcare providers, hospitals, clinics, laboratories, pharmacies, and small pharmaceutical companies unite in this network. In that case, we can create that much-needed alternative to Big Pharma's current monopoly. The alternative to BigPharma would guarantee the population therapies, treatments, medicines, and care that conform to the Hippocratic Oath and respect the ethical principles of the art of medicine.

Obviously, it would not be a matter of bringing all these groups together into a single entity that would erase their specificities. Still, bringing together healthcare professionals dedicated to a genuine concept of human rights would create the basis for a future common project of public health reform. If all these professionals unite and collaborate, they will not only be able to concretely help the millions of people who legitimately want to be treated according to science and conscience. So united, these health professionals will also be able to identify the globally recurring elements that made possible the pandemic fraud of criminally administering to billions of people a drug that health authorities knew to be harmful, deadly, and sterilizing.

This healthcare network will eventually be able to make arrangements with ethical insurance companies, allowing citizens to be treated at member clinics or by physicians. A healthcare network formed under the banner of the Hippocratic Oath would take the patient-doctor out of the control of the government and Big Pharma, returning control over medical decisions to the doctor and the patient, where genuine respect for human rights demands medical decisions must be made. This healthcare network would be able to collaborate with groups of lawyers and magistrates to assist its adherents (both doctors and patients) and to coordinate legal and conscientious objection actions.

The Mouth of Truth

Among the initiatives the Anti-Globalist Alliance intends to promote, we cannot fail to mention the "Mouth of Truth." In Venice, during the Republic of the Doges, there were letter holes where citizens could submit secret (but not anonymous) complaints to report corruption crimes committed by public administrators. There are still many visible around Venice: one of them, still in existence, bears the words *Denoncie contra la Sanità* (Report crimes against public health). The citizens of Venice called these potholes "lion mouths" because they were usually carved in the form of a lion's head. Still, since the Mouth of Truth (*Bocca della Verità*) found in Rome is better known for its simplicity and communication effectiveness, the expression "Mouth of Truth" seems more appropriate and easier to understand.

The goal of the Mouth of Truth Project is to collect sworn testimony from nurses, doctors, and health administrators about crimes or violations of human rights during the COVID-19 psycho-pandemic farce or any similar "medical emergency" psycho-pandemic farce the Deep State decides to stage in the future. A pool of lawyers will be able to assist these whistleblowers and collect their sworn testimonies. By putting these testimonies together from around the world, it will be possible to understand that all the actions taken by the health agencies of different nations—and by every public hospital or private clinic—are consistent with a single direction and script, and thus demonstrate a common thread of Deep State malice and premeditation being broadcast internationally by the government-controlled media echo chamber.

The Mouth of Truth initiative makes it possible to encourage many doctors and health personnel to denounce the orders they receive, considering that in many cases, the subordination of medical personnel resembles military subordination (e.g., in the World War II Nuremberg trials, in which soldiers and low-ranking officers were neither tried nor convicted of human rights violations). The pool of lawyers would also obtain sworn testimonies to use at trial. Key witnesses would be protected and safeguarded through grants of immunity.

The Mouth of Truth Project will be particularly useful in identifying psycho-pandemic abuses, including the exposure of creating "dramatizations" of crowded emergency rooms or piles of body bags with piles of COVID-19 patients awaiting cremation. Abuses of the elderly should also be vulnerable to discovery when, for instance, an elderly care facility begins administering drugs to euthanize the infected as an alternative to providing the type of expensive medical care that may be needed. We must expose cases where COVID-19-infected seniors were simply left to die, or where family and friends were kept from entering nursing home facilities in which their loved ones were left to die alone.

The Food Network

Creating a food network is undoubtedly among the first concrete and most viable initiatives we should implement immediately. The food network involves, on the one hand, farmers, ranchers, fishermen, farms, and artisans in the sector, as well as the end customers, households, and small entrepreneurs in the restaurant and food distribution sectors.

The World Economic Forum seems intent on concentrating food production and distribution into agribusiness multinational corporate control, utilizing technology to produce genetically modified and bio-engineered laboratory-produced food. At the same time, small farms are systematically being driven from the market. The World Economic Forum's concerns are always couched in Agency 2030 "sustainability" language, combined with the message that traditional methods of farming, the use of nitrogen-based fertilizers, and the consumption of meat are all to be restricted in pursuit of achieving net zero levels of CO_2 production. The World Economic Forum's so-called Food Innovation Hubs (FUBs)—located in various parts of the world, have generated the "No Farms, No Food" farm protests across Europe. These protests have tied up major cities like Berlin and Paris with farm tractors driven into the central business districts from the fares.

Criminal policies endanger the existence of farmers, but this attack—based on climate fraud and the alleged negative environmental impact of farming and ranching—can only be thwarted if citizens know what is happening and engage together in a concrete action that is relatively easy to accomplish. Remember that the insane regulations imposed by regional governments like the European Union are accompanied by scandalous speculation by large retailers, with the courtly complicity of farmers' unions. The prices at which fruits and vegetables are sold in supermarkets come to be as much as ten times higher than the cost at which those products are purchased from farmers, with speculation that benefits large retailers and increasingly impoverishes growers who are already challenged by green delusions and the systematic destruction of crops and livestock by arson, geoengineering, and livestock pandemics. Avian flu—like the swine flu plague a decade ago—is now being used as an excuse to wipe out entire farms, cause a shortage of meat, eggs, and dairy products, and thus have the pretext to put on the market synthetic foods, insect meal, beetle milk, and lab-produced meat.

The idea of the food network is based on organizing a supply/demand exchange between producers and end customers, guaranteeing that natural products are not genetically modified and not subjected to harmful treatments. This "ethical market" could occur locally, periodically, to create "temporary communities" of exchange and discussion. We would call them *agoras*, after the Greek name for the squares where citizens gathered in ancient times. There should be markets for healthy, fresh food sold without intermediaries and at prices that allow legitimate profits for the producer and reasonable savings (compared to supermarket prices) for families. The benefit would be immediate on both fronts, allowing for diversification and increased supply.

Suppose a farmer knows that he has a loyal local customer base. In that case, he can produce, for example, several varieties of fruit by non-intensive methods instead of just one variety to sell at meager prices to the wholesaler. Farmers can raise pigs and cows outdoors and with natural processes instead of investing in intensive farms that require many animals and minimize quality. Bakers, butchers, cheese and dairy vendors, and small artisans could also be found in these agoras: depending on the context in which each of these communities develops, those activities that are most present in the local area could be favored and, if some products are not locally available, exchange relationships could be created with other agoras, so that each person could sell what they have in abundance and buy (or simply barter) what they do not have.

You can well imagine that this exchange of products also implies an exchange of ideas, a sharing of ideals and principles, and a shared vision that goes beyond the sale of vegetables and jams: it allows for socialization and the creation of territorially organized groups, capable of actions with social and political impact, especially at the local level. The mayor of a rural community cares more about his election by helping his constituents than about pandering to the follies of government technocrats. Given the cost-of-living increases caused by programmed inflation, the mayor of a non-rural town has every interest in helping his citizens by offering them the opportunity to buy directly from producers, or at least not preventing them from organizing. And suppose a mayor or governor does not want to encourage and support these initiatives. In that case, there will undoubtedly be a candidate who will want to ride this battle—which is entirely laudable—by making these agoras known even where these were not yet widespread. **A website or an app could give the possibility to coordinate these realities, to enter one's activity, and to know where and when markets are organized.**

It is foreseeable that as citizens begin to exercise their rights as responsible consumers critically, there could be chain stores or supermarkets that decide to support this initiative and agree with farmers and breeders on ethical contracts, committing to share the anti-globalist vision and to favor natural and healthy farming and ranching.

The Agora App could also allow the sale of products online, enabling even those without a nearby community to support participating farms. Of course, with electronic commerce, we are always in enemy land. We will have to remember always to favor cash transactions and direct and personal contact with those who share our ideas: we may meet teachers with whom we can organize parent schools for our children, or doctors from whom we can get treatment without fear of being harmed; we may meet people with whom we can meet again, and maybe in those places there is also a space for children to play, a tent for Sunday Mass, a corner for those who want to play music, or an area dedicated to barbecue. It will be nice to see how little it takes, in those moments, to have a cell phone to make friends and to discover that, in the end, we are not as few and as strange as the mainstream would like.

The food network can be a decisive element in building resistance because we all need to eat, and we cannot put our own and our children's health at risk by believing that the products on the market in large-scale distribution are not poisoned or manipulated, moreover at exorbitant prices. And suppose a company cares so much about proclaiming itself environmentally sustainable and adhering to Agenda 2030. In that case, it should not be surprising if that is enough for us to decide to boycott it, and doing so will be accessible when a list of brands is available on the Alliance website. **As the climate narrative collapses, few businesses will decide to distance themselves from globalism and stand on the opposite side.** At that point—and it will be the agoras' main merit—it will become fashionable to be an anti-globalist.

The Educational and Training Network

This network is dedicated to school and vocational education and includes anti-system media and counter-information. **We want to counterbalance the monopoly of information, entertainment, school and university education, and employment-specific educa-tion.** There are huge wasted potentials of journalists, intellectuals, pro-fessors, academics, artists, actors, and sportsmen who are penalized in newsrooms, foundations, schools, universities, theaters, cinemas, and stadiums because they are not "woke." Those who believe in God have to jump through hoops not to be "found out" and fired, not to be accused of "white supremacism," or homophobia. Professionals with traditional values must self-censor or risk being ostracized by the System.

Yet these same God-fearing traditionalists will have an incred-ible opportunity when the Anti-Globalist Alliance allows them to become the protagonists and implementers of a "parallel" system of education, information, and entertainment. Just think about it: If sportsmen and women started organizing themselves into avowedly no-woke teams and agreed to compete only in no-woke leagues, do you think sponsors would not consider this? And if sports activities for chil-dren and adolescents were organized in facilities that guarantee good morals and principled instructors, wouldn't the parents benefit first and foremost, as well as society?

Countless families find themselves exasperated by woke gender indoctrination to which their children, from the youngest to the old-est, are subjected. Why not create avowedly **anti-globalist schools,** where parents are sure to see their children educated according to traditional curricula and with respect for religion and homeland history? Why can't the money we give to campuses to see our children corrupted and perverted go to colleges that banish woke culture and pass on the healthy values and principles we hold dear? And why, instead of paying subscription fees to Netflix or Amazon, don't we create **our own thematic channels** or help existing ones grow so that we can offer information and entertainment that is not infected with LGBTQ+ perversion and cancel culture? And what prevents a chain of movie theaters from endorsing the Anti-Globalist Alliance and offering only morally and ideologically sound film production? If the elite has censored good things and given space to vices and violence, why should we not censor vices and violence and give their rightful space back to good things? Again, I stress that **being an anti-globalist will indeed become fashionable** if only we resist the woke globalist elite by reforming our educational and training networks.

Beyond the undeniable improvement in the quality of services provided—whether schools, newsrooms, or otherwise—we must consider the additional benefit to individuals and society: giving an alternative to education, information, and entertainment professionals so that they can leave the limbo (or hell) in which they work, so they can find employment in new realities where they can give their best in keeping with the ideals and aims of anti-globalism. The case of Tucker Carlson is an example. Tucker could have continued his broadcasting job peacefully, knowing that he was making an essential contribution to improving the current situation, with a decent salary and job security—so long as he did not cross certain red lines. Tucker found that not crossing those red lines was morally impossible for him. Tucker's solution was to create his own alternative network—one in which he was censorship-free.

Saying "No!" is not something to be underestimated. By natural law, we pursue happiness—happiness the globalist elite do not want to experience. **The globalist demons know that in sadness and loneliness, we face the temptation to take refuge in drugs, psychotropic drugs, virtual reality, and pornography—all virtual reality markets in the hands of multinational corporations and the usual investment funds. The globalist elite dystopian dream is to force millions, if not billions, of people to live an existence designed specifically to demoralize them.** The goal of the globalist demons is to engage in a psychological operation of social engineering such that the masses seeking to live a serene and peaceful life have as their only alternative to enter the dark virtual metaverse of drugs and lies the globalist elite have devised to manipulate them into slavery.

The anti-globalist alternative involves us retaking control of our lives and our future to build a new edifice with the stones of our broken homes. These stones come from afar and carry the marks of the past, our lives, and history. We do not want globalist "magic" to transform our world into a promised utopian paradise. We want to return to a livable life because it is morally less prone to evil. After all, it is God-centric and less likely to be self-destructive because education and training systems are based on truth. **And for this path of reclaiming what has been usurped from us—if only the right to have a blue sky, pure water, and natural food—we must start small, creating networks, weaving relationships with one another, and building communities locally—but all the while knowing how to think big.**

The Bank of Arts and Crafts

The Alliance plans to establish a Bank of Arts and Crafts to preserve and save the priceless treasure of knowledge handed down over the centuries. The globalist elite are deliberately wiping out treasures in our art museums and libraries for the flat uniformity of multinational corporations.

The Bank of Arts and Crafts will allow vocational training to the younger generation, which will soon find itself without job outlets due to the coming employment crisis, particularly in the service sector. Until today, those who have scraped together a paltry salary as call center operators or Uber drivers will soon be replaced by AI operators, drones, and self-driving cars, as is already happening. Those earning a living as help in a fast food restaurant or a worker in a warehouse will soon see themselves replaced by robots. Multinational corporations are investing an enormous sum of money in technology designed to replace human workers with machines—even if the machines do not meet with the appreciation of customers, who are still accustomed—fortunately—to the value of human interaction.

Given the "Reset" that will hit Western countries and the consequent exponential rise in unemployment, **an anti-globalist alternative to the globalist proposal of universal income linked to social credits must also be created in this area.** Therefore, preparing a concrete, viable response that represents a real prospect of work and subsistence is necessary. For this reason, while the elite aims to centralize the management of the economy, trade, agribusiness, and healthcare industries, **we must implement a systematic decentralization**, favoring small businesses, handicrafts, small farms, livestock raising, local fishing, etc.—all those labor activities that guarantee economic independence and, along with it, the possibility of escaping the control of the globalist Leviathan, **because the more numerous and autonomous these anti-globalist employment realities become, the more complicated it will be for the globalist demons to push the entrepreneur and the family-run business into oblivion.**

If we look back to our past, we discover many jobs and trades have been all but wiped out because they are considered **a dangerous benchmark for the paltry supply of big business.** Once upon a time, when a couple was getting married and setting up a house, it was inconceivable to choose mass-produced furnishings. Every city and every town, even the most remote, had artisans capable of customizing any furniture or household fixture. If you wanted a sideboard with two doors instead of one or a table of cherry wood instead of walnut, all you had to do was agree with the cabinetmaker to craft what you wanted at an honest price. Repairing any damage to handcrafted works for the home was also quick and easy.

The intrusion of large-scale distribution has destroyed this human-scale business model. Gone are the personal relationships and esteem for local artisans, who were known as members of the community—friends and neighbors. Today, multinational corporations force us to settle for mass-produced models constructed with often shoddy materials designed to last a short time—planned for breakdown and obsolescence—planned not to be repaired on breakdown but to be replaced. And when that model of chair with an unpronounceable name that we bought at a package store goes out of the catalog, we can no longer order another one.

The abandonment of craft and art applies to all—I repeat, *All* areas of handicrafts and the minor arts, but it also extends even to the techniques of cultivating fields and raising livestock. Ancient knowledge, handed down for centuries and varying from region to region, is disappearing to make way for intensive GMO crops and synthetic production of surrogates, which are harmful to our health while also having a very high negative environmental impact. Seeds, too, are not exempt from this destructive operation: Monsanto and other multinational corporations produce sterile, genetically modified seeds under patent so that farmers are forced to depend on an agribusiness when traditionally nature would allow them to have new seeds to plant every time from the previous harvest.

I am not talking about marginal jobs done by underpaid or incompetent labor in some Third World village, but about **a heritage of**

meaningful activity that has been the pride of many generations in first world nations. Not surprisingly, the globalist elite demons view the survival of the crafts in so many human endeavors as a threat to mass-produced artifacts in China, India, or Pakistan.

Vocational training that looks at the preservation and innovation of crafts and trades guarantees independence for those who start a business, be it a workshop, forge, laboratory, or farm. This anti-globalist rebirth of the social fabric based on arts and crafts also restores honesty to work as human productivity—on the desire to make products executed skillfully, in which to express one's talent and manual skills. **Professionals in the arts and crafts—in the true sense—are at their best when they see their work formed in their own hands, knowing that their handiwork is made from suitable materials, worked with passion to build something that will last, not something designed to break down shortly after that, according to the cynical principle of planned obsolescence.**

In agriculture and animal husbandry, the Alliance will contribute to preserving and passing on the knowledge of our fathers, combining that knowledge with what healthy progress can simplify and make less burdensome. In this sense, respect for Creation—of which we are the careful steward of material assets for which we are accountable to the Creator—will have to be guided by moral principles, as it has always been, rather than by bureaucratic fulfillments designed to favor large landowners and multinational corporations.

In this sector, too, if we can get young people to understand how much more beautiful and fulfilling it is to feel clods of earth in their hands, to return home tired but proud of their work, following the rhythms of the seasons and the alternation of toil with rest, and sowing with harvest, we **will have an army of people willing to learn, and perhaps even many grandfathers and fathers eager to pass on their knowledge, their experience, their secrets.** This personal satisfaction would strengthen relationships between different generations, helping to counter the isolation between youth and adults that the System uses to dominate one another.

I think of the satisfaction of a printer who has decided to reprint fine books, or the work of the bookbinder working in genuine leather, the scent of the pages that each of us smells when we open a hand-crafted volume. We contemplate the joy of the blacksmith, the carpenter, and the weaver, who are no longer underpaid clerks but valued makers of unique artifacts and custodians of age-old crafts to which they will add their talents.

An artisan who works well or a farmer who respects nature will find new customers in the various anti-globalist networks who understand and value their passion and commitment. The community will express joy at creating **an alternative to the globalist market**—an alternative that shifts the critical mass toward a new way of understanding the market—that is, the ethical market—an alternative that will inevitably have a significant impact on botht employment and the quality of supply.

Let us not forget that, in all that we undertake to accomplish, the little that our disorganization and inexperience will allow us to accomplish will certainly be compensated by the value God will add to our work, provided we have the humility of our fathers to pray to Him, to thank Him, to ask Him for forgiveness, and, above all, to obey His Commandments. This divine order is the order broken by the anti-globalist elite that we must restore. As anti-globalists, we must recognize ourselves as creatures of God. We must acknowledge that God is the Creator of all. We must never forget that God is genuinely Sovereign and that Jesus Christ is King.

The Financial Network

The System's main strength is, at the same time, its weakness. We are in a transition phase to a technocratic totalitarian system, and in this transition, some indispensable steps, such as digital ID and digital currency, have not yet been taken. The System controls the economy and finances in virtually all aspects except paper currency cash transactions.

The West, subservient to the globalist dictatorship, uses economic leverage that, while it does not share globalism's ideological underpinnings and its criminal aims, supports it at least temporarily in pursuing its short-term goals. The sellers of Plexiglas, masks, and tampons who did a brisk business during the psycho-pandemic are not necessarily neo-Malthusians like Bill Gates or Klaus Schwab, just as some brands that adapt corporate communication to eco-sustainability and net-zero policy are not necessarily globalists, but tomorrow may find it more attractive to focus on product quality and the choice of local suppliers.

The perspective from which a business owner sees the creation of this "anti-globalist alternative" is the same as that of the artisan who makes custom-made clothes in a market dominated by the lowest quality ready-to-wear gear. Even if 90 percent of the population dresses in rags, 10 percent still want to dress elegantly. This small percentage still creates a lot of customers for tailors ready to make custom clothes. Given that the non-woke percentage of the population outnumbers the woke, the first firms to make non-woke, higher-quality attire will find themselves in a niche destined to expand. **There are thousands of *woke* companies sharing a huge marked, while there are very few for the *non-woke* market.** But in a niche that is certainly much larger than the tiny percentage of the woke market that one firm among a thousand other equals can hope to achieve.

Companies will abandon Agenda 2030 virtue signaling as the woke agenda begins to fail. **The inevitable collapse of climate fraud is already foreseen: just look at how the major car manufacturers are discontinuing electric and reverting to the gasoline engine; this means that this market "migration" will happen anyway, as**

far-sighted entrepreneurs know. Companies that moved to wake to virtue signal only to increase sales will abandon Agenda 2030, DEI, ESG, eco-sustainability, and net zero emissions policies once projects like forcing all cars to be electric vehicles fail to gain consumer acceptance. That is why we must expect that shortly, we will see a repositioning away from corporate woke globalism for which we must be prepared.

In finance, the Anti-Globalist Alliance's alternative to international banking conglomerates **involves restoring community banks financed largely by customers' deposits. Community banks are dedicated to granting lines of credit to small- and medium-sized local enterprises comparable to the effort to combat globalism by supporting local craftsmen and artisans.** If citizens begin to move their savings to these savings banks, with the certainty that their money will not be converted into digital currency or made subject to lending criteria based on the questionable parameters of eco-sustainability, the immediate effect would be a reduction in the liquidity of the banks in the hands of the globalist elite.

Along with this real reappropriation of savings, forms of resistance based on **local currencies, i.e., units of exchange used voluntarily, with which goods and services can be exchanged,** could be explored. These local currencies are designed to facilitate transactions and not for savings or investment: they are, therefore, to be used as an alternative or complementary to the official currency and have a parity exchange ratio with it; their issuance could be centralized at induced value, with zero debt: the amount of local currency issued would then be divided into equal parts among the members of the community who recognize its value, in this case the members of the Alliance or those who adhere to particular projects consistent with it.

Experiments in banks issuing local currency or merchants accepting cryptocurrency would also break central banks' hold on money creation. Exchange units similar to credit vouchers could be denominated in local currency. **The exchange units could be purchased by businesses or local governments and given to their employees in addition to the wages they already receive. Once issued, the exchange units could be spent in stores, supermarkets, restaurants, bars, etc., on everything including babysitting. The mere fact that people could exchange units for payments would constitute a recognition of their value.** With exchange units issued by employers as a part of employee compensation, the employee would have an extra amount to spend in their paycheck, creating an immediate positive impact on the family budget.

If, then, businesses joining the Alliance were to accept payments in local money (units of exchange)—for example, by allowing them to pay for electricity bills, gasoline, and food supplies from the local markets—there would be an immediate benefit, on top of the significant savings from ethical pricing adopted by members of the various networks.

I believe that the forthcoming launch of the Anti-Globalist Alliance—which will accompany the publication of this Manifesto—will allow for the development of an ambitious—and morally praiseworthy—project, thanks to the contribution of all those who wish to participate. **The idea that moves the Alliance is to constitute a point of reference that allows for the implementation of forms of resistance to the World Economic Forum coup without necessarily wanting to impose a solution valid for all realities in all countries. The important thing on launch is to provide an Anti-Globalist Alliance forum to share our inspiring principles and understand the rationale that must govern concrete action.**

The Energy Network

Rising energy prices serve the destruction of the socioeconomic fabric of Western nations and outrageous speculation on both traditional

and renewable sources. The Amsterdam energy exchange gives multinational corporations substantial profit margins. At the same time,
contracts with the Russian Federation and other producers before the
Ukrainian crisis and economic sanctions provided reliable natural gas
supplies at agreed prices. Wind power and photovoltaics do not guarantee reserves or continuity, in addition to having a huge environmental impact and not being recyclable: if Agenda 2030 imposes the green
transition, it is only because, in this way, it centralizes control over the
supply of energy to users—to whom it can technically be suspended
or reduced remotely—and allows enormous profits for the construction and maintenance of wind and solar farms. On the other hand, to
cooperate with big energy companies in this destruction of the national
economy, the Deep State had to make them join the banquet by guaranteeing them huge profits.

Of course, when the globalist elite decided to digitize all our lives—
transactions, interactions, relationships, interests, entertainment—they
knew full well that this would entail an exorbitant amount of energy
for the data centers and cloud facilities on which to house these many
infinite data points: videos, audio, images, texts, phone calls, databases,
purchases, health records, tax data, bank and credit card accounts—and
all this for every citizen, for every moment of their life. Where do we
expect to obtain this energy that was not needed until now, especially
if we restrict the use of hydrocarbon fuels and nuclear power? From us,
of course. We are the ones who have to use less energy, and what little
we are given must cost more, so we are forced to reduce consumption
anyway to benefit the globalist lobby.

The deception is even more paradoxical when we consider that,
while they are pushing us to install solar photovoltaic systems, their
accomplice Bill Gates has just begun experimenting with dimming
the sun to reduce the temperature of the Earth. If Gates succeeds in
his project, how will the reduction resulting from solar photovoltaics

impact energy availability? It is the same deception as the green narrative: they cry about CO_2 reduction but destroy entire forests that also feed on CO_2 to produce oxygen. And this is what the lobby wants: to force us to accept fraud as such, abdicating our reason.

Considering that the energy suppliers have no intention of giving up their shameful earnings and that the governments are complicit with the World Economic Forum, we need to organize ourselves to have our own energy supplier, which can be done through an energy consortium.

This consortium will unite companies to buy energy on the market, bypassing supplier speculation; a targeted advertising campaign will make it known to companies and individuals. The consortium will also form a nucleus of civil resistance of companies against the criminal aggression of the government, which uses the energy emergency as a tool to force smaller businesses into bankruptcy and to lay off their employees (who are forced into perpetual unemployment and to be recipients of the universal income that will turn them into slaves of the state).

An initial group of founding members will lead the way for the hundreds of thousands of medium-small businesses, giving them significant bargaining power in purchasing gas, electricity, and raw materials. All these companies united in consortium structures will create a united front to avoid bankruptcy, suspension of production, and layoffs. As soon as the consortium enters into supply contracts at more favorable prices, production will be able to restart, and this will also affect the final prices of products and the maintenance of employees' salaries. Thousands of households will benefit immediately, demonstrating the speciousness of the government's criminal action at the behest of the World Economic Forum. It will also benefit all supply chain companies and households because electricity and gas operators for individuals will also be able to join the consortium.

CONCLUSION

Humanity has been the victim of a criminal plan by a subversive lobby that has managed to penetrate the top of the civil and religious institutions of the Western world: this is what I have tried to explain and demonstrate in the first part of this Manifesto. The only reason this destructive action has successfully penetrated Western institutions is that the global elite's diabolical cunning elite has consisted in the exploitation of entire sections of the population, used unscrupulously to achieve a short-term goal, and then left to their own devices. And here, these victims of the globalist coup d'état must become aware that they have been shamelessly deceived. I am referring in particular to those social categories that the System has gradually instrumentalized to demolish traditional society with the illusion of DEI: a "diverse" utopian society in which everyone would achieve "equity" (i.e., everyone would receive a distribution of economic goods according to their needs) in a manner that would be "inclusive" (i.e., in which all differences, including LGBTQ+, would be celebrated). Of course, the woke DEI utopia did not include those who believe in God, those who believe in the traditional family, and those who support Donald Trump.

The feminist movement has destroyed the female figure, tearing women away from their role as wives and mothers while throwing them into the competitive world of work. The anti-racist movement has sharpened the differences in ethnicity, culture, and religion—not for peaceful coexistence but for their homogenization. The ethnic replacement plan led by George Soros's foundations and NGOs aims at the erasure of national identities through the uncontrolled invasion of illegal immigrants, who sooner or later will constitute an enemy army within our nations. Western nations welcome into once-Christian lands hordes of fanatical Muslims who insist on living under Sharia Law, without Christ, in preparation for the New World Order. The LGBTQ+ movement claims to fight for gay rights while using them to demolish the family and society in a hedonistic retreat into self, going so far as to erase the very complementary differentiation of the sexes to further the gender transition industry. The green movement elevates the climate fraud that falsely blames humans for the causes of alleged global warming to the level of a cult-like secular religion. Finally, the woke ideology sums up the worst of all these movements by creating a mass of hopeless lunatics suffering from eco-anxiety and convinced they are fighting a battle in defense of the planet while being financed by the elite.

I wonder: Do feminists, people of color, believers of various religions, homosexuals, lesbians, transsexuals, climate radicals, and their fellow-traveler adherents of neo-Marxist critical theory realize that they are being used and will shortly be ignored to make room for new fashions, new and increasingly absurd claims?

When the globalist elite takes over, the self-appointed oligarchs aspiring to transhuman status will not welcome further disruption or challenge. In a world run by New World Order transhumans, the DEI, ESG, and woke LGBTQ+ will be the first to be eliminated—followed closely by climate cult fanatics.

Does the woman who fights for gender equality know that the model societies of the globalist dystopia contemplate the sterile androgyne and transhumanism that unites man and machine in an obscene chimera? Does the African of Islamic religion realize that the illusion of conquering and subduing the West serves only to destroy Christianity and that the next victim of religious purges and destruction of places of worship will be Islam itself? Does the Catholic or Protestant who agrees to change his beliefs to be politically correct and compatible with woke LGBTQ+ ideology understand that he is digging his own grave and destined for extinction? Does the homosexual or lesbian who claims to be married to a person of the same sex, with a right to adopt children, know that their claims only serve to pave the way for the aberrations of pedophilia, bestiality, necrophilia, marriage to animals, marriage to things, and a host of other such absurdities?

These are not exaggerations. The Overton window is already open on the acceptance of pedophilia, and it is the World Health Organization itself that is calling on member states to lower the age of consent for minors. At the same time, the pornography industry waits impatiently for a chance to get rich by exploiting this promising new market. "Minor-attracted adults"? Do you think the System will have a problem labeling homosexuals, lesbians, transvestites, and trangenders as "retrograde" when they will refuse to have relations with minors? And do the idiots who glue their hands to paintings in museums or glue themselves to highways in order to stop traffic know that their sponsors were the first to speculate on the failed Green New Deal for the purpose of enriching themselves while concentrating control of energy and food sources in their own hands? Have the woke sect believers realized that cancel culture ultimately results in canceling the cancel culture radicals themselves? **Above all, what can and should be our efforts to open the eyes of those who still believe in the lies of the globalist elite just because they do not want to be discriminated against or because they are ashamed of having lent their consent to a colossal lie?**

I have no trouble understanding that, in a world that perceives all reality as subjective, a necessary consequence is the denial and negation of all true ideals—the destruction of all sound moral principles and the ridicule of all genuine spiritual perceptions. But once we understand that the System is inherently rotten, corrupt, and dedicated to evil, we cannot continue to fight battles that are absurd in premise, means, and end. We must find the courage not to accept this *danse macabre* toward the abyss. We must find the determination not to be exploited by an elite that wants us to believe that real progress demands our collective suicide. We must see that the globalist elite's embrace of evil because it is evil involves only the negation of all that is true, all that is holy, and all that is good. We must reject the globalist elite's insistence that we will be happy to own nothing, that we will be blessed to know nothing, to believe nothing, and to love no one. We must refuse to walk voluntarily into a hopeless slavery structured to poison ourselves in body and soul until the day the state decides that our life is not sustainable.

Let us regain our dignity as human beings, as God's creatures, as people made of body and soul destined for happiness. Let us reject the globalist elite's hell on earth. If the globalist elite chose eternal damnation, we do not have to go along with them. Let us learn to discipline ourselves, to set limits, to make sacrifices, and to think with our intellectual faculties and not with our bellies. Let us rediscover the pride of honest work, the serenity in our steadfast belief in God's sovereignty, and our righteousness in obedience to God's commandments. Let us rediscover a zest for life, an enthusiasm for interpersonal relationships, and a selfless generosity.

I cannot and will not believe that the peoples of the West are willing to trade the Christian Civilization founded on Greco-Roman culture for a world of alienated people enslaved by sex, drugs, and video games. **The exploitation and destruction of our children must end, and it must end with a collective rising of the shield, with a firm and courageous protest, and a resounding movement of resistance and civil disobedience.**

As Archbishop Viganò points out in Appendix C, "The Technocratic

Dystopia," Aldous Huxley's 1932 book *Brave New World* was an example of "predictive programing," a psychological technique of preparing the world for a future event while appearing to warn the world against the coming event. In 1937, Aldous Huxley acknowledged there was only one technique that could defeat the coming dystopia—a technique he knew would succeed, though he appears to have ultimately doubted we would have the courage to succeed:

> The only methods by which a people can protect itself against the tryanny of rullers possessing a modern police force are the non-violent methods of massive non-co-operation and civil disobedience. Such methods are the only ones which give the people a chance of taking advantage of its numerical superiority to the ruling caste and to discount its manifest inferiority in armaments. For this reason it is enormously important that the principles of non-violence should be propagated rapidly and over the widest possible area. For it is only by means of well and widely organized movements of non-violence that the populations of the world can hope to avoid that enslavement to the state which in so many countries is already an accomplished fact and which the threat of war and the advancement of technology are in process of accomplishing elsewhere.[343]

Let's build social networks constructed along principles of community, which I would like to be precisely the goal of the Anti-Globalist Alliance internationally. We want to join forces with similar initiatives that have sprung up in recent years, giving them the opportunity to join forces with us to defeat the globalist elite transhuman *ubërmench* by rejecting their Satanic lies. We will take Huxley's advice, and with the help of

343 Aldous Huxley, "Individual Work for Reform," in *Ends and Means: An Enquiry into the Nature of Ideals and Into the Methods employed for their Realization* (London: Chatto & Windus, 1937). From the 1946 edition, Chapter X, pp. 126–160, at p. 155–156.

God, we will succeed in defeating the dystopian future Huxley ultimately felt was too powerful and too inevitable to fail. As noted earlier, in the final analysis, God always wins!

APPENDICES

Appendix A

MESSAGE
of Archbishop Carlo Maria Viganò
to the participants of the
"Medical Doctors for Covid Ethics International" Zoom Meeting
January 2, 2024

Dear Dr. Frost, dear Friends, at the beginning of this new year, allow me to address my best wishes to all of you. I am grateful to have this opportunity to share with you some thoughts regarding the present situation.

For the past four years we have been witnessing the implementation of a criminal plan of world depopulation, achieved through the creation of a false pandemic and the imposition of a false vaccine, which we now know to be a biological weapon of mass destruction, designed with the aim of destroying the immune system of the entire population, causing sterility and the onset of deadly diseases. Many of our friends and acquaintances have died or been severely damaged by the adverse effects of this experimental gene serum. Many have discovered, too late, that they have been the victims of a global plan with a single script under a single direction.

What is even more serious is that this neo-Malthusian project of mass extermination, to which is added the will to control each of us through graphene oxide nanostructures, has been announced to us for some time by those in the World Health Organization and the World Economic Forum who conceived and implemented it. The rulers of all Western states, hostage to Bill Gates and Klaus Schwab, have become accomplices to this crime, demonstrating their malice and premeditation by their behavior: falsifying data on alleged infections, doctoring statistics that attribute deaths and adverse effects to Covid-19 but not to the gene serum, prohibiting effective treatments, imposing harmful protocols that have no scientific basis, banning autopsies, and preventing or thwarting accurate reports to health authorities.

In this attack, unprecedented in the history of the human race, we have witnessed the complicity of all national and international institutions, the entire medical profession, and the media. A social engineering operation has been carried out to manipulate consensus through terror, threats, blackmail, and the violation of citizens' most sacrosanct fundamental rights. The judiciary has been silent, the armed forces have looked the other way, and teachers and priests have zealously cooperated.

We are well aware of the perpetrators of this crime against God and humanity. Of course, the multinational pharmaceutical corporations have profited disproportionately from mass vaccination, and they are now preparing to accumulate still more billions of dollars from the sale of treatments against the turbocancer that their serums have caused. Those who peddle the vaccine have profited from administering these poisons to pregnant women, children, and the elderly. They have funded the self-styled experts, paying them to propagandize false efficacy and safety on the mainstream media. Multinationals have profited and, due to the lockdowns, have taken the place of small businesses, restaurants, and local shops. Energy suppliers have profited and are still profiting, and thanks to the crisis created by the system, they have made huge profits, while the costs of electricity and gas are forcing businesses to increase prices and close. Those who took advantage of the restrictions to work from home, those who sold masks that were not only useless but actually harmful, those who provided Plexiglas barriers and hand sanitizer, and those who managed the measurement of fever in public places also took their cut of profit. Many of them, who understood perfectly well what was happening, preferred to remain silent so as not to miss the opportunity to make money off of the lives and health of the rest of us.

But it's not just money that is the motive for this crime. Behind the lust for enrichment motivating many is the will to power of the subversive Davos elite, which aims to establish the New World Order. The psycho-pandemic has been a dress rehearsal for the attack they are now making against the economy, the social fabric, and indeed the very life of humanity. Fifteen-minute cities, digital identity, electronic money, and the destruction of agriculture and ranching all serve the same purpose, stated in the Agenda 2030 and the Rockefeller Foundation's "Great Reset" project. The wars in Ukraine and Palestine also have the same purpose: to destabilize the international order, create permanent crises, and fuel conflicts that will impoverish individual nations and feed the globalist leviathan. Gaza's huge oil fields are tempting targets for those who want to appropriate them in order to keep Europe and the United States under blackmail, especially when the same people are imposing insane energy policies in the name of a fake climate emergency.

Today, the perpetrators of these crimes have a name and a face. Their accomplices in governments and institutions, who are guilty of high treason and very serious crimes, all come from the *World Economic Forum* and were students of its program called "Young Global Leaders for Tomorrow." Others, like George Soros, support them by means of philanthropic foundations that fuel social strife, civil war, and color revolutions around the world.

This global coup d'état must be denounced, and those responsible must be tried and judged by an international court. But above all, it is necessary for all of us to understand that this all-out war against humanity is not motivated only by the lust for wealth and power, but mainly by a religious motive—a *theological* reason. This reason is Satan's hatred: hatred of God, hatred of God's Creation, and hatred of man, who is created in the Image and Likeness of God. Bill Gates, Klaus Schwab, George Soros, and the hundreds of servants whom they blackmail in governments all hate God. They hate life, which only God can give. They hate love, which comes only from God. They hate peace, which can reign only where Christ reigns. As Tucker Carlson said a few days ago, we are facing people who serve Satan and the demons of hell, just as normal people worship and serve God.

This, then, is a battle in which body and soul, matter and spirit are made the object of a mortal attack by men and spiritual powers. But let us not forget that, if our enemy avails himself of the help of infernal spirits, we have on our side the Lord God of the armies arrayed—*Dominus Deus Sabaoth*—and all the hosts of Angels and Saints, infinitely more powerful. God is Almighty: let us never forget that. And He is Father: He does not abandon His children in times of trial.

I therefore exhort you, dear friends, to fight this battle with the spiritual weapons that God places at your disposal: prayer, trust in the Lord, and the awareness that this enemy will not be defeated where it is most organized and fearsome, but by striking it where it is weak. This weakness comes from its corruption, from its being subservient to evil, from the execrable sins that it has committed and still commits against God's little children. Because I tell you that the men and women who in these four years have submitted and endured lockdowns, violations of their rights, job deprivation and social segregation are not willing to tolerate the crimes that this cursed network of perverts and pedophiles commits against children. Therefore, bring to light and courageously denounce the network of complicity and crimes of politicians, bankers, actors, journalists, prelates, and famous people who are united by their *blood pact*, and the whole castle of lies and deceptions that they have hatched will collapse, dragging with it the entire globalist plan, woke ideology, gender theory, the fake climate emergency, health fraud, and digital currency. *Simul stabunt, simul cadent,* says the Latin maxim: just as they stand together, so also they will collapse together.

Stay strong, therefore, under the banner of Christ and in the army of God, Who is Almighty, and Who on the Cross has already won the war that is now entering its final stages. Gather around the Lord, call on His Holy Name, and He will give impetus to your battle. Remember the words of Saint Paul: "*I can do all things through him who strengthens me*" (Phil 4:13).

+ Carlo Maria Viganò, *Archbishop*
January 2, 2024
Most Holy Name of Jesus

Appendix B

MESSAGE
of Archbishop Carlo Maria Viganò
For the **First Health Holocaust Remembrance Day**
lest we forget the victims sacrificed in the name of covid
and the victims of the vaccine genocide

11 March 2024

Dear Friends,

I am grateful for the invitation of Professor Massimo Citro della Riva to offer my greetings to the participants in the *Health Holocaust Remembrance Day*. You know well that I have never been shy in offering my interventions since the beginning of the psycho-pandemic farce, and that my complaint—since May 2020—anticipated everything that has emerged in these four years regarding the criminal management of this social-engineering experiment of neo-Malthusian origin.

What appears today in all its evidence is the subversive plan of a global coup d'état, aimed at the decimation of the world population and the enslavement of the survivors. The pressure for the approval of the WHO Pandemic Treaty and for the health passport—accompanied by the activation of the digital wallet—demonstrate that the authors of this coup have no intention of giving up their criminal intentions, and will not do so unless they are faced with firm and determined opposition from the population and those few of its representatives who are not sold out to the World Economic Forum, by those who courageously do not fail in their duties.

We have seen the *false Bergoglian church* totally subservient to the genetic treatment agenda, a treatment that was produced using aborted fetuses. We have seen doctors and paramedics killing frail and elderly people in intensive care through the use of anesthesia. We have seen rulers, magistrates, and police forces unleash an unprecedented criminalization of those who did not allow themselves to be "marked." We know who is behind these people, who pays them, and who blackmails them: their names are well known. These murderers will soon find themselves answering for their crimes, if not before the tribunal of the world, then certainly before God, Whom they hate and Whom they would like to replace, in a mad delirium of omnipotence that is an inexorable prelude to their eternal defeat. The *children of darkness*, the conspirators of the *World Economic Forum*, and the globalist cabal want to establish the kingdom of the Antichrist on earth, as an obscene counterfeit of the Kingdom of Christ Our Lord.

Look at their work: only lies, deception, horror, sin, vice, violence, and monstrosity. And always for a price, because everything they do is an object of exchange, of commerce: you pay to have children, you pay to kill them, you pay to sell their organs, you pay to abuse them, you pay to impose lethal treatments, you pay to live and to die, you pay for the lies of the media and the obscenities of the internet, you pay for the simulation of love and friendship, you pay for the chimera of a digital eternity. You also pay to end up in hell, to damn your soul. While with the things of God, everything is free—it is the fruit of charity, generosity, and magnificence.

You are rightly denouncing the *health holocaust*: with this term you highlight on the one hand the extent of the crime committed by the servants of the WHO, and on the other the desire to "sacrifice" millions of victims to the globalist Moloch. Do not lose sight of this fundamental element: the extermination—in ways not dissimilar to those that the totalitarian regimes of the last century caused—shows us the ritual aspect of the Great Reset and reveals the culture of death embraced by those who promote it. The death of babies in the mother's womb; the death of sick and elderly people in hospitals; the death of young people torn from life by drugs; the death of the family in the name of perversions and betrayals; the death of beauty, knowledge, and science. It is a death that affects not only the body, but also the soul, killing the flame of hope within it. And it is significant that those who deny the existence of an otherworldly hell seem to want to do everything to recreate it on this earth, as if to take revenge on us for the fate that inexorably awaits these psychopathic murderers.

Therefore, continue in your courageous commitment, but never lose sight of the overall picture of this epochal battle, in which the forces of Good and Evil are preparing for a decisive clash. It is important to understand that the psycho-pandemic farce was only one of the means of imposing this infernal plan, and that it is accompanied by other threats that follow the same script under the same direction. Demonstrate to people this overall coherence and even the most distracted will understand and rebel against what has been imposed on them through fraud and violence.

Our Lord said, *The truth will set you free*. He who said of Himself: *I am the Way, the Truth, the Life*. It is only the Truth of Christ that can free us from the chains of lies and the falsity of the enemy of mankind. Therefore, fight this battle in the awareness that your and our adversary can only be defeated with the weapons of Truth. Saint Paul exhorts us, *Do not let yourself be overcome by evil, but overcome evil with good*. Act with freedom within the bounds of what is good, and the Lord will bless your commitment, as he has always done throughout history for those who love Him and obey His commandments. If you yield on this, you will expose your flank to the Enemy, and all your effort will have been in vain. And remember the words of the Lord: *Do not be afraid, I have overcome the world.*

I bless you with all my heart.

+ Carlo Maria Viganò, *Archbishop*

Appendix C: Message of Archbishop Carlos Maria Viganò, "The Technocratic Dystopia" (April 30, 2023)

"The Technocratic Dystopia"

Are the novels of Huxley and Orwell an unheeded warning or instead an example of predictive programming?

When we speak of "dystopia," we mean the opposite of a utopia, that is, the description of an imaginary reality with respect to time or space—a *non-place*—that unlike utopia, which is considered desirable and positive, is instead perceived as undesirable and frightening. Two of the best-known dystopian novels, Aldous Huxley's *Brave New World* (1932) and George Orwell's *1984* (1949), represent precisely the example of two tyrannical and anti-human models of society that, if they found full realization, would be considered a kind of hell on earth. In the face of this prospect, taken for granted to be unrealizable, the function of the dystopian novel should be to create a warning for those who read it, so that the threat remains confined to the realm of the imaginary.

For the sake of completeness, we cannot disregard another lesser-known essay by Huxley, *Brave New World Revisited* (1958), translated in Italy as *Ritorno al mondo nuovo* (1961),[344] in which the author addresses the issue of world overpopulation, noting that increased life prospects for people with genetic diseases and advances in medicine

---

344 The fixation on Malthusianism also recurs in *Island* (1962), in which the (strictly anti-Christian) social organization provides for contraception, artificial insemination, and euthanasia; boys are initiated into drug use and all forms of sexual deviation, from sodomy to promiscuity, without neglecting the nudity flaunted in clothing and a disturbing attention to the sexuality of minors that evidently alludes to a form of legitimization of pedophilia. Another novel—very revealing because it was written forty years earlier—is *Crome Yellow* (1921), translated into Italian as *Giallo cromo* (1932), in which Huxley anticipates themes of state birth control, sexualization, and drug use among the masses, along with a caste division of the population. "An impersonal generation will take the place of Nature's hideous system" (*Crome Yellow*, ch. 5).

end up increasing this problem. Huxley describes the centralization of economic power in multinational corporations, the problems of social organization and labor associated with technological development, and the use of propaganda and marketing techniques in the political sphere; he also does not neglect the world of synthetic drugs, psychotropic drugs, and LSD (similar to soma in the novel),[345] which he considers to be tools that an overt or covert dictatorship could use as a method of political control, along with the psychological manipulation of subliminal persuasion and hypnosis.

Many are persuaded that Huxley and Orwell, with their novels, intended to warn humanity of the danger of dictatorship, and that their unheeded warnings should alarm us and—in the face of many elements of the two dystopias we see unfolding before our eyes—lead us to denounce the coup d'état of the globalist technocratic elite. Instead, with this paper I would like to argue the opposite thesis, namely, that the description of the *Brave New World* and *Oceania* society constitutes the anticipation by literary, and then cinematic, means of a precise subversive project, conceived in circles in which Freemasonry and its esoteric and gnostic philosophies unite and coordinate the activity of cultural circles, academic institutions, theosophical sects, writers, intellectuals, filmmakers, and eugenicist scientists. It is not possible that Huxley and Orwell—both of whom belonged to Freemasonry, both of whom were

---

345 Wells introduced Huxley to Aleister Crowley (1875–1947), who initiated him into the *Golden Dawn* and who in 1929 made him experiment with psychedelic drugs. During those years, Huxley, along with Christopher Isherwood (1904–1986), Thomas Mann (1875–1955) and his daughter Elisabeth Mann-Borgese (1918–2002), laid the groundwork for what would become the LSD culture, as part of the Golden Dawn's Isis cult. The launch of LSD as a tool for dissolving youth—a product of the Sandoz pharmaceutical company owned by the Israelite financiers the Warburgs—occurred through Aldous Huxley, University of Chicago Chancellor Robert Flutchins, and Allen Dulles (1893–1969), then head of the CIA, as part of a plan hatched by the CIA itself during the period between 1948 and 1962. Huxley described the effects of LSD in his two essays *The Doors of Perception* (1954) and *Heaven and Hell* (1956); those doors inspired the name of the rock band *The Doors*.

at Oxford in relationship with the Freemason Herbert G. Wells (1866–1946), a member of the *Golden Dawn*, an advocate of a world government and a friend of the Satanist Aleister Crowley—did not share the cultural and ideological setting of that milieu in which Aldous's grandfather, Thomas Henry Huxley (1825–1895) was an active proponent of Darwinian evolutionary theory and among the founders of the para-masonic Round Table organization,[346] as well as a member—at only twenty-six years of age—of the Royal Society.[347] Aldous's brother Julian Huxley (1887–1975), who was George Orwell's professor, was a genetic biologist, author of *Evolution, The Modern Synthesis* (1942), a member of the Eugenics Society,[348] the first president of UNESCO and one of the three founders of WWF; was also connected to the Fabian Society and a friend of Margaret Sanger (1879–1966), the theorist of birth control and founder of the clinics—generously funded by the Rockefellers—that later evolved into Planned Parenthood, of which Sanger was president from 1952 to 1959.

It thus becomes clear that the *milieu* that Huxley assiduously frequented and by which Orwell was influenced is the crucible in which the subversive plan of a world government in the hands of a tyrannical elite was conceived, in which science becomes the instrument with which to shape reality: the technocratic elite takes the place of God, creating its own paradise and keeping the masses in ignorance, according to the dictates of Weishaupt's *Illuminati*.[349] A science that claims

---

346 The *Royal Institute of International Affairs* (established in London in 1919) and the *Council on Foreign Relations* (founded in 1921 in New York) are two powerful think tanks of the *Round Table*.

347 The *British Royal Society* played a key role in the spread of scientism that would later lead to the "scientific dictatorship." All of its founders and members were Freemasons, which could thus use a prestigious institution to lend credibility to a version of "science" based on the esoteric doctrine of the Lodges.

348 In 1989, the Eugenics Society changed its name to the *Galton Institute*. Since 2021, it has been called *Adelphi Genetics Forum*.

349 Johann Adam Weishaupt (1748–1830), Jesuit-educated, German philosopher, founder of the Order of the Illuminati, with the aim of establishing a "new order"

irrational assent: "Orthodoxy means not thinking, not needing to think. Orthodoxy and unconsciousness are one and the same," Orwell wrote in *1984*.

An example of perfect "orthodoxy" to the *depositum scientiæ* of the Masonic elite was first and foremost Modernism, which introduced doubt, which is proper to the sphere of the empirical sciences, into theological speculation after the Masonic Enlightenment had sanctioned the divorce between science and faith in the name of rationalist thought. The "goddess of Reason" enthroned by the revolutionaries on the high altar of Notre Dame later entered Saint Peter's Basilica with the Second Vatican Council, which ratified the supposed opposition between science and faith, ousting the Church from civil society and ceding to the new priests of technocratic religion the hierarchical superiority of one over the other. Bergoglio, promoting the gene serum and pandering to the psycho-pandemic narrative, has done still worse: he has deified science by making it religion, and at the same time he has humanized (*de-divinized*, I would say) Religion, subjecting it to the scrutiny of scientist rationalism.

War is peace; freedom is slavery; ignorance is strength. In the Orwellian novel, the orthodoxy of the citizens is tested daily by the Ministry of Truth through two elements of forced manipulation of reality: neolanguage and biplanning. Neolanguage—of which the party is the controller—involves the use of neologisms and the deletion of all words expressing traditional thought; it includes *psycho-religion*, which the *psychopolice* prosecute and punish in the *nonperson* who performs it.[350]

---

leading to the abolition of governments, religions, private property, and marriage. He was initiated into Freemasonry in Munich in 1777; linked to the *Golden Dawn*, esotericism, and theosophism. Weishaupt's thought influenced the Revolution, the Commune, Utopian Socialism, and Karl Marx.

350 Is it not *neo-language* to refer to the killing of a helpless child in the womb as "termination of pregnancy," the imposition of contraception and abortion on Third World countries as "reproductive health," the genital mutilation of minors as "gender transition," the buying of children from poor women as "surrogacy," pedophiles as

The other tool of social control is provided by the adoption of *bip-ensarianism*, which forces the people of Oceania to believe any concept and its opposite to be true, depending on the will of the party, and instantly forgetting the change of opinion and the very act of having forgotten. On the basis of *double thinking*, the state modifies historical events of the past (through tampering with newspapers and books) and by adapting them to the changing present situation, no more or less than *cancel culture* theorizes today.

Malthusian thought and Darwinian theory are the application of Masonic principles and the ideological premise of transhumanism, a term coined by Julian Huxley. In the evolutionary delusion of these neo-Malthusians, man should evolve into a transhuman creature (the person integrated with the machine, but also the biological body separated from gender, as per transgenderism) and then become the *post-human man* (the machine made into a person or the person transferred to "the cloud" and connected to artificial intelligence). Transhumanism considers the convergence of nanotechnology, biotechnology, computer science, and cognitive science to be decisive for the depersonalization of the individual: it is in this key that the attempt to create a kind of global neural network in which all individuals are forcibly connected to each other and controllable should be read.

The statements of Klaus Schwab and Yuval Noah Harari are perfectly consistent with the application of the doctrine of "becoming" professed by Freemasonry. So too is the project of creating a *collective consciousness*, a hive mind, erasing (indeed, atrophying) free will in the name of the "good of the community," the Planet or any cause as absurd as it is imposed to be believed as a dogma promulgated by technocrats: global warming, the water emergency, zero CO_2 impact. The rest, on the other hand, is already before our eyes: mass sterilization (in

---

"people attracted to minors," and cities where citizens are no longer free to move beyond a certain distance as "smart cities?"

part induced by vaccines) and the consequent increase in the business of assisted reproduction and surrogacy;[351] the legalization of adoption for same-sex couples and the new market for surrogate wombs; gender indoctrination especially of children and young people and the creation *ex nihilo* of a huge business for clinics practicing gender transition; the blaming of life itself as "unsustainable" in order to legitimize its suppression by euthanasia offered by special clinics and pharmaceutical companies with the complicity of the health industry. Even the perversions and vices that are made available to the populace to corrupt them and keep them subjugated are always—without exception—mediated by a parasitic corporation that reaps untold profits from them. It is the monetization of every aspect of human life, especially if it is functional to the System, that is being pursued through a process of privatization that, in parallel with the imposition of limitations on natural rights, makes them purchasable for a fee, including the ability to produce CO_2 by paying emission rights to the European Union.[352]

The political foundation that enables the establishment of a technocracy is a *monstrum* of socialist collectivism and liberal mercantilism, for the benefit of a private "central committee" that holds world economic control through two very powerful investment funds and has its own emissaries at the top of governments, public institutions, and international bodies, in addition to owning the major media outlets. Let us not forget that technocratic dictatorship was theorized by Saint-Simon (1760–1825),[353] an ideologue of socialist thought. The combination of

---

351 In addition to the increase of pathologies related to gestation and childbirth, to which the Tavistock Institute is no stranger. Cf. https://www.medicinenon.it/tavistock-listituto-del-controllo-delle-masse.

352 On April 20, 2023, the European Parliament (with the vote of a Left not represented in the member countries but totally subservient to the diktats of the World Economic Forum) approved the rule that applies carbon emission taxes under the ETS to domestic consumption as well: gasoline, diesel, LPG and natural gas for automotive and home heating purposes.

353 Cf. Claude-Henri de Rouvroy de Saint-Simon, *Reorganization of the European Society*, 1814.

Malthusian population control with Social Darwinism has produced national socialism, Marxist international socialism, and multinational international capitalism.

What *Brave New World* and *1984* describe corresponds to the same processes of *predictive programming* that we find in numerous movies having as their theme pandemics, dictatorial regimes after climate crises, and plots by pharmaceutical companies, high finance, and secret services—that is, to the use of the fictional literary genre as a tool for mass mental programming in order to make the population more willing to accept planned future events. The fate of Popé in *Brave New World* and Winston in *1984*, not surprisingly, serve as a warning to those who would try to rebel, showing the failure of all opposition.

By small steps, initially, and then at an increasingly rapid pace: the reaction before a scientific dictatorship *not preceded by its representation* would lead us to rebel. We have seen and experienced this during the psycho-pandemic farce of the past three years: billions of people placed under seizure by the same oligarchy of technocrats who in recent decades—since the days of Huxley's grandfather—have been enfeebling universities and scientific institutions with their Masonic brethren to spread Darwinian and Malthusian theories—that is, theories of population reduction and demographic control—to be pursued through wars, famines, pandemics, mass vaccinations, and economic crises. Anglican pastor Thomas Robert Malthus (1766–1834) was the first to theorize the spread of promiscuity, homosexuality, and adultery as methods of depopulation, along with the drastic reduction of sanitary and hygienic conditions in the poorer classes. It was he who first spoke of "useless eaters," and it is significant that this expression—after its eugenic applications by the dictatorships of the twentieth century—is eloquently taken up in equal measure by Henry Kissinger, Jacques Attali, and Klaus Schwab, after Aurelio Peccei's *Club of Rome* in 1968 had sounded the alarm to Western governments about the threat of the unsustainable exponential increase in world population, gaining cooperation and funding in the promotion of "reproductive health"—*i.e.*, abortion, in the expression of Orwellian neo-language—and "disease prevention," which consists of the mass vaccination plan—with related disease chronification—by the pharmaceutical industry.

The apparent condemnation of the dystopia narrated in Huxley's and Orwell's novels proposes a scenario presented as *inevitable*, which it would be useless to resist and which, on the contrary, it is better to accept by trying to identify its positive aspects, exactly as happened during the pandemic farce. What the elite expects from its victims—that is, from all of us—is unconditional surrender, based on deception and illusion. The continuous siege of the media, the ideological hammering of international organizations, the complicity of religious leaders, and the mercenary silence of accomplices is intended to create the perception of an inevitability of programmed destiny and bring about, in most people, a kind of fatalistic renunciation of rebellion, resistance, and combat. To reassure the obedient, the term *resilience* has recently been coined, by which the ability of the individual and society to "transform an adverse experience into an opportunity" is elevated to "civic virtue," according to the hypocritical vocabulary of neolanguage.

Just as every Catholic knows and believes that he cannot change anything, by his own strength, of God's inscrutable plans—which are always aimed at our material and spiritual good—and therefore relies on His Holy Providence; so too the elite demands that we regard its plans—human and infernal, aimed at evil and our physical and moral destruction—as impossible to control and avert, demanding our total resignation and helplessness. The dystopia of literary fiction should not lead us to believe that reality meekly goes along with the elite's delusion. Indeed, we must be the first not to enter into globalist dystopia, just as we did previously with the blandishments of socialist or liberal utopia, which proved to be failures on a par with all human and anti-Christian ideologies.

In a collectivized world where individualities are obliterated in order to cancel them out in the mass consciousness imposed by the System, we must be champions of Christ, His courageous Knights, denouncing the global coup and opposing to it a model of society that is as far from utopia as it gets: the *societas christiana* that we saw was feasible and was in fact realized before the Revolution struck our Civilization to the heart. And even if we should individually succumb, we will still be victorious together with the One who first engaged this battle and indeed has already won it.

This time the first to fall for the Serpent's deception will be the very synarchs of globalism, intoxicated with their belief that they can be *sicut dii* (Gen 3:5), like gods, because this infernal sham—as realistic and impressive as it is—changes nothing about reality, nor about the final destiny of the good and the wicked, since Christ has overcome Satan and the world.

+ Carlo Maria Viganò, *Archbishop*

April 30, 2023
Sunday III after Easter
Commemoratio S. Catharinæ Senensis Virginis